1913

An End and a Beginning

1913

An End and a Beginning

by Virginia Cowles

1817

HARPER & ROW, PUBLISHERS

NEW YORK AND EVANSTON

CONTENTS

Contents

ILLUSTRATIONS

St Petersburg

Vienna

Paris Fashions

John Sloan, *Sunday, Women drying their hair*, 1913. Addison Gallery of American Art, Phillips Academy, Andover, Mass. (*Victoria and Albert Museum*)

Poster for the 69th Regt. Armory Show. The Joseph H. Hirschorn Collection, New York (*Victoria and Albert Museum*)

Irving Berlin (*Brown Brothers*)

Two stills from Zukor's *Quo Vadis; Daheim*, 22 February (*Liverpool Public Library*)

Mr and Mrs Vernon Castle (*Culver Pictures*)

'Modern Dances'; *Elegante Welt*, 29 January (*Bert, Manuel – Tasiemka*)

Paul Chabas, *September Morn* (*Brown Brothers*)

All artists' rights reserved
Picture research by Georgia Tennant
Layout of illustrations by Sheila Sherwen

Acknowledgment

The author and publishers would like to thank the artists and photographers mentioned above for kind permission to use their work, and, in particular, Georges Sirot and Hans Tasiemka, who made valuable collections of photographs available for this book.

ONE

LONDON

The year 1913 marked the close of an era. Yet it was no tame sheep trotting obediently at the end of the queue. It had a character and personality of its own that was neither Victorian nor Edwardian and made itself felt from one end of Europe to the other. It was brash and defiant, turbulent, adventurous and moody. It marched through Time like a huge procession carrying hundreds of banners clearly announcing the way to a new age, but the words were invisible to contemporary eyes. They could be read only by a future generation endowed with the wisdom of hindsight.

Indeed, in 1913 many people regarded England's way of life as permanent as her rain-swept skies. London was the gayest, richest and largest capital in the world. It was the focal point of an empire which spread over a quarter of the earth's surface and embraced a quarter of the earth's people; it controlled the elaborate game of European power politics; it served as a meeting place for international society; it dominated the literary world and attracted to its stage the most celebrated artists of the day. Even more amazing, it preserved an ancient monarchy, operated a modern democracy, and at the same time managed to keep its aristocracy firmly in the saddle. Foreigners regarded this pattern as nothing less than magic, and probably that is what it was. Nevertheless change was in the air, and nowhere was the breeze blowing fresher than in London.

1913 was ushered in to the tune of ragtime. The prosperous middle-class crowds which filled the fashionable London hotels protested when the orchestras struck up the strains of the customary cotillions and demanded 'modern' music. 'At the Cecil and Waldorf,' reported *The Times* correspondent lugubriously, 'there was ragtime during supper and ragtime afterwards, and at most places that boasted orchestras guests danced to ragtime until the small hours of the morning.'

At midnight traditional tableaux were staged. The Hotel Metropole depicted Father Time moving across a wintry threshold. Then came 1912 in the form of a chrysalis which, on the stroke of twelve, turned into a butterfly. Winter faded into a garden laden with flowers marked Abundance, Happiness, Luck, Wealth and Health. Nothing so sentimental for the Waldorf. This hotel staged a terrifying scene, which managed to put a halt to all merriment for at least ten minutes. Father Time wheeled in a submarine marked 1913 which began to bombard an old ship marked 1912. The ship sank as the clock struck twelve. To heighten the effect the room was plunged into darkness with only the submarine searchlights playing around the ceiling.

Most hotels adhered to the custom of distributing souvenirs to their guests in honour of the new year. The Piccadilly gave lorgnettes on a silver stem to the ladies and handsome leather card cases to the gentlemen. Only the Savoy refused to play. At a business meeting a few days earlier the directors had decided to put an end to costly gifts.

Any revellers dutiful enough to read *The Times* on New-Year's Day must have had their spirits dampened by the leading article which condemned 'the craze for costly and luxurious living which has wrought so much mischief in England in recent years'. 'An even greater evil,' it continued, 'is the incessant craving for movement and excitement which permeates every class.' The solution? 'Calmer and simpler ideals and a wholesome conception of duty to the State.'

But not even the leader writer of *The Times* could halt the advance of a new day. Everywhere slings and arrows were being hurled at revered formulas and ingrained taboos. Despite much controversy, the first performance in England of Richard Strauss' *Der Rosenkavalier* took place in January. The opera had been considered for the Gala Performance in 1911 to celebrate the coronation of King George and Queen Mary, but was turned down on grounds of indecency. 'I hope,' wrote Queen Mary's aunt, the Grand Duchess of Mecklenburg-Strelitz, 'this novelty will not be selected for it is the most improper opera in existence, even the *male* singers declared their horror at having to sing such words, and the females were more than scandalized!' [1]* In January 1913, Covent Garden Opera House was sold out, and the conductor, Mr Thomas Beecham, received a standing ovation.

That same month Mr Asquith's Liberal government announced the final arrangements for nationalizing the Telephone Company, which had been in private hands since 1880; and six thousand taxi-drivers staged their first ever strike in protest against the decision of their employers to make them

* Notes begin on page 255.

contribute towards the cost of petrol. In February London was deeply shocked to learn that Captain Scott, leader of the Antarctic Expedition, had perished with three of his companions on his return journey from the South Pole, one hundred and fifty miles from his base at Camp Evans. News of a more routine nature was the assassination of King George of Greece, a brother of the Dowager Queen Alexandra, who was murdered in Athens in March. His death marked the fourth political assassination of the year. The others were Hussein Nazim Pasha, commander-in-chief of the Turkish army, and the deposed President and Vice-President of Mexico. The following month an abortive attempt took place on the life of the King of Spain.

That spring motor-cars, cricket and pigtails were all under fire. 'In pre-motor days,' wrote Mr G. S. Street in the *Daily Mail*, 'Piccadilly was an agreeable place to live. I should as soon think of living there now as in Waterloo Station . . . It is absurd to suppose that all these new and violent shocks are not affecting our lives for evil.' [2] 'In my opinion,' wrote a member of the Liverpool Cricket Club, 'one of the chief reasons why the crowd is so disgusted with modern cricket . . . is the abominable way in which many batsmen walk about in front of the wicket and play the ball with almost every part of their body – but not the bat . . . The public will not go to see it. The public is right.' [3] And as for pigtails . . . a North Devon schoolmistress refused to allow her pupils to wear 'loose hair', whereupon a North Devon doctor raised a storm by declaring that the pigtail was un-hygienic. Hair, he said, required aeration. This started a controversy which was taken up by the press and even debated from the platform.

Women were delighted by the new 'vacuum dust extractors' which, although invented ten years earlier, were now on the market for six pounds. At the same time they were disturbed by the shortage of cook-generals. The rich had no problems, for servants had an annoying habit of gravitating to large houses where their duties were clearly defined. Modest, middle-class families who only kept two or three servants and expected their cooks to 'help in the house' were finding it increasingly difficult to obtain assistance. They grumbled that they were having to pay cook-generals twenty-six pounds a year and to promise in their advertisements 'no outside windows and no washing'.

Women also discussed the horrors of the 'white slave traffic', the subject of many magazine and newspaper articles in the early months of 1913, due to the propaganda efforts of the suffragettes. The term 'white slaver' was not limited to men who exported girls to foreign brothels but included all procurers who lived off the earnings of prostitutes. Early in 1913 Mr Justice Darling took advantage of a new bill reintroducing flogging for offenders, and sentenced a man who had sent his wife onto the streets to a term of imprisonment and thirty strokes of the dreaded 'cat' in one beating.

Even the English court was bowing to new pressures. In April, King George and Queen Mary made a three-day visit to the industrial area of Staffordshire. They stayed at Crewe Hall as the guests of the Marquess of Crewe, Secretary of State for India, who had helped to organize the royal trip to Delhi the previous winter. Apparently much preparation was required to make the visit befittingly regal. 'Though it lasts only three days,' wrote Lord Crewe, 'it seems to take almost as much arranging as the Durbar.' [4]

The tour was part of a new look for royalty. Never, before 1912, had a sovereign embarked on a purely 'industrial' tour. But the cost of living was rising and wages were not keeping pace. Since 1909 Britain had been torn by strikes and fierce dissensions; indeed, in the first eight months of 1913 there were more trade disputes than in any previous year.

Consequently royal visits were arranged to coal-mines, railway workshops, factories, foundries, potteries and dairies. On one of these trips the Queen even popped into a council house unannounced and had tea with the owner. On another she visited a coal-mine. Her ninety-year-old aunt, the Grand Duchess of Mecklenburg-Strelitz, wrote ecstatically from Germany, 'I followed you all along even into the coal-mine, for I have been in one, in Wales in 1849, wearing a *hood* over my head, not a hat with *white* feathers! That will have suffered!' Queen Mary replied that the hat was all right as she had merely seen the 'surface working of a mine'. [5]

Although by 1913 George and Mary had been on the throne for three years, they were far from popular with fashionable society, which still lamented the death of the genial King Edward. George v had adored his father, yet no two men could have been more different. George was bluff and unimaginative with only two hobbies: stamp-collecting and shooting. Much to his wife's regret he could not even be prevailed upon to go sight-seeing, for Mary had a passion for antiques of all kinds, from churches to china.

Although George v was an upright, hard-working man of simple tastes, all sorts of malicious stories were circulated about him during the first years of his reign. An allegation that he had been married to the daughter of a British admiral when he was a midshipman in Malta in 1890 even found its way into print in a seditious Paris newspaper. The crown sued, and the libeller, Mr Edward Mylius, was sent to prison for a year.

London

At the Whitsun holiday Hampstead Heath became London's fairground.

In September, the Prince of Wales
went to Germany as the King's
representative for the wedding of
ex-king Manoel of Portugal to
Princess Augusta Victoria of
Hohenzollern at Sigmaringen.
Here he is seen in the wedding
procession with the Duchess of
Aosta.

In June, Poincaré, who had
become President of France in
January, paid a state visit to
London. He arrived, like many
other distinguished visitors, at
Victoria Station, his train suitably
decorated with emblems of the
French Republic.

In the heat-wave of the summer 1913, when society flocked to Hyde Park, Kensington Gardens was a favourite place for nursemaids to bring the children in their care.

Assembling for dinner in the entrance hall of the Savoy Hotel.

Opposite. The cold spell during the winter tempted skaters on to the ice at Wimbledon.

Left. The most esoteric of English sports, the Eton wall game, the annual contest between collegers and oppidans, was celebrated as usual on St Andrew's Day, November 30.

In December France dealt a blow to England's sporting prestige, when young Georges Carpentier knocked out Bombadier Wells in seventy-seven seconds at the National Sporting Club. He was 25 pounds lighter than the 6′ 3″ tall Englishman, and is here seen being chaired by his supporters after the knock-out.

Sea-bathing during the summer heat-wave.

A dramatic photograph of Emily Davison, the suffragette who threw herself under the king's horse at Tattenham Corner during the Derby on June 4. The jockey, Jones, escaped with minor injuries, but Miss Davison died in hospital.

The funeral of Emily Davison, impressively organised by the suffragettes. 'The great public responded to the appeal of a life deliberately given for an impersonal end.'

Christabel Pankhurst, daughter of the suffragettes' leader, with their paper *The Suffragette*. When the 'Cat and Mouse' Act, which came into force in 1913, hampered the activities of the suffragettes in London, Christabel controlled their activities from her refuge in Paris.

Sylvia Pankhurst, Mrs Pankhurst's younger daughter, taken through enormous crowds to the police station after her speech in Trafalgar Square on July 28.

Winston Churchill, First Lord of the Admiralty, riding with his wife. His part in the Marconi affair and his Admiralty estimates kept his name in the news in 1913.

Lloyd George, Chancellor of the Exchequer, addressing a meeting of strikers at Birmingham. 1913 set a new record in trade disputes.

Asquith, leader of the Liberal government since 1906, and one of the most implacable opponents of the suffragettes.

Sir Edward Grey, the Foreign Secretary, who had to abandon his country pursuits to preside over the Conference of Ambassadors and the Balkan Peace Conference in London.

Walter Hines Page, the new American Ambassador, one of the most acute critics of London life and society in 1913.

More rumours spread. People said that the King drank and that the Queen was frightened of him. Apparently the drink story emanated from the fact that George V had a mottled skin and a loud voice, but in truth he was an abstemious man. As for Queen Mary, tales about her loveless marriage were not to be wondered at, as she first had been engaged to George's elder brother, the Duke of Clarence. When her fiancé died her hand had been transferred to Prince George. However, this mechanical operation did not mean that she was a neglected wife. 'My love grows stronger for you every day mixed with admiration,' wrote George V shortly after the coronation, 'and I thank God every day that he has given me such a darling devoted wife as you are . . . God bless you my sweet Angel May . . .' [6]

The smart set could not forgive the new King and Queen their lack of interest in society. Whereas Edward VII had been present at every lighted candle, had adored rich men and pretty women, clothes, bridge, French cooking and grand week-end parties, King George seemed to loathe them all. The aristocracy dubbed the royal couple 'provincial'; Max Beerbohm even wrote a poem which was circulated from hand to hand, the verses ending alternatively, 'The King is duller than the Queen', 'The Queen is duller than the King'. [7]

Even the kitchen staff at Buckingham Palace was slightly dismayed to be told in 1913 (as a result of the King's visit to India in 1912) that when George V was dining alone with the Queen he wished to be served at every meal some form of curry and Bombay duck. However, the chef took heart when he was assured that state banquets and formal dinners would continue to follow the pattern laid down by King Edward.

Some people thought that the nineteen-year-old Prince of Wales, an undergraduate at Magdalen College, Oxford, might follow his father in a dislike of society. After a party in Buckingham Palace in March 1913, the Prince wrote in his diary, '. . . three hundred people came for a private dance . . . I had to dance, a thing I hate. However, I started off with Miss B. and was frightfully nervous . . . the whole thing was a great strain . . . I was *very* glad when it was over . . .' [8]

While the King and Queen were touring the Staffordshire Potteries that spring the Prince was sent on a tour to Germany 'to improve his knowledge of the language'. He visited Count Zeppelin's airship plant at Friedrichshafen on Lake Constance, and the old man, still vigorous at seventy-four, showed him his latest dirigible, the Z4. He also visited his great-aunt, the Grand Duchess of Mecklenburg-Strelitz; his cousin the Duke of Saxe-Coburg and

Gotha; King William and Queen Charlotte of Würtemberg and Prince Henry of Prussia.

Before leaving Germany he also paid a brief visit to Kaiser William II at the Königliches Schloss in Berlin.

Arriving in the late afternoon [wrote the Prince] I was taken at once to the Emperor's room. He was sitting in a uniform behind an extraordinarily high desk; and in greeting me he rose in a most curious manner, as if dismounting from a horse. Upon drawing closer I saw to my astonishment that he had risen from a wooden block shaped like a horse's body; to this was girthed a military saddle, complete with stirrups. Noting my startled expression, the Emperor smiled and explained condescendingly that he was so accustomed to sitting on a horse he found a saddle more conducive to clear, concise thinking than a chair.

I dined that night with him, the Empress and several other members of the family. The Kaiser, in a different and more colourful uniform, led the conversation in German to test my fluency. Satisfied that I had not been wasting my time, he relapsed into English, which he spoke well, and asked all sorts of questions about my parents and his English relatives.

Dinner over, he excused himself, only to reappear almost immediately in the most dazzling uniform of all, and whisked me off alone to the opera for a performance of *Aïda*. We swept through the streets in a gleaming limousine; a *Jäger*, in a rich green uniform, with gilt hunting dagger and plumed hat, rode in front, while distinctive notes on the horn warned the police to hold the traffic for the Emperor. [9]

King George and Queen Mary – unlike Edward VII and Alexandra – were well disposed towards Germany and the German Emperor. They were delighted to travel to Berlin in May 1913, to attend the wedding of the Kaiser's only daughter, Princess Victoria Louise, to the Duke of Brunswick, a relation of the British royal family. At the ceremony Queen Mary appeared in a gown of Indian cloth of gold with a train made of fine Irish lace lined with gold tissue. She wore magnificent jewels. On her head was a crown of pearls and diamonds; around her neck a diamond collar, with the large crown diamond necklace beneath this, and the lesser Stars of Africa as a pendant.

She found time to pay a few hours' visit to Aunt Augusta at Neu Strelitz, taking the King with her, accompanied by a large suite. Aunt Augusta was thrilled, but slightly put out by the 'film men' present – an innovation she was not used to. 'Fancy our going *kissing* all over the world,' she wrote to Queen Mary, 'but it is impossible to stop those horrid kino-men.' And Mary replied, 'Too amusing George and you appearing in a photo embracing! I believe it already appeared in a London paper.' [10]

When the King returned to London he dropped a line to Sir Charles Cust, a close friend and equerry, who was ill and had been unable to make the trip. 'Our visit to Berlin has, I think, been a great success in every way, and I trust that it may tend to improve the relations between the two countries. Nothing could have exceeded the kindness of the Emperor and Empress. He went out of his way to entertain us and to do everything in his power to make our visit a pleasant one . . .'

In May a fresh note was struck by the arrival of a new American Ambassador – Mr Walter Hines Page. Mr Page was not a conventional choice. He was neither rich nor socially prominent. He came from North Carolina and had begun his career as a journalist, gravitating to the editorship of the *Atlantic Monthly*. In 1899 he had founded, in partnership with Frank Doubleday, the famous publishing firm of Doubleday, Page Inc.

Mr Page's staff consisted of five people; a secretary of embassy, two assistant secretaries, a military and a naval attaché. Upon his arrival he was taken to the Coburg Hotel in Carlos Place (now the Connaught) which was supposed to serve as a permanent home, since the United States did not possess an official residence. However, as soon as Mr Page's sharp eyes noted the grandeur of Old World diplomacy – the magnificent houses and lavish entertaining – he found the Coburg Hotel intolerable. As for the Embassy Chancellery, it was nothing less than 'a nightmare'.

My heart sank [he wrote] . . . the moment I entered that dark and dingy hall at 123 Victoria Street, between two cheap stores – the same entrance that the dwellers in the cheap flat above used – I knew that Uncle Sam had no fit dwelling there. And the Ambassador's room greatly depressed me – dingy with twenty-nine years of dirt and darkness, and utterly undignified. And the rooms for the secretaries and attachés were the little bedrooms, kitchen, etc. of that cheap flat; that's all it was. For the place we paid $1,500 a year. I did not understand then and I do not understand yet how Lowell, Bayard, Phelps, Hay, Choate and Reid endured that cheap hole. Of course they stayed there only about an hour a day; but they sometimes saw important people there. And, whether they ever saw anybody there or not, the offices of the United States Government in London ought at least to be as good as a common lawyer's office in a country town in a rural state of our Union . . . [11]

Even King George, at the first audience, murmured to Mr Page that he thought a rich country like America ought to provide its envoys with better amenities. 'It is not fair on an ambassador,' pronounced the sovereign.

Within a few months Mr Page had rectified the position. The Chancellery was moved to Grosvenor Gardens, and the Page family moved into a house in Grosvenor Square.

. . . a splendid, big old house [he wrote to his brother] not in any way pretentious – a commonplace house in fact for fashionable London and the least showy and costly of the Embassies. But it does very well – it's big and elegantly plain and dignified. We have fifteen servants in the house . . . They pretty nearly run themselves and the place. The servant question is admirably solved here. They divide the work according to a fixed and unchangeable system and they do it remarkably well – in their own slow English way. [12]

The American Ambassador presented his credentials to the King at the height of the season. Nowhere in the world was so much concentrated entertaining crammed into three months as in the British capital. This was because the English aristocracy had its roots in the land; and the only time that most of them were willing to quit their country estates for a prolonged period was the thirteen weeks from the first of May to the end of July when fox-hunting and shooting were in abeyance. Town houses were flung open, dust-sheets were removed, ballroom floors polished, wives, servants, children and dogs all moved en masse to Mayfair.

In 1913 the aristocracy and their kinsfolk, the landed gentry, constituted a ruling class which ruled, not only through the House of Lords, but through the Commons where it held nearly all the Conservative and seventy per cent of the Liberal seats. It dominated the rural areas through the ownership of agricultural land; many of the industrial areas through the ownership of coal mines and quarries; and the City of London through its control of the banks. The secret of its success lay in the fact that it was far from being a closed shop. Its doors were wide-open to success, particularly in the field of politics and finance. Cabinet ministers and newspaper proprietors became part of the establishment through the creation of new peerages, while the sons of rich industrialists gained admittance by attending public schools.

The rich industrialists themselves sometimes managed to crash the barriers by spending money, despite the hostility of dowagers bent on maintaining the status quo. The older generation frequently complained that Edward VII's weakness for luxury and rich adventurers had 'started the rot'. But the new money and new talent injected into the stiffening arteries of the aristocracy not only revitalized it but transformed it into a world-wide phenomenon: a well-bred plutocracy.

Many ducal families lived in almost Oriental splendour. The Duke of Portland had a house – Welbeck Abbey – so vast that he built an underground railway to carry food from the kitchen to the dining-room. He had twelve tennis courts placed in different positions so that his guests could play at any hour of the day undisturbed by the glare of the sun. The Duke of Bedford had an income of over two hundred thousand pounds a year (a million dollars in 1913). At his fabulous house, Woburn Abbey, he had an indoor riding school, but as a concession to the modern age he employed eight chauffeurs, and always provided motor transport for guests travelling the sixty miles from London, changing cars at various stage-points *en route* as was done with horses in the old days. The Duke of Westminster owned land in Belgravia and Pimlico; possessed one of the largest yachts in the world and a huge country house with greenhouses full of orchids. The Dukes of Devonshire and Marlborough had palaces in the middle of the countryside, like royal domains complete with their own electricians, carpenters, their own night watchmen, dairymaids and wine specialists. Marlborough frequently imported the Blue Hungarian Band from London to play to his dinner guests, who were waited on by six-foot-tall footmen in maroon plush breeches, maroon coats, waistcoats with silver braid, silver-coloured stockings and silver-buckled shoes. His gamekeepers wore Irish green velvet coats with brass buttons and black billycock hats; and his lodge-keepers wore black coats, garters and top hats. He had his own cricket ground and employed a professional to instruct him in the art of the game.

During the season these noblemen and many more – the Derbys, Londonderrys, Roxburghes, Norfolks, Portlands and Northumberlands, the Lonsdales, Sutherlands and Ilchesters – moved into London and opened up their vast town houses, maintaining the same regal standards as in the country. The footmen wore powdered hair and the special livery of their house – for each house had its own colours. The hair was no mean achievement, for it had to be washed with soap, combed out and set in waves before applying the powder. It was then left to harden, like cement. The powder was a combination of violet dust and flour which the footmen mixed themselves.

Apart from the great houses, some of which were the size of hotels and employed from twenty-five to thirty-five servants, there were hundreds of ordinary houses with staffs numbering from ten to fifteen. All of them were geared to the function of entertaining: luncheons, garden parties, dinners and private dances galore. The Court contributed to the glitter with levees, presentations, state balls, while the sporting world staged such traditional events as Ascot, the Derby, Lords, Goodwood.

Food was taken seriously. Formal dinners ran to twelve courses, often beginning with caviar and turtle soup, followed by fillets of sole and *saumon au court bouillon,* reinforced by cutlets of snipe, saddle of lamb, ham in champagne, roast duck, and finally ending with sweets and *soufflés,* ices and savouries. Some hostesses allowed their chefs to run riot in the elaborate presentation of the food. At a dinner given by Lady Michelham at Strawberry Hill the entrées were illuminated by night-lights, and one course was made to resemble lighthouses, surrounded by ortolans to represent sea gulls, with surf made of white sauce breaking over them.

The London season glittered and glowed with so much vitality that it drew the rich and powerful and adventurous from all over the globe. 'London is no longer the capital of Britain,' pronounced *The Times* solemnly, 'but of the world.' Smoke-stained Victoria Station witnessed the arrival of Russian grand dukes, German princes, Spanish grandees, Austrian archduchesses; of shahs and pashas and sheiks and maharajas; of American industrialists, Central European financiers and Japanese potentates. The Diplomatic Corps contributed its huge embassies to the general festivity, and the Court provided unforgettable splendour with its series of levees, receptions and balls. The American Ambassador was fascinated by the Court functions.

The diplomatic ladies [he wrote to a friend] sit on a row of seats on one side of the throne room, the Duchesses on a row opposite. The King and Queen sit on a raised platform with the royal family. The Ambassadors come in first and bow and the King shakes hands with them. Then come the forty or more Ministers – no shake for them. In front of the King are a few officers in gaudy uniforms, some Indians of high rank (from India) and the court officials are all round about, with pages who hold up the Queen's train. Whenever the Queen and King move, two court officials back before them, one carrying a gold stick and the other a silver stick ...

The ladies to be presented come along. They curtsey to the King, then to the Queen, and disappear in the rooms farther on. The Ambassadors (all in gaudy uniforms but me) stand near the throne – stand through the whole performance. One night after an hour or two of ladies coming along and curtsying and disappearing, I whispered to the Spanish Ambassador, 'There must be five hundred of these ladies.' 'U-m,' said he, as he shifted his weight to the other foot, 'I'm sure there are five thousand' ...

At a levee, the King receives only gentlemen. Here they come in all kinds of uniforms. If you are not entitled to wear a uniform, you have a dark suit, knee breeches, and a funny little tin sword. I'm going to adopt the knee breeches part of it for good when I go home – golf breeches in the day time and knee breeches at night. You've no idea how nice and comfortable they are – though it is a devil of a lot of trouble to put 'em on. Of course every sort of man here but the American wears some sort of decorations around his neck or on his stomach, at these functions. For my part, I like it – here. The women sparkle with diamonds, the men strut; the King is a fine man with a big bass voice and he talks very well and is most agreeable; the Queen is very gracious; the royal ladies (Queen Victoria's daughters, chiefly) are nice; you see all the big Generals and all the big Admirals and the great folk of every sort – fine show. [13]

However, it was not necessary to be a king to provide spectacular settings in 1913. 'Fancy dress balls were the rage, and there was one almost every night,' wrote Prince Felix Yusupov, a handsome young Russian of fabulous wealth (destined to be the killer of Rasputin), who had been sent to Oxford University but spent most of his time in London. People who could afford it often paid four hundred pounds to Léon Bakst or Paul Poiret to design them a costume, while money gushed like a geyser to transform the Albert Hall into some exotic setting. The most memorable occasion of 1913 was the Versailles Ball held for charity at the Albert Hall in June. The *mise en scène* was a reception held by Louis XIV in 1680, the year of the marriage of the Dauphin.

I was to be Louis XIV [wrote Yusupov], and even went to Paris to have my outfit made. But, at the last minute, the costume struck me as altogether too ostentatious, so I passed it on to the Duke of Mecklenburg-Strelitz, and attended the ball not as the King of France but as the humblest of his subjects, a simple French sailor. The German Prince looked magnificent; gold brocade, precious stones and feathers galore. [14]

Louis XIV received sixteen sovereigns and their courts from Europe and the East. The part of Marie-Thérèse was played by the Countess of Dudley; Charles II by Captain Harry Lindsey; Catherine of Braganza by Lady March; the Papal Nuncio by Lord Alington; the Great Mogul by Baroness Goldschmidt. The Court of England was organized by Lady Paget; of Russia by Lady Maud Warrender; of Spain by the Duchess of Somerset; the Holy Roman Empire by Lady Drogheda; China by Lady Mond; Holland by Lady Downshire, etc. Anna Pavlova, the great Russian ballerina, danced a waltz and a minuet supported by the Russian ballet.

The King and Queen attended the ball, and although the journalists sent to cover the event did not think that the Albert Hall resembled Versailles very closely, they were enchanted by the beauty of Charles II's favourites, as depicted by Lady Curzon, Lady Lytton, Lady Ingestre and Lady Diana Manners. They were also impressed by the vast assembly of rank and wealth.

I can unhesitatingly affirm [wrote Mr Valentine Williams] that London has become the premier social capital of Europe. One has only to scan the newspapers and note the yearly increasing list of foreign notabilities who regularly figure in the events of the social season to realize the attraction London exercises on society abroad . . . The *bal masqué* was in its hey-day in Paris of the Second Empire when the City of Light was the social centre of the world. Is not London's rise to social pre-eminence among her sister capitals shown by the ever increasing vogue of these splendid costume fêtes, each one more magnificent than the last? [15]

Members of the older generation did not view things in such a rosy light. They loathed seeing London 'the centre of the world'. Society was being ruined by foreigners and millionaires. The salon was a thing of the past; wit and refinement and even conversation were disappearing from the English scene. 'The cultivation of the senses came in when the cultivation of the mind went out', wrote a lady, who signed herself 'A Hostess in Three Reigns', in the *Daily Mail* of 7 July. The present generation, she asserted, did not even remember the elegance and esprit of yesteryear 'which disappeared with the sudden crop of millionaires that shot up in a night in the golden soil of Australia and South Africa, in the nitrate plains of South America, in the rubber plantations of the Malay States, in the oil fields of Eastern Europe and the prairies of Canada.'

Complaints about the 'decay' of society went on continually throughout the year. However, the lamentations proffered by this particular lady had already been dealt with by the humorist Charles Jerningham, who pointed out with considerable wisdom, 'In these days of greatly increased luxury and the greatly increased cost of luxuries they who merely know how to spend money cannot for long compete with those who mainly know how to make it . . . Is it decay or merely change?' [16]

Some changes were accepted without demur. The fact that the doors of society were open to the great dancers and singers and musicians of the day – an innovation of the past five years – was no longer regarded as freakish or even daring. Mrs Hwfa Williams, a fashionable lady who lived at Coombe Springs, often entertained Caruso and the Australian singer, Nellie Melba. Mrs Williams named a pet crow after the famous soprano because it always insisted on joining in when the real Melba, who often entertained the Williams' guests, began to sing. One day the feathered Melba gave everyone a fright.

She flatly refused to speak or sing [wrote Mrs Williams], and we really did not know what to do. We decided to send for the doctor, when suddenly Melba hopped on to a chair and, as she gave out a piercingly shrill note, a large mouse came out of her beak. Some days afterwards my sister-in-law told the story to a friend who, as she thought, knew both Melbas. But she was mistaken. We had almost forgotten the incident, when one afternoon our butler announced Madame Melba. As I went to greet her Nellie burst into the room in a storm of rage. 'At last I have traced this monstrous story to its source!' she cried. 'I have been accused of many things before, but never, until now, of swallowing mice!' [17]

But it was really the wife of the best shot in England, the Marquess of Ripon, who led the way. Lady Ripon encouraged the great Russian impresario, Diaghilev, to bring to London the operas and ballets that transformed the taste of a generation. In 1913 Diaghilev produced three operas and took the capital by storm: *Boris Godunov* and *Khovanshchina* by Moussorgsky and *Ivan the Terrible* by Rimsky-Korsakov. Chaliapin sang the main role in *Boris Godunov* and over-night became the darling of society; his performance was described by contemporary papers as 'magnificent', 'superb', 'breath-taking'. He was entertained by Lady Ripon and Mrs Hwfa Williams, and fell in love with Lady Diana Manners.

The time-revered old Italian opera in its buskins and farthingales, its tights and its cap-doffing, had wearied an audience older than me [wrote Lady Diana]. Boxes at Covent Garden were hired for the season, but not for the music. The darkness hid many sleepers. Wagner nights were more musically alert, because only enthusiasts could stand them. Now came a blast to awaken the dead, a blaze of blinding gold, the Kremlin bells clanged and crashed, and Boris was there, a humble giant on his way to be crowned . . . I think he was pleased with me, for I was perhaps a little shield against the onset of what I then called 'rapacious women'. He would bow to me from the stage as he must have done to the Czar. He would bring flowers to the box when he was not singing, he encouraged me in amusing pranks, such as dressing as a peasant or a boyard's wife and singing in the chorus. Hearing him sing so near to me on the stage made the stalls pall and the box an anti-climax.[18]

That year Diaghilev also presented three new ballets in London: Florent Schmitt's *La Tragédie de Salome*, Debussy's *Jeux*, and Stravinsky's *Le Sacre du Printemps*. The last two ballets had been choreographed by Nijinsky. Although *Le Sacre du Printemps* had suffered a very rough reception in Paris, London received it with polite amazement. Lady Ripon entertained Nijinsky and Karsavina at Coombe Court, and the popularity of Britain's entente with Russia soared among the artistically inclined members of the Establishment.

When Diaghilev had visited London earlier in the year, he had engaged as a dancer a young English girl, Hilda Munnings. He later christened her Sokolova after the Russian ballerina. 'She made her name at a time when Diaghilev had the whole Maryinsky to choose from, when Fokine was *maître de ballet*, Karsavina and Nijinsky in their prime,' wrote Diaghilev's biographer. 'These English are fine dancers,' said the great Russian impresario, 'one day they will form a school of their own.' [19]

A spell of hot weather in the summer of 1913 revived the popularity of Hyde Park as a meeting place. Fashionable people cantered gently in Rotten Row; others strolled along the stretch between Achilles Statue and Grosvenor Gate; still others gossiped on the park benches.

Another thing very noticeable this summer [reported the *Daily Mail*] is the number of well-appointed carriages that one sees in the Park, and in the fashionable thoroughfares generally. Five or six years ago one saw far too many ramshackle and dilapidated turnouts. This year greater attention is paid to horses, carriages and liveries, and it is quite likely that ladies are beginning to realize that their smart toilettes are really not seen in motor cars, and for this purpose nothing is so effective as a landau or a barouche.[20]

The 'smart toilettes' cost the ladies of 1913 many a tedious hour. Make-up was still taboo, and the effort required to 'coax nature' was most exhausting. Hours were spent brushing hair, and as a white skin was regarded as the most essential attribute to beauty, more hours given to experiments with sour milk and fruit juice.

With the V-shaped corsage and blouse now in fashion [wrote a beauty expert smugly] the neck and throat should not show traces of sunburn. To keep the neck white is a simple enough matter. . . When taking the daily warm bath, dip a towel into hot water and lemon juice or borax, wring it out and wrap round the neck, keeping it on for a few minutes. Then rub the neck with the tip of the fingers until it is well massaged and finish by washing well with a soft brush and plenty of good soap. [21]

Clothes also demanded deep concentration. Although Paris set the trend it had not yet established itself as the tyrannical dictator of fashion. Ladies – and particularly duchesses who were a law unto themselves – simply got together with their dressmakers and improvised. They discussed materials and cuts and invented their own creations. 'We would have died,' said Lady Diana Cooper,* 'if we had met someone at a party wearing the same dress.' Lady Diana's mother, the Duchess of Rutland, was singularly independent.

I remember black tulle over moonlight blue [wrote Lady Diana] and flesh-pink satin stuck over with sequins or bunches of rosebuds, always the creation of some little dressmaker, never Paquin or Worth . . . The noble family tiara was worn back to front, holding up the Grecian handle of hair. Nothing was used for its true purpose. The diamond eighteen-inch-waistbelt that had sparkled at great London

* *Nee* Manners.

houses when the beautiful Duchesses of Devonshire and Rutland laced themselves mercilessly to achieve the smallest waist, was divided into two pieces and formed her shoulder straps. Nell Gwynn's Lely pearl necklace hung in a festoon between two sensational diamond drop ear-rings from her shoulder...[22]

Despite the absence of a fashion dictator, 1913 had a line of its own. Hats were very high and laden with birds or feathers. The young wore plumes that shot two feet in the air and swayed when they walked. Clothes were revolutionary. The wasp waist had disappeared; so had puffed shoulders and beribboned sleeves. Materials were soft and transparent; necklines almost as low by day as by night; and skirts long and straight and very tight. English ladies, much to the despair of French couturiers, made their own innovations. 'At the Ascot races,' reported *The Times* fashion writer, 'almost every dress seen in the paddock supported a train.'

The older generation was appalled by the low necks and skin-tight skirts. In *The Times* on 16 July an anonymous correspondent wrote scathingly of 'ladies' undress', likening the current fashion to a 'Bacchanal rage'.

It is no exaggeration to say that we are in the height of a revolution in feminine clothes, such as not seen since that other revolution gave sanction to the excesses of women in the Directoire and the Empire [the letter began]. Five years ago women still wore skirts and bodices which covered them, stockings thick enough not to show the colour of their skin and sufficient stays and petticoats to conceal the details of their persons. Nowadays women wear almost nothing under their gowns even in the day time.

Petticoats went some time back and were replaced by tights – or not replaced at all. The stockings are of such diaphanous silk as to embarrass the beholder who sees, even in the street, so much of them, and they are not covered by any but court shoes. So much for the foundation. Over this is worn a filmy sheath of half-transparent material, cut almost as low by day as by night, and with such slashings and liftings in the skirt as may fully display the leg half-way to the knee and which show every movement of the limbs – almost of the muscles...

It is interesting to note that the Bacchanal rage has fallen upon women at a time when much is in the melting-pot, at a time of world restlessness, of war abroad, of constitutional crisis at home, of social misery everywhere. It is difficult to see the connection between fashions and such things, or to say which is cause and what effect, or to determine how much our almost bare feet and quite bare arms and neck owe to Mr Asquith's indifference to stable government or to the anarchy in the political and artistic world. But it says a great deal for the length of road we have travelled that the old-fashioned people (perhaps there are none left) have not lifted up their voices in the Press to rebuke a generation which would have made their fathers gasp and stare and presently resort to prayer to avert a thunderbolt.

Although men's clothes were not so controversial as the ladies', they were nearly as much of a preoccupation. The punctiliousness promoted by Edward VII continued with George V. Gentlemen went to the City or the House of Commons in morning coats (which had tails), striped trousers and tall silk hats. Even eight-year-old boys were sent off to school in this outfit. The frock coat, which also had tails, was worn with trousers of the same colour and used for garden parties or weddings.

The dinner jacket was worn only on the most formal occasions, such as dining at home. Tails and a white tie were *de rigueur* for all dinner parties. The lounge suit (tailless) was regarded as a sports outfit and worn to racing events such as Goodwood. Tweed jackets and plus fours were worn in the country.

No 'gentleman' ever bought ready made hats or gloves or shirts or shoes or even handkerchiefs. All were made to his own taste and specification. Brown boots could not be worn with black suits. Straw hats and brown and white shoes could be sported at Goodwood, but grey frock coats and grey top hats were required for Ascot.

Indeed, what to wear and how to behave was so complicated that in July 1913, London University laid on a holiday course in etiquette for foreigners. Two hundred and fifty visitors from seventeen countries enrolled. Miss Violet Partington, one of the instructors, told reporters that the German students were the most argumentative.

One German girl, she said, was very surprised when told that she must make the first sign of recognition when meeting a man acquaintance on the street. 'I think it most immodest,' she said. 'The man always bows first in my country.'

Another German girl asked: 'Do women take off their hats when they go to afternoon tea as in Germany?'

'Never at afternoon tea, but you may for luncheon.'

'Should you take soup from the end of the spoon as in Germany?'

'No. You must take it from the middle.'

And a German boy asked: 'Is it polite to make a call after dinner?'

'It is very polite.'

'Should you leave your hat and stick in the hall when you pay a call or take them into the room with you?'

'Never leave your hat and stick in the hall. It is too familiar and suggests that you have the run of the house.'

'How absurd. A hat and stick is very uncomfortable in the drawing room.'

'Never mind. In England it is better to feel uncomfortable than to be thought presumptuous.'[23]

While foreigners were being schooled in deportment that July, the English themselves were whooping it up in no mean fashion. Eton beat Harrow at Lords by nine wickets; and on the Saturday night after the match boys from both schools accompanied by parents, sisters, cousins and friends invaded the Imperial Services Exhibition at Earl's Court and had what the press described as 'a joy night'. They swept across the huge hall, often with arms linked, shouting 'E-ton' or 'Har-row'.

The boys had light or dark blue bands around their hats [wrote the *Daily Mail*], while the girls had coloured quills in their hair or in their dresses. One party of six girls and a dozen boys commandeered the moving stairway. Another group tried to capture it with the result that many silk hats were battered and many skirts torn.

Then a group of young girls led a party of boys a steeplechase over a five-foot gate barring the bridge over the lake. The girls, despite narrow skirts, vaulted the gate with as much agility as their brothers. Girls also led a furious onslaught on the china at the Breaking Up and Happy Home Booth.

The giant roundabout with its gaily coloured ostriches was packed, each ostrich being ridden by five boys and girls, some standing on the heads of the birds shouting, 'E-ton' or 'Har-row'. From the roundabout to the mountain railway, the rolling tubs, the joy wheel, the water shoot, the shooting gallery went the crowds. Many people were caught up in the circles of boys and girls singing: Here we go round the mulberry bush.[24]

Meanwhile Europe hovered on the brink of war. The Balkans had ignited in 1912 when Bulgaria, Serbia, Montenegro and Greece had launched a joint attack on Turkey to wrest away the latter's European possessions. The war continued intermittently throughout the first seven months of 1913. Would Austria intervene to prevent her deadly rival, Serbia, from acquiring too much territory? Or would Russia decide that the moment had arrived to make a bid for the Turkish straits? 'The details,' wrote Sir Edward Grey, the British Foreign Secretary, 'with which we dealt were insignificant – in themselves mere sparks; but we were sitting on a powder magazine.' [25]

In order to prevent a world conflagration Sir Edward Grey called a Conference of Ambassadors, representing the four great continental powers, France, Germany, Russia and Austria, which met every day at the British Foreign Office under Grey's chairmanship. The object was to iron out disagreements among themselves, and to form a joint policy which they could impose on the Balkans. The meetings were very informal because three of the ambassadors – and the three most important – were related to one another. Prince Lichnowsky of Germany and Count Benckendorff of Russia were first cousins, while Count Mensdorff of Austria-Hungary was related to Benckendorff by marriage.

For many weeks the press and parliament speculated on the likelihood of the war spreading. In April, Mr H. G. Wells came out against military conscription for Britain; not because he was a Socialist, he said, but because if a war broke out involving the great powers of Europe, he was convinced that only small, mobile units would be used. 'The large amateur army,' he declared, 'is a thing of the past.' [26]

Sir Edward Grey often found the daily sessions numbing. He had a passion for fishing and bird-watching and hated being forced to spend so much time in London. The fact that he was a country gentleman and an amateur endeared him to the British public, although foreigners often found his character puzzling. In the middle of April he turned over the chairmanship of the conference for a few days to Sir Arthur Nicolson, head of the Foreign Office.

There is some prospect of rain and if so the sport will be very good [he wrote from the country]. It seems almost too much to expect that everything including the Balkan crises and salmon should go well simultaneously, but things seem to prosper so well in my absence that it would not be in the public interest for me to curtail it. I am in rude health with an appetite for everything except office work.[27]

Foreigners could not believe that Sir Edward Grey's character was as simple as it seemed. The Austro-Hungarian military attaché suspected him of scheming behind their backs. Even Prince Lichnowsky, one of the most popular ambassadors in London, imagined that he had something to hide and wrote ironically, 'I have just had an interview with Sir Edward Grey in which we discussed the situation fully. He regards it with his usual imperturbability and ice calm. He even found time to tell me all about the fish he caught on his holiday.' [28]

That same April an armistice was signed between Turkey and the aggressor states, and the delegates from all the countries involved took their seats in St James's Palace to work out the peace terms. The Turks began to renegue on the conditions they had accepted, and the Balkan allies began to bicker among themselves. Sir Edward Grey became impatient. The aspirations of the half-savage little states with their complicated demands for transfers of population and outlets to the sea could be very trying. On 25 May he summoned the delegates to his room at the Foreign Office and tried to explain the urgent necessity of signing peace.

The delegates of Serbia, Bulgaria, Greece, Montenegro and Turkey, somewhat sheepish in their frock coats, were ranged one by one upon the carpet [wrote Harold Nicolson, whose father, Sir Arthur Nicolson, was present at the meeting]. Sir Edward Grey advanced towards them and fixed them with his eagle eye; he pointed towards them with an outstretched and imperative finger: he summoned to his assistance the total resources of his Wykhamist French. '*Ou signer,*' he shouted at them, '*ou partir.*' The Treaty of London was signed between Turkey and the Balkan states on 30th May. [29]

In 1913 Sir Edward Grey was lucky, for both the Kaiser and the Czar were determined to prevent a European war. Although a second Balkan war broke out in June – this time between two of the victors, Bulgaria and Serbia, in a quarrel over the spoils – it lasted less than two months and Europe settled down once more to an uneasy peace.

At the height of the season, an event occurred which knocked the Balkan wars off the front page, and riveted the attention of the world. At the famous Derby, run at Epsom Downs in June, thirty-five-year-old Miss Emily Davison ran on to the track at Tattenham Corner, in the face of thundering hooves: she grabbed the reins of the King's horse, bringing down the horse and jockey. She was injured so badly that she never regained consciousness and died a few days later.

Miss Davison was a militant suffragette. She had taken a Bachelor of Arts degree at London University and a degree in English at Oxford. She had campaigned for votes for women for seven years. Although up until now she had done nothing more violent than set fire to a letter box, and on another occasion hidden herself in the House of Commons to demonstrate in the gallery, she had been imprisoned several times and forcibly fed. Indeed, in order to escape this ordeal she had tried to kill herself by throwing herself headlong from one of the upper galleries of the prison, but only sustained cruel injuries. On another occasion, when she had barricaded her cell against the prison doctors, a hose pipe was turned on her from the window, and she was nearly drowned in icy water while workmen were breaking her cell door.

From that time onwards, Miss Davison was convinced that England would not grant women their rights unless one of them made a dramatic sacrifice that caught the attention of the world. Miss Davison's fantastically brave act certainly captured global headlines, although in England the upper class was furiously indignant. Queen Mary referred to her in her diary as 'that horrid woman' and lamented the fact that the jockey had been knocked about.

How they execrated Emily Davison! [wrote the famous music composer, Dame Ethel Smyth] Some critics actually remarked, 'Such bad manners to the King!' apparently not grasping that the King's horse would call attention as no other animal could to the strange fact that, for the sake of women in general, one particular woman was ready to let herself be trampled to death. Again others said, 'Why, she might have killed the jockey!' though after all, this one must have seen what was coming, and jockeys are trained to fall. 'Pure self-advertisement,' cried the specially foolish, 'although to seek a horrible death is a form of it not likely to be widely imitated!'[30]

The suffragettes organized a huge funeral procession to do her honour.

The call to women [wrote Sylvia Pankhurst], to come garbed in black carrying purple irises, in purple with crimson peonies, in white bearing laurel wreaths [the Suffragette colours] received a response from thousands who gathered from all parts of the country. Graduates and clergy marched in their robes, suffragette societies, trade unionists from the East End, unattached people. The streets were densely lined by silent respectful crowds. The great public responded to the appeal of a life deliberately given for an impersonal end. The police had issued a notice which was virtually a prohibition of the procession, but at the same time constables were enjoined to reverent conduct . . .[31]

Despite the fact that thousands of intelligent people in England favoured votes for women, the Liberal government, headed by Mr Asquith, was adamant. 'Would our standard in manners,' he superciliously asked the House of Commons, '. . . and in manners I include the old fashioned virtues of chivalry, courtesy, and all the reciprocal dependence and reliance of the two sexes – would that standard be raised and refined if women were politically enfranchised?' [32]

Mr Asquith's sword was unsheathed against a slender, rather beautiful woman in her sixties, Mrs Emmeline Pankhurst. Mrs Pankhurst had spent a lifetime doing social work and was convinced that the horrifying, 'sweated labour' conditions under which many women worked would not be alleviated until they got the vote. They were not only paid far less than men, making it impossible for them to save money for their old age, but even married women often found themselves penniless when their husbands died, as widows were rarely provided for by pensions.

Mrs Pankhurst formed the Women's Political and Social Union in conjunction with her two daughters, Christabel and Sylvia, in 1903. Their hopes soared when the Liberal government was elected in 1906, but Mr Asquith's implacable opposition proved decisive. Although a majority of the House of

London Theatre

A scene from *Eightpence a Mile*, the revue at the Alhambra Theatre, with costumes and sets by Paul Poiret.

Gladys Cooper, of Drury Lane Theatre, who
followed the fashion for expensive jewellery.
The diadem she is wearing contains
one of the largest existing diamonds.

Two sophisticated versions of the latest dances, from *The Girl on the Film* at the
Gaiety Theatre. M. Oy-Ra and Miss Dorma Leigh (*left*) give a new twist to the tango,
while Mr George Grossmith and Miss Kitty Mason do the Maxixe.

A sketch from the revue, *Keep Smiling*, celebrating the recovery in Rome in
November of the *Mona Lisa*, which had been stolen from the Louvre in 1911.

'Mock heroics, Mr Bernard Shaw's realism during a rehearsal [of *Androcles and the
Lion*] gives Mr Granville Barker anxiety for the safety of Lavinia, his wife.'
Photograph by Alvin Langdon Coburn.

'The most improper opera in existence', Richard Strauss's *Der Rosenkavalier*, finally received its first performance in London in January. The Marschallin and her young lover, Oktavian were played by Eva van der Osten and Margarete Siems, who had created the rôles in Dresden.

Below. Serge Diaghilev, impresario and genius of the Russian Ballet.

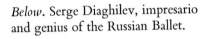

Left. Chaliapin as Boris. The Russian bass, who was brought to London by Diaghilev, captivated musical public and society. A signed photograph dedicated to Lady Diana Manners.

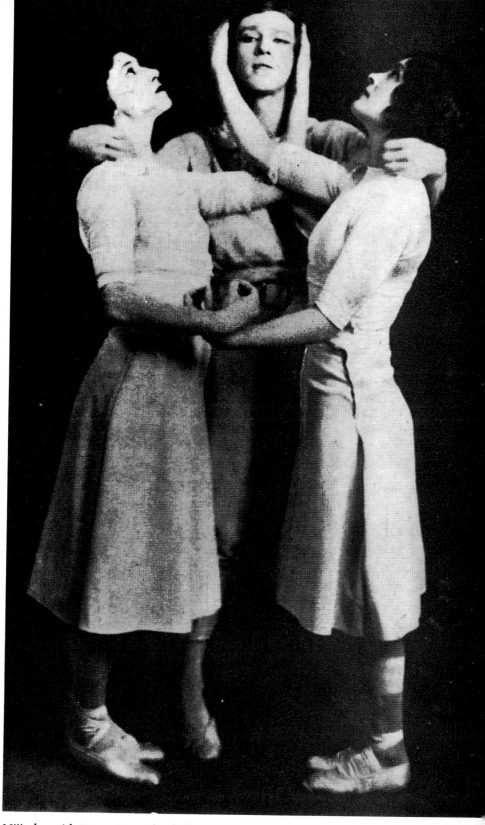

Nijinsky with Karsavina and Schollas in a scene from *Jeux*,
Nijinsky's ballet to Debussy's music.

'Crowning glories: the head-dress in its latest shapes', which include 'the Nun',
a 'cap of Mail', a 'Dutch cap' and an 'Eastern head-dress'.

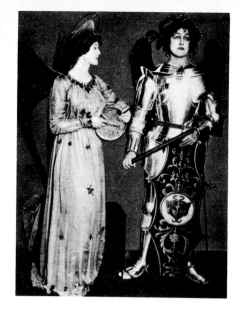

Four of the guests at the ball of living paintings at the Albert Hall: Mrs Lavery as Flora (after Botticelli's *La Primavera*); Mrs Asquith as an Angel (after Fra Angelico) and Miss Penant as St Michael (after Ghirlandaio); and Mrs Dickinson as an Angel (after Melozzo).

Louis XIV and Queen Marie-Thérèse (the Duke of Mecklenburg-Strelitz and the Countess of Dudley) at the great 'Versailles' ball.

Right. Sarah Bernhardt as Racine's 'Phèdre' in a charity performance at the London Coliseum; 'she had rarely played with more passion and fire.' *Below*. A picture taken at the farewell banquet in London for J. Forbes-Robertson and F. R. Benson, which shows (left to right) Sir Herbert Beerbohm-Tree, Sir Squire Bancroft, Sir Sidney Lee, Sir J. Forbes-Robertson and Mr F. R. Benson (seated). 'With the exception of Sir Sidney Lee, President of the English Shakespeare Society, all the gentlemen are England's finest interpreters of Shakespearean roles.'

Commons favoured female suffrage, the Prime Minister twisted and turned, blocking every private amendment by fair means or foul. During this period the women were not yet 'militant', but becoming increasingly aggressive. They sent deputations to Parliament, rang dinner bells at political meetings, heckled and shouted and created disturbances in the House of Commons gallery. Occasionally they broke windows. For these misdemeanors they received anything from six weeks' to several months' imprisonment – and in those days imprisonment meant solitary confinement.

In 1909 Mrs Leigh, who had demonstrated against Mr Asquith's meeting in Manchester – climbing on to a roof and throwing slates on to the hood of the car below – was sent to prison for four months. When she was placed in the cell she broke her window and was then sent to the dark, cold punishment cell. 'Her hands were handcuffed, behind her during the day, and at night in front of her body *with the palms out*,' wrote Mrs Pankhurst. [33] When she refused to eat, a battalion of wardresses and doctors entered her cell, pinned her on to the bed, and forcibly fed her by stuffing a tube up her nostrils, causing her excruciating pain.

The treatment meted out to women, coupled with allegations by politicians that there was no 'popular national movement' behind the suffrage leaders, determined Mrs Pankhurst to adopt more aggressive tactics. Thus, from the end of 1911 onwards, militancy was the watch-word. Property was the target; it was attacked in many different forms but extreme care was taken not to endanger human life.

The activities of the militant suffragettes kept all England agog in 1913. In January and February shop windows in the West End of London were smashed by hammers which women carried in their muffs; golf course greens at Sandwich and Pontypool were destroyed by acid; pillar boxes were burned by inflammable chemicals; telegraph and telephone wires were cut; two orchid houses at Kew were broken into; pungent snuff was posted to Members of Parliament; windows on Victoria Street were smashed by young ladies equipped with powerful catapults riding on buses; a house being built for Mr Lloyd George at Walton-on-Heath was partially destroyed by fire. In March two railway stations on the Great Western were burned down and pictures damaged in the Manchester Art Gallery. In April and May an empty train was set alight at Teddington; two empty houses were burnt; a bomb was found under the Bishop's Throne at St Paul's; a valuable Pekinese dog was poisoned. Then came the Derby sensation.

As forcible feeding had been denounced by the medical profession and the whole of the clergy as physically dangerous and morally degrading the Cat and Mouse Bill was passed in 1913 to break the spirit of the suffragettes. Those who resorted to hunger strikes were released upon the verge of death and allowed to go home; once they had recovered they were re-arrested to serve the remainder of their sentence. This Act, combined with a final legislative disappointment, when the Speaker ruled a suffrage amendment out of order, increased militancy all over England.

In 1913 the diehard opponents of woman suffrage both in the Conservative and Liberal parties voiced unchanging sentiments. 'If by any chance,' Lord Rothschild told a City Conservative meeting, 'this ill-fated measure, with woman suffrage, became law the electors of the City of London would be mainly charwomen, who would probably send to Parliament members who were not at all qualified to represent the interests of the finance and commerce of this great Empire.' [34]

The 'great Empire' was the note struck again and again in Parliamentary debates; women simply were not equipped to cope with an Empire. 'It would make Britain a laughing stock among nations,' said Lord Curzon. Occasionally other arguments were used: women should not have the vote because (a) they did not fight in wars; (b) they did not work in coal mines; (c) they might vote as a sex and wrest all power from the hands of the men by electing a wholly female House of Commons; (d) they had intuition but no ability to reason; (e) they were radical by nature and the only party that would benefit would be the Labour Party, or perhaps the Communist Party. Mr Asquith did not think 'our legislation' would be more 'respected' or 'our social and domestic life' more 'enriched' if women had the vote; while the famous barrister, F. E. Smith, said bluntly: 'I venture to say that the total sum of human happiness, knowledge and achievement would remain unaffected if ... Sappho had never sung, Joan of Arc had never fought, Siddons had never played and if George Eliot had never written.' [35]

Many ladies of high social position fought for the suffragettes. Lady Constance Lytton, the sister of the Earl of Lytton, was a militant supporter; so was Lady Sybil Smith, the daughter of the Earl of Antrim. The Duchess of Bedford, the owner of Prince's Skating Rink, refused to pay tax in protest against forcible feeding. And although the Duchess of Marlborough was not a member of the movement, she lent her house to women trade unionists to alleviate the conditions under which women worked.

The Duchess's American mother, Mrs Oliver Belmont, who paid a visit to her daughter at the end of April, was less equivocal. She gave an interview to the press saying that she 'would not spend one cent in England'. She would cut her stay as short as possible because of the disgusting way the British were treating the suffragettes. When reporters asked her how she would avoid paying for the Louis XVI suite of rooms she had engaged at the London Ritz she replied:

Of course I shall have to spend money. How ridiculous of you to pay any attention to that remark of mine. How I hate and loathe your brutal treatment of your women – your forcible feeding torture in the prisons; the shameful ill-treatment by mobs! How can Englishmen look on callously and not lift one finger to protest? We in America are disgusted with you! Mrs Pankhurst is one of the greatest women of the age. You will probably treat her as you treated Joan of Arc, and then fifty years hence erect statues to her illustrious memory. I don't understand how you can tolerate such a tyrannical government as you have. [36]

While the sensational death of Emily Davison at the Derby drew clucks of disapproval from fashionable circles, Dame Ethel Smyth emphasized the grandeur of the sacrifice.

The common herd [she wrote] will always have difficulty in detecting the principle that lies behind an outrageous action, but sometimes unexpected individuals will. The jockey himself gauged the super-human courage of that woman and understood why she acted as she did, for he came to Mrs Pankhurst's funeral [many years later] with a little wreath that bore the inscription: 'To do honour to the memory of Mrs Pankhurst and Miss Emily Davison'.[37]

Another event that titillated the political and social world from March to June was the Marconi scandal. Ugly rumours that Cabinet ministers had been gambling in Marconi shares (the British Marconi Company had signed the contract with the government to erect wireless stations throughout the British Empire) had been in circulation for some months. Mr Rufus Isaacs, the Attorney General, and Mr Lloyd George, the Chancellor of the Exchequer, had been accused on the floor of the House of 'disgraceful, scandalous gambling in these shares' but had denied it categorically.

In the spring of 1913, the Postmaster General sued the French paper *Le Matin* for libel. Mr Rufus Isaacs joined him. When the case was heard in March, Isaacs disclosed that he and Lloyd George and Lord Murray, the Liberal Chief Whip, had bought shares in the *American* Company which, although a subsidiary of the British Company, did not stand to benefit by the contract. 'Lamentable conduct,' Prime Minister Asquith told the King, 'and so difficult to defend.'

The House of Commons went into an uproar, claiming that the Cabinet

Ministers had attempted to deceive the House by denying that they had gambled in *British* Marconi shares and admitting that they had bought *American* shares. A select committee was appointed to investigate the matter; and one of the highlights of the drama came when Mr Winston Churchill was named as being involved in the share dealing. He was summoned before the committee and arrived quivering with rage. Thumping the table and almost shouting he denounced as insulting 'the charge that, having had dealings in Marconi shares, I sat silent while my friends came forward and voluntarily disclosed their exact position – that I sat silent while they were subjected to gross ill-usage and covered with every species of calumny and insult – that all the time I skulked in the background, keeping my guilty knowledge to myself and desiring to conceal it from your Committee.'

The Chairman tried to smooth him down, insisting that he had been called merely to allow him an opportunity of clearing his name. Churchill refused to be placated and proffered his denial with the force of a cyclone, adding: 'And if at any time anyone has said so, then he is a liar and slanderer! And if anyone has repeated it, and has no evidence, the only difference between that person and the liar and slanderer is that he is a coward as well!' He then snapped, 'May I now assume my examination is finished?' [38]

The Select Committee reported on 13 June; and reported on strictly party lines. The Liberal majority gave Lloyd George and Mr Rufus Isaacs a complete vindication. The Conservative minority criticized the handling of the share issue and found 'grave impropriety' in the conduct of Lloyd George and Isaacs. The Chairman compromised, saying that it was a pity the men had ever bought the shares in the first place, and an even greater pity that they had not made a clean breast of it to the House in October.

Not long after the end of this affair, Mr Asquith named Rufus Isaacs to fill the post of Lord Chief Justice. Rudyard Kipling did not allow the appointment to pass unnoticed and penned one of the most savage political diatribes of his career, which began with the words:

> Whence comest thou Gehazi
> So reverend to behold
> In scarlet and in ermine
> And chain of England's gold?

The verse compared Isaacs to Gehazi, the servant of the prophet Elisha, who ran after Naaman and by false pretences 'extracted somewhat of him' – for which the prophet struck him with leprosy.

Thou mirror of uprightness
What ails thee at thy vows?
What means the risen whiteness
of the skin between thy brows?[39]

Speculation about the Marconi scandal, suffragette sensations and ladies' 'undress' were interlarded with more mundane gossip. That summer people also talked about the staggering price of forty-one thousand pounds paid for Romney's portrait of Anne, Lady de la Pole; the penal fine of two pounds imposed on a woman taxi-driver, Alice Neville, for driving at twenty-one miles an hour in a ten-mile-an-hour limit at Storrington, Surrey; the new novel *Sons and Lovers* by D. H. Lawrence; the record gate of ten thousand at the Lawn Tennis Championships at Wimbledon. Mr A. F. Wilding, the New Zealand holder, beat his American opponent, Mr M. E. McLoughlin 8–6, 6–3, 10–8. The ladies' singles ended in a walk-over for Mrs Lambert Chambers of England as her opponent, Mrs D. R. Larcombe, was forced to retire due to an accident to one of her eyes. It was Mrs Chambers' seventh win since 1903.

People talked about the Japanese contention that the English did not know how to make tea; the pigeon race from Big Ben to the respective constituencies of two MPs; the man who called at Mr Winston Churchill's residence, Admiralty House, pretending to be a laundryman, and made off with the family washing; the headmaster of the Market Boswell Grammar School who said: 'Boys of today lack initiative . . . Everything must be served up to them in an interesting, pleasant fashion'; the parliamentary delegation that called on Prime Minister Asquith in August to discuss the proposed Channel Tunnel between England and France. Nearly one hundred members of Parliament of all parties signed a paper urging the Prime Minister to withdraw the veto placed on the construction of the tunnel, which actually had been begun a few weeks earlier, and was being built at a cost of sixteen million pounds. The Government had prohibited the continuation for fear it might be a source of invasion from the continent. The progress of flying, the deputation argued, had altered strategic considerations; but the Government refused to reverse its decision.

People also talked about the new plays which opened in London in September: *Androcles and the Lion* by George Bernard Shaw and *The Adored One* by James Barrie. Neither received good reviews. Shaw's mixture of seriousness and farce annoyed his first-night audience. 'Was ever beast so fortunate?' wrote *The Times*. 'We do not mean in getting the thorn pulled out of his paw by Androcles; we mean in being the one character in the whole range of Shavian drama who never talks.' [40] As for Barrie, 'The house was *not* amused,' reported *The Times*, 'and the curtain fell to the accompaniment of groans which drowned the cheers.' [41]

People talked about the farewell performance of the great Russian ballerina Pavlova at the Covent Garden Opera House in October before leaving on a world tour. She danced in *Giselle*, which *The Times* declared a fitting choice, as 'she has bewitched us too . . . and we shall never be ourselves again till she comes back to us once more.' That same month the sixty-eight-year-old Madame Sarah Bernhardt appeared in a charity performance at the London Coliseum organized by the Earl of Lonsdale. She gave an extract from Racine's *Phèdre* which, said *The Times*, 'she has rarely played with more passion and fire.'

People talked about the interest in 'the occult' revealed by the autumn book list. Over twelve thousand new titles were published in Britain in 1913. Those which attracted the greatest attention in the non-fiction field dealt with mysticism in varying forms. Some of the titles were: *Mysticism in English Literature* by Caroline Spurgeon; *Ibsen, Poet, Mystic and Moralist* by H. Ross; *Native Mysticism* by the Bishop of Tasmania; *A Handbook of Mystical Theology* by D. H. S. Nicholson; *Jewish Mysticism* by J. Abelson; *The Mystical Personality of the Church* by Mr De Barry.

In November and December people talked about the sale by the Duke of Bedford of his Covent Garden estate of twenty-six acres to Mr H. Mallaby-Deeley, M.P., for two million seven hundred and fifty thousand pounds; the announcement by Sir Edward Shackleton that he intended to lead a new Antarctic Expedition in 1914; the sale of the Earl of Crawford's collection of British postage stamps for twenty thousand pounds; the Rede lecture delivered by Lord Curzon of Kedleston on the subject of 'Eloquence'; the failure of the Duke of Westminster's attempt to raise a hundred thousand pounds to select and train competitors for the Olympic Games to be held in Berlin in 1916. The sum subscribed was less than eleven thousand pounds of which only five thousand pounds was promised unconditionally. The effort was criticized as 'tending to encourage a limited and over-specialized athleticism'.

And people talked and talked about the tango. This dance was a novelty in the spring, a craze in the summer, an obsession in the autumn, all of which drew rebukes from the pulpit. What *was* the world coming to? Critics re-ferred to 'the contortions of this immodest dance', but the younger generation refused to listen. Hostesses gave tango 'at homes'. The hotels followed suit, the Trocadero breaking new ground with tango suppers. *The Times* correspondence column frequently printed a *cri de coeur*. 'My grandmother has often told me of the shock she experienced on first beholding the polka,' wrote 'A Peeress', somewhat enigmatically, on 20 May, 'but I wonder what she would have said had she been asked to introduce a well-brought-up girl of eighteen to the . . . horrors of American and South American negroid origin . . .'

The Times did not deign to pronounce on the controversy until 10 November. Then it came down on the side of rebellion.

The Tango [it lectured] has clearly made a stir in the dancing world comparable only to the polka and the waltz. M. Richepin [a member of the French Academy] has recently warned us not to despise the Tango for its lowly origin . . . It may be added that by now reputable teachers of dancing have eliminated from the Tango any traces of vulgarity which it once possessed and have thus done much to legiti-mize its success. The rage for the Tango is part of our new sense of pageantry . . . a revival of Royal ceremonial . . . Feminine apparel has a note of exotic fantasy, while the staid yellow and brown brick of our streets is being replaced by Baby-lonian palaces with majestic columns.

So the tango was respectable after all; and people could reserve their energies for more important altercations.

Less reconcilable were the political differences between Conservatives and Liberals. Although income tax was not raised by Mr Lloyd George in 1913 and remained at approximately one shilling in the pound, the fifteen per cent duty on estates valued at over a million pounds was regarded by Conservative landowners as scandalous. Even more resented was the Parliament Act of 1911 which had stripped the Tory-dominated House of Lords of its right to veto. And in the autumn came the Irish Home Rule Bill which, Tories declared passionately, would lead to civil war, for the Protestant north of Ireland was determined not to fall under the domination of the Catholic south.

Mr Page was amazed at the acrimony he found.

A Tory Lady [he wrote to President Wilson in October] told me with tears in her eyes that she could no longer invite her liberal friends to her house: 'I have lost them – they are robbing us, you know.' I made the mistake of saying a word in praise of Sir Edward Grey to a Duke. 'Yes, yes, no doubt an able man; but you must understand, sir, that I don't train with that gang.' A bishop explained to me at elaborate length why the very monarchy is doomed unless something befalls Lloyd George and his programme. Every dinner party is made up with strict reference to the party politics of the guests. Sometimes you imagine you see something like civil war; and money is flowing out of the kingdom into Canada in the greatest volume ever known and I am told that a number of families are investing their fortunes in African lands.

To his brother Page wrote: '. . . all the Cabinet are all the time going about making speeches on Ireland. They talk to me about it ."What would you do?" "Send 'em all to the United States", says I. "No, no." They have had the Irish question three hundred years and they wouldn't be happy without it.' [42]

Like many others in the rebellious England of 1913, Mr Page was fascinated by novelty. But what was novel to him was not the new but the old.

You've no idea [he wrote] how much time and money they spend on shooting. The King has been shooting most of the time for three months. He's said to be a very good shot. He has sent me, on different occasions, grouse, a haunch of venison, and pheasants.

But except on these occasions, you never think about the King. The people go about their business as if he didn't exist, of course. They begin work much later than we do. You'll not find any of the shops open till about ten o'clock. The sun doesn't shine except once in a while and you don't know it's daylight till about ten. You know the House of Commons has night sessions always. Nobody is in the Government offices, except clerks and secretaries, till the afternoon. We dine at eight, and when we have a big dinner, at eight thirty.

Except that part of life which is ministered to in mechanical ways, they resist conveniences. They don't really like bathrooms yet. They prefer great tin tubs, and they use bowls and pitchers when a bathroom is next door. The telephone – Lord deliver us! – I've given it up. They know nothing about it. (It is a government concern, but so are the telegraph and the post office, and they are remarkably swift.) You can't buy a newspaper on the street, except in the afternoon. Cigar-stores are as scarce as hen's teeth. Barbershops are all 'hairdressers' – dirty and wretched beyond description. You can't get a decent pen; their newspapers are as big as table-cloths. In this aquarium in which we live (it rains every day) they have only three vegetables and two of them are cabbages. They grow all kinds of fruit in hot-houses, and (I can't explain this) good land in admirable cultivation thirty miles from London sells for about half what good corn land in Iowa brings. Lloyd George has scared the landowners to death.[43]

Meanwhile the struggle between the old and the new was at its fiercest in the international sphere. Established, powerful Britain was being challenged in her role as mistress of the seas by a vigorous, coldly ambitious Germany;

while the United States, another young giant, watched passively, confident that in due course the sceptre would pass automatically into her own hands. 'What are we to do with this England?' wrote Mr Page to President Woodrow Wilson in October 1913, 'when economic forces unmistakably put the leadership of the race in our hands?'

London, however, was not concerned with American pretensions. The naval race with Germany absorbed the attention of Whitehall, and finally caused sharp differences between members of the British Cabinet. Shrouded from public view, a tense battle of wills was taking place between Winston Churchill, First Lord of the Admiralty, who wanted money for more ships, and Lloyd George, Chancellor of the Exchequer, who wanted money for social services. There was not enough for both. For two years Churchill had been urging Germany to agree to limitation, suggesting that both countries take 'a naval holiday'. But Berlin's repeated refusals left Churchill no choice but expansion. His naval estimate for 1911–12 had been forty-three million pounds; for 1912–13, forty-four million pounds. Now he was asking for fifty-one million pounds.

At a Cabinet meeting on 16 December 1913, Churchill pushed a note across the table to Lloyd George. 'I consider that you are going back on your word; trying to drive me out after we have settled, and you promised to support the estimates.' To which Lloyd George retaliated: 'I agreed to the figure for this year and I stood by it and *carried it*, much to the disappointment of my economical friends. But I told you distinctly I would press for a reduction of new programme with a view to 1915 and I think quite respectfully you are unnecessarily stubborn. It is only a question of six months' postponement of laying down. That cannot endanger our safety.' 'No,' retorted Churchill. 'You said you would *support* the estimates. The estimates included the new programme.' [44]

Finally Asquith intervened and Churchill got his way. But before the struggle ended, Lloyd George did all he could to cut the ground from under Churchill's feet. On the last day of 1913 he prepared an interview, which appeared in the *Daily Chronicle* on 1 January, castigating an increase in armaments as pure 'folly'. The prospects for the world, he said, had seldom been more peaceful. There was scarcely a cloud on the horizon. 'Never', he insisted, 'has the sky been more perfectly blue.'

TWO

BERLIN

When the Kaiser strode into the royal box of the Berlin Opera House on the night of 27 January for the gala in honour of his fifty-fourth birthday, he received an emotional ovation. 1913 was 'a Hohenzollern year'; not only did it mark the centenary of the Battle of Leipzig, at which Prussia, Russia and Austria had inflicted a decisive defeat on Napoleon's army, but the twenty-fifth anniversary of the Kaiser's accession to the throne.

William II had taken great pains to provide the audience with entertainment which would do credit to a remarkable year. He loved music and knew a great deal about it – although his dogmatic views often offended intellectuals and caused secret derision. He did not like Wagner 'because he was too noisy'; nor Strauss 'because he was too unmelodious'. He liked Bach and Handel, Gluck and Weber. He often strode over to the Opera House and conducted rehearsals himself. He would seat himself at a table in the stalls with an imposing array of pencils in front of him. Whenever he had a suggestion, an aide standing beside him would raise his hand and the performance would stop. Sometimes he made humorous comments from the darkness. When *La Prophète* was in rehearsal and the heroine, Fräulein Hempel, candle in hand, was about to seat herself next to a large cask, the imperial voice boomed out: 'Fräulein Hempel, it is obvious you have not had a military training or you wouldn't take a light so near a barrel of gunpowder!' [1]

For the gala performance in January the Kaiser had waved aside classical opera and outlined a two-act *Lustspiel*, inspired and executed under his personal direction. The first part consisted of folk songs and dances from Corfu, the island which he visited every year and where he owned the Achilleion Palace, originally built by Elizabeth of Austria. The second part reflected William's passion for archeology, for the setting was the Gorgon Temple, excavated at Paleopolis in 1911. The score was based on fragments of ancient Greek music and the story written by the Kaiser's favourite play-wright, Josef Lauff. Lauff pleased the Kaiser because he was always ready to adapt himself to the imperial will. A few years earlier he had produced a play entitled *Frederick of the Iron Tooth*, which dealt with the Elector of Brandenburg, the Kaiser's ancestor. In order to liven things up, he had intro-duced a love theme, but William II had struck out the episode with the comment: 'A courtesan has no place in a Hohenzollern drama.' [2]

In 1913 Lauff did not commit a *faux pas* of this sort; and although the evening was not exciting, the critics were generous. In between the acts the Kaiser held a Cercle in the foyer, his aides-de-camp singling out worthy subjects and leading them to him. Although mistresses were taboo for Hohenzollern kings, the Kaiser apparently was in a flirtatious mood. Baron Beyens, the Belgian military attaché, was impressed by his attentions to the ladies. He kissed their hands, looked rapturously into their faces, flattered and soothed them and sent them back to their seats with beatific smiles on their faces.

As he received the homage of his people that night, William II seemed the very embodiment of majesty and might. His white uniform glittering with gold, his erect carriage, his finely chiselled features, even his provocative upturned moustaches, gave an impression of superb self-confidence. Yet this was far from the truth. He was deeply perturbed lest the Balkan wars lead to a world conflagration. Inside the breast glittering with decorations was a gnawing anxiety which frequently broke into hysteria. Poincaré's victory in the French presidential election depressed him, and he told people darkly that France and Russia and England were plotting to destroy him. 'From the beginning of 1913', wrote the Chancellor, Herr von Bethmann-Hollweg, 'he spoke to me of the coalition which, like that of Kaunitz, was forming against us and which would fall on us.' [3]

Although William II loved to pose as a war lord, war was not what he wanted. He wanted the acclamation that power bestows, not the dangers and anxieties. But his sights were limitless, for the possession of the greatest army in the world was not sufficient; he had to build a navy as well. And when Britain retaliated by forming an *entente* with Russia and France, he promptly accused her of jealousy and ill-will. In January 1913, with Austria threaten-ing to attack Serbia, and Germany pledged to defend Austria; with Russia itching to intervene and France pledged to support Russia, the situation looked as black as possible. The Kaiser seized upon the fact that although Britain was part of the Triple Entente she had no military treaty with France.

Would she enter the conflict or remain neutral? He knew the answer, for his ambassador in London, Prince Lichnowsky, had been writing to the Wilhelmstrasse for weeks stating flatly that England would support France. 'A real nation of shopkeepers . . . the final struggle between the Slav and Germanic races finds the Anglo-Saxons on the side of the Slavs!' William had written on the margin. [4] Yet he had such a capacity for self-deception that when Prince Lichnowsky returned to Berlin in January and reported to him in person, the Kaiser pretended to be shocked and dismayed. It was nothing less than a conspiracy organized by England, through hatred and envy. When England gave the nod to Russia, Russia would strike and France would fall into line. The German Ambassador in St Petersburg, Count Pourtalès, did his best to reassure his sovereign. He wrote that Russia's rulers were not men who looked far ahead and that to predict what would happen several years in advance required the gift of second sight. 'There is such a gift!' replied William. 'Sovereigns often have it, statesmen seldom, diplomats never!' [5]

Although the Kaiser worked feverishly behind the scenes to restrain Austria, sending personal letters to the Emperor and to the Archduke Franz Ferdinand begging them to use their influence for peace, his alarm made him appear more bellicose than he had for years. On 9 February he attended a ceremony at Berlin University in commemoration of the war of 1813. He was not expected to speak but just as the Rector of the University was about to begin he stepped up to the rostrum, crashed his fist on the desk and said that the renaissance of Prussia, which had enabled her to crush the foreign tyrant, was no mere human deed but 'an act of God'. The Fatherland of 1913, armed with well-tried weapons, intended to pursue its own way. God was with the Germans before; he was with them now. It could be said today as truly as when Bismarck proclaimed it: 'We Germans fear God and nothing else in the world.'

This was followed in March by an announcement that the Kaiser had approved a new Army Law which would be laid before the Reichstag in April, demanding a huge increase in the army. The bill added eighteen infantry regiments and new regiments of cavalry and heavy artillery. It meant that Germany would have a peace strength of eight hundred and seventy thousand men, and in the event of war could put five and a half million men in the field. It also meant that a capital levy would be imposed on all property valued at ten thousand marks or over (five hundred pounds), starting at a rate of one half per cent and rising to one and a half per cent. The new tax, it was estimated, would cost the Krupp family five million marks or the equivalent of a quarter of a million pounds. But the Krupps could afford it.

Other people would feel the pinch. 'The resort to a tax on fortunes', declared the *Vossische Zeitung* angrily, 'is a declaration of bankruptcy.' The *Berliner Tageblatt* directed a back-hand shaft at the Kaiser. 'It smacks strongly of an impulsive suggestion which sprang from some romantic recollection of Napoleonic wars.' The Socialists did not attack the levy, but made a fuss in the Reichstag about the rebuilding of the Kaiser's yacht. This unnecessary expense, they said, added ten million marks to the defence estimates.

The protests were negligible, the Bill became law, and the Kaiser seemed to be more popular with his people than ever before. That winter he frequently rode through the streets of Berlin on a huge white thoroughbred, wearing the spectacular black and white uniform of the Death's Head Hussars. He usually went to the Tiergarten, and when his glittering retinue passed through the Brandenburger Tor foreigners hurried to their windows in the Adlon hotel to watch the crowds along the Linden running to the edge of the street, waving and cheering in spontaneous delight.

At long last the German people had taken William II to their hearts. No longer dismayed by bombastic speeches interlarded with references to sharp swords blessed by the Deity, nor to indiscretions which invariably set Europe by the ears, his failings seemed to charm them. 'He wants to be the bride at every wedding,' observed a Hamburg wit, 'the corpse at every funeral.' The truth was that despite his weakness for theatricals, the Kaiser had given Germany a quarter of a century of peace, and unprecedented prosperity. The population had increased from forty to sixty-six millions; production had trebled, income doubled. Germany led all Europe in chemistry and applied science; her railway system was the best in the world, her shipping and electrical industries expanding rapidly. She had surpassed Britain in the production of pig-iron, iron-ore and steel, and was close behind her in coal. Her emigration had become a mere trickle, and many German firms were importing labour from abroad. Colonies no longer were an economic necessity, merely a question of status.

Berlin reflected the rise of the new colossus. When the Kaiser rode through his capital he was traversing a city that had sprung up under his own hand. In twenty-five years the population had leapt from one to two and a quarter millions, accompanied by dozens of mushroom suburbs, hundreds of new buildings, miles of new streets, acres of squares and gardens. Not a single municipal building had gone up without the Kaiser's approval, while much of the statuary which adorned Berlin in overwhelming profusion was the result of his inspiration. On the balustrades of his castle his grandfather, Emperor William, was posed as Jupiter; the Empress Augusta as Juno; his father, Emperor Frederick, as Mars, and his mother, the former Princess Royal of England, as Minerva. The rows of kings and electors of the Hohenzollern line, who stood in the Sieges Allee, larger than life, in blinding white marble, had been commissioned by him and presented to the city as his personal gift. He had directed the work and, when it was done, gathered the sculptors together, lectured them on the true purpose of art, bid them retain a 'high and chaste' standard and congratulated them on giving Berlin a proud new status. Not everyone agreed. Max Liebermann, one of Germany's foremost painters, who had a studio overlooking the Tiergarten, wailed to the *Daily Mail* correspondent: 'All I can do is to wear blue goggles; but it is a life-sentence.' [6] Sometimes the statues were defaced in the night; the Kaiser blamed the socialists, but others smiled knowingly and described it as 'a protest'.

William II never doubted his artistic judgement. He felt qualified to pronounce on everything, from music to drama, painting to sculpture, poetry to architecture. Although he had quarrelled deeply with his blue-stocking, politically-minded mother, the eldest daughter of Queen Victoria and Prince Albert, he respected her knowledge of the arts. 'My mother was an artist,' he told people, 'and from my earliest youth I have been surrounded by beautiful things.' [7] His tastes were classical and veered to the Roman rather than the Greek. He loathed all modern tendencies. On 23 October 1913, the *North German Gazette* reported that he had thrown two hundred and seventy-one designs for a new German Embassy in Washington into the waste-basket. Among them was the prize-winning award done by one of Germany's leading architects, Herr Mohering. He had now appointed Herr von Ihne, the court architect, to draw him a plan.

The Kaiser's ideas were never picayune. He insisted that the expansion of Berlin should take place on a grand scale. The avenues were immensely wide; houses and shops and blocks of flats were required by law to have three yards of garden frontage; parks, benches and trees abounded. There was an exuberance of private building in which the young architects had scope to express themselves. Although after the war it became the fashion to deride German taste, M. Paul Poiret, the famous French dress and stage designer, who visited Berlin in the spring of 1913, was impressed by the ingenuity. 'I spent whole days in visiting modern interiors, built and arranged with such a wealth of new ideas that I had seen nothing like them at home. The villas around Berlin, standing in pine forests, on the borders of lakes, surrounded by gardens full of surprises, seemed to me delicious . . .' [8]

The Kaiser fretted because the ungainly crowds on the streets did not seem to fit into the twentieth century sweep of the new city. Apart from the Prussian officers, tall, handsome and arrogant, walking along the pavements like lords of creation, the majority had the rough hands and faces of peasants. The capital had expanded so fast that thousands of its inhabitants, fresh from the farms, had not had time to become urbanized. Foreigners laughed at Berlin's uncouth manners, and journalists wrote about the garish clothes; melon-shaped hats with thick velvet bands, frock coats with gaudy waist-coats, brown boots with black suits, knitted ties with evening clothes. They described people in the cafés who tucked their napkins under their chins and gobbled up their food. One journalist wrote that the populace straggled about on the street like chickens and geese on a country road; that they gaped and stared; cropped their hair and walked with their toes pointing out.

The Kaiser did his best to 'smarten up' his subjects. He longed to make Berlin as fashionable a capital as London. In 1913 he had moving pictures taken of people drinking tea in the Adlon Hotel which he sent to America to dispel the idea that Berlin was provincial. He tried to turn Kiel Week into Cowes – without much success – and even attempted to institute a *corso* in the Tiergarten in imitation of the afternoon procession of carriages in Hyde Park at the height of the season. Although William drove daily in the park in his coach and four, and ordered his Master of the Horse and other members of his court to do likewise, the experiment was a failure. He had overlooked the fact that apart from himself very few people owned smart equipages. The rich aristocrats who came to Berlin from the country did not bring their carriages with them; and the rich Berlin shop-keepers and Jewish manu-facturers, who might have owned them, were not received in society and therefore saw no point in it.

Berlin society was dominated by the land-owning Junkers, who consti-tuted both an officer and a ruling class. Unlike the English landed gentry, the Junkers refused to welcome the rich self-made industrialists, with the result that the upper class was far from luxurious. Although a handful of sophisti-cated hostesses and many aristocratic ladies from other parts of Germany entertained in the capital, Berlin society was swamped by the proud, poor, dowdy, dull squirearchy. Even opera audiences were depressing. 'They come,' wrote an American journalist, Price Collier, in 1913, 'in the clothes they have worn all day ... They have many of them a meal of meat, bread and beer during the long pause between two of the acts always provided for this purpose. Some of them bring little bags with their own provisions, and only buy a glass of beer ...' [9]

The Kaiser made it clear that when his presence was announced beforehand, no one would be admitted to the Opera who was not in evening dress.

This order was for a time not strictly enforced [wrote Miss Anne Topham, the English governess employed to instruct the Kaiser's daughter], and a good proportion of the audience even after repeated warnings habitually ignored it; but on one occasion all those whose dress did not come up to the required standard – ladies whose gowns were not *ausgeschnitten*, men who had omitted to put on the regulation suit – were politely but firmly refused admission and advised to go home again and change. There was much anger and heart-burning but no one now fails to obey the imperial mandate. [10]

The Kaiser even issued directives about the dancing at Court Balls. He disliked such 'modern' dances as the waltz and polka, and reversed a century to the minuet and the gavotte. These were the only dances permitted; and no one could attend a Court Ball who had not previously attended a *Tanz-Probe* held by the Court dancing mistress, whose nod of approval was the card of admittance. He was outraged when, in the autumn of 1913, he learned that the Countess Schwerin-Löwitz, wife of the Speaker of the Prussian Parliament, had used the official parliamentary reception rooms to give a 'tango' tea which was attended by diplomats and high officials. He promptly slapped down an edict forbidding any man in uniform to dance the tango, or to be seen in a house where other people danced it.

The authoritarianism of the Kaiser seemed to be contagious, for rules and regulations seeped into every aspect of Berlin's public life. No capital in the world had so many signs saying *Nicht gestattet* or *Verboten*; or offered so much gratuitous advice. The restaurant menu advised you how to pour out your wine so that you would not spill it on the table cloth and the post boxes bore signs saying: 'Do not forget to stamp and address your envelope'. 'In one cab I rode in,' wrote a visitor, 'I was cautioned not to expectorate, not to put my feet on the cushions, not to tap on the glass with stick or umbrella, not to open the window but to ask the driver to do it, and not to open the door until the auto-taxi had stopped; one hardly has time to learn the rules before the journey is over.' [11] In April 1913, more rules came into effect. People were not allowed to walk on the pavements more than three abreast; nor swing

The Hohenzollern

The Emperor, the Crown Prince, Princess Victoria Louise and the Crown Princess with the 'Death's Head Hussars' in Danzig.

There were large-scale manœuvres in Germany, France, England and Austria in 1913.
The illustration shows a cavalry charge during the German manœuvres at Döberitz.

Centenary parade outside the Royal Palace in Berlin—celebrating the Prussian defeat
of the French in 1813.

General Podbielski memorizing his speech for the opening of the Olympic Stadium.

The procession of athletes at the opening of the new stadium.

The procession of chimney-sweeps in Berlin to celebrate the Kaiser's jubilee.

His Majesty's contribution to defence: 'His Majesty has no time for Europe. His Majesty is designing a uniform for service chaplains.' The design of army uniforms was one of the many small matters on which the Kaiser liked to dictate his own views.

The Kaiser's study, showing the saddle he used at his desk, in preference to a chair.

Court Hunting – at Konopischt and Potsdam. The Crown Prince was notorious for his reckless driving.

The Kaiser and Archduke Franz Ferdinand of Austria hunting with Prince Fürstenberg.

'Fidgety Phil': Crown Prince William, the Hohenzollern Struwelpeter.

The Crown Prince, darling of the army and the militarists, inspecting a regiment of *Jäger* in historical costume.

Right. The youngest children of the Crown Prince paddling at the seaside at Zoppot on the Baltic.

Below. The Crown Prince photographed in a tennis tournament at Zoppot, with his partner Fräulein Müller-Beck.

'Guelph and Hohenzollern reconciled': Prince Ernest Augustus and Princess Victoria Louise on their way to the Royal Palace on their wedding-day.

The battery of press photographers at the royal wedding.

their canes and umbrellas as they walked; nor drag their garments in the street; nor sing nor whistle.

The Kaiser's dictatorial nature was not thought strange in a state dominated by the military. For a young man there was nothing more glorious than a commission in the army. Officers were a race apart, members of an exclusive club with high social standing and privileges that compelled deference from ordinary civilians. The only two ways, in 1913, of achieving this goal were by attending a Cadet School or by being recommended by a Regimental Commanding Officer as a volunteer 'aspirant'. Neither way was automatic, for if the aspirant did not receive the *imprimatur* of his regimental comrades he could not hope to receive a commission. For example, no Social Democrat was ever likely to become an officer.

Officers were not subject to the jurisdiction of civil courts or the public police. But they stood in awe of their own Courts of Honour. Most breaches of military discipline were punishable by fortress detention; but far worse was an offence against the code of an officer and a gentleman, for this could mean expulsion from the army and a return to civilian status.

Stripped of his commission [wrote Brigadier-General Morgan], despoiled of all his prerogatives as an officer, deprived of his right to wear uniform he was an outcast. The places that had known him knew him no more. As a soldier he was dead or worse than dead, for in Germany it is not better to be a living dog than a dead lion. The only course open to him, if he wished to avoid a life-long disgrace, was to shoot himself. He usually did.[12]

Public opinion, however, was hardening against the duel. In a debate in the Reichstag a Socialist motion demanded that officers should not lose their commissions by refusing a challenge, while a Radical motion called for duels to be declared illegal. The matter was referred to the Federal Council of Princes, who put out a statement in January 1913 saying that no drastic alterations of the law could be made. Three months later an announcement was made on behalf of the Emperor saying that His Majesty had discussed the subject with his generals on New Year's Day; that he hoped duelling would disappear of its own accord, and felt that the answer lay in a higher standard of education. He pointed out that in recent years no duels had taken place because of minor disputes. The fact that serious provocation resulted in duelling should teach officers self-restraint, and he could see no reason to deprive Courts of Honour of the function of deciding whether or not challenges should be given or accepted.

Not one major duel was reported in the German press in 1913. More duels in fact took place in Austria and France that year than in Germany. Nevertheless, faces scarred by steel blades were still fashionable, and very easy to acquire as all universities encouraged rapier contests between members of the corps and other student associations. Indeed rapier wounds were such a symbol of prestige that in June 1913, a Hamburg newspaper declared that a new business had sprung up in many towns in Germany. The object: to make men interesting to women. 'German women,' declared one advertisement, 'prefer an interesting man to a handsome one.' How to be interesting? The firm would provide rapier cuts 'without pain or interruption to business'. 'An accurate resemblance,' continued the honeyed inducement, 'to the real thing is guaranteed.' [13] The real thing required courage; although there was no danger to life, wounds were plentiful and often sewn up without anaesthetics.

For safety's sake [wrote Mr William Dawson, an Englishman residing in Germany], the hands, eyes, neck and breast are protected – the hands by means of baskets, the eyes by means of iron spectacles, and the other parts by means of silk bandages and shields. The face and skull are thus the parts really exposed to the cuts of the glittering blade. At every *mensur* a medical student is present, and it is his business to attend to the wounds, and stop the encounter if it promises to become serious. He discharges his duty well, and many are the stories of the surgical feats which are performed in emergencies of this kind – of how nose ends and ear-tips are gathered expeditiously from the ground and replaced so skilfully as not to betray the temporary excision, nay, of how science has even remedied the defects of nature by making crooked noses straight in the act of restoration. [14]

Although the army was the pride of the nation, when anything went wrong with its machine-like efficiency the average civilian found it irresistibly funny. Such was the case on 5 February when the German commander of the Strasbourg Garrison received a telegram from the Kaiser: 'Arrive twelve o'clock. Am coming by motor car. Proceeding to parade ground. Entire garrison to be alarmed.' The message sent fife and drum scurrying through the streets, giving the signal for all soldiers on leave to hurry back to barracks. Prince Oscar of Prussia, the Kaiser's fifth son, leapt up from a half-finished luncheon to hasten to the Polygon ground. Rumours of mobilization spread from door to door; tears and farewell embraces were plentiful. Finally eighteen thousand troops with bayonets, guns, rifles and lances were assembled in the midday sun. But no Kaiser. After three hours the Chief of Police telephoned Berlin to ask what had gone wrong. He was told that the Kaiser was at Königsberg, a thousand miles away.

It was discovered that a slow-witted, twenty-five-year-old ex-sergeant, recently discharged from the army for inefficiency, had disguised himself as a messenger and delivered the telegram. He had spent an interesting day quietly watching the confusion and excitement. When he was arrested he told his superiors that he had perpetrated the hoax because he wanted to impress the army with his ability. He was sent to a lunatic asylum.

Everything that happened in 1913 seemed to reflect the glare of the throne. Even the eight caged lions that escaped from Barnum's Circus in Leipzig after a collision with a tramcar seemed symbolic of the restless, explosive reign of William II. Although Herr Sudermann sold his novel *Der Katzensteg* to Hollywood for the unprecedented sum of fifteen thousand dollars, although Douglas Fairbanks went up in a Zeppelin and M. Saint-Saëns conducted a performance of *Samson and Delilah* in Berlin and found the Kaiser charming, although opera singer Emmy Destinn lost five pounds dieting on potatoes and Professor Otto Lummer of Berlin announced that diamonds could be manufactured, everything seemed irrelevant except for the military parades on the Tempelhofer Feld, and the mammoth opening of the mammoth stadium at Grünewald built for the 1916 Olympic Games. Meanwhile William II was so unpredictable that nothing about him was disbelieved. On 6 April the New York *Tribune* solemnly published that the Kaiser was planning to put an illuminated flag, painted on glass, on his car with the words *God Be With Us* so that people could see him coming from a long way off.

Nevertheless, 1913 fell into two parts, like a play. The first part was filled with martial music, waving banners, torchlight processions, cheers and laughter; the second part was a tale of woe. The great event of May was the wedding of the Kaiser's only daughter, twenty-one-year-old Princess Victoria Louise, to the Duke of Brunswick of the Guelph line. Newspapers concentrated on the Romeo and Juliet aspect of the romance; 'Guelph and Hohenzollern reconciled' was a world headline. The quarrel between the two families had started in 1866 when Prussia, under Bismarck, had annexed Hanover and deposed the King, the bridegroom's grandfather. When the Duke of Cumberland became head of the family he still refused to renounce his claim to the Hanoverian throne, and as a result the Hohenzollerns would not permit him to succeed to another inheritance, the throne of Brunswick, a petty state with an area little larger than Lancashire.

No Guelph had set foot in Berlin since 1886. The Kaiser frequently tried to patch up the quarrel but Cumberland avoided meeting him so often that he was nick-named 'the vanishing Duke'. Now Cumberland's son, the Guelph

heir, was to marry the Hohenzollern princess and all was forgiven and for-
gotten. Ernest Augustus would take an oath of allegiance to William II, and
the Kaiser in turn would restore Brunswick to the Prince as a wedding present.
The couple had met in dramatic circumstances. A year earlier the Duke of
Cumberland's eldest son had been killed in a motor crash, not far from
Potsdam, on his way to the King of Denmark's funeral. As soon as the
Kaiser heard the news he sent the Crown Prince and Prince Eitel Fritz to give
what assistance they could. The body of the dead boy lay for two nights in
the village church while the two princes watched by the coffin, finally escort-
ing it to the burial place. In order to thank the Kaiser for his kindness, the
Duke sent his second son, Prince Ernest Augustus – now his heir – to Potsdam.
The young man fell in love with Princess Victoria Louise on sight.

The wedding festivities began on 22 May with a state banquet at the Berlin
Castle, and the ceremony took place two days later. The King and Queen of
England arrived early on the 22nd and were received with appropriate
honours, but their reception seemed a simple affair compared to the welcome
deemed necessary for the Emperor of Russia. The Czar and Czarina pulled
into Anhalter Station in an armoured Court train consisting of ten saloon
cars. An hour before their arrival the station was swamped by uniformed
men. 'It looked like a constabulary camp,' wrote a reporter, 'police and
detectives were everywhere. On a platform fifty feet from that at which
the Czar's train was to come in was a line of infantrymen stretching far
beyond the end of the station. They had rifles loaded with ball cartridge.' [15]
The Duke and Duchess of Cumberland, the bridegroom's parents, who had
never before visited Berlin, because of the feud, were nettled to find that
their entrance, which should have been dramatic, was totally eclipsed by the
arrival of the Russians.

There were two hundred and fifty guests at the banquet and the room
glittered with resplendent uniforms and flashing jewels. The Kaiser in the full
dress uniform of the English Royal Dragoons with the Russian Andreas Order
across his shoulder led in Queen Mary of England. King George of England
in the uniform of the Prussian Dragoons and wearing the Prussian Black
Eagle Insignia followed with the Kaiserin. The Czar, who also wore a Prussian
Dragoon uniform decorated with the Order of the Black Eagle, escorted the
Dowager Grand Duchess of Baden, the Kaiser's aunt. The Duke of
Cumberland, the bridegroom's father, had the German Crown Princess on
his arm. The Crown Prince escorted the Duchess of Cumberland. Prince
Ernest entered with his fiancée, Princess Victoria Louise.

The highlight of the wedding day was not the actual ceremony but the centuries-old Torch Dance which always concluded nuptials at the Prussian Court. It took place in the famous White Hall, which, as its name implied, was entirely white, the mouldings being silvered instead of gilt. The Hall had a glistening parquet floor with a crowned Prussian eagle in the middle of it. Apparently the eagle was a source of immense pride to the palace attendants, who kept it in such a high state of polish it was as slippery as ice.

Woe betide the unfortunate dancer who set his foot on it [wrote Lord Frederick Hamilton]. He was almost certain to fall; and to fall down at a Berlin State ball was an unpardonable offence. If a German officer, the delinquent had his name struck off the list of those invited for a whole year. If a member of the Corps Diplomatique, he received strong hints to avoid dancing again.[16]

Prussian princesses, however, were expected to overcome such hazards and always did. The Torch Dance began to the strains of an old-world melody intermingled with the high notes of a trumpet. Accompanied by her bride-groom, and preceded by a Master of Ceremonies and twelve scarlet-clad pages bearing long flaming torches, she moved round and round the Hall in stately promenade. At each circling the bride led out two of the male royalties while the bridegroom did the same with the ladies. 'There was a wonderful sweeping of Court trains on the floor,' wrote an onlooker, 'that of the bride in white and silver being carried by four young maidens in shorter ones of rose colour.'

No one who saw the radiant bride, skirting the treacherous eagle so light-heartedly, would have guessed what agitation had gripped her in the past few months. Like her father, she was obsessed with a premonition of war. The conflict in the Balkans appalled her and she told her mother that she felt her wedding would never take place. 'The poor child did nothing but cry after she was engaged,' the Empress confided to Anne Topham, the princess's English governess. 'She was always imagining that war would break out – extraordinary, wasn't it? Always thinking that Prince Ernest would have to go away and fight and they would never meet again. She was continually crying when he was away, and grew so thin and miserable – always fretting and unhappy.' But when at last the eve of the wedding came she decided that perhaps the Fates would be kind to her. 'I was born on a Friday and on the thirteenth of the month,' she said laughingly, 'but my luck hasn't been so very bad, has it?' [17]

The Torch Dance was performed perfectly, guests and onlookers behaved impeccably, but apparently when the evening was over and the lights were being extinguished, the conduct of some of the younger army officers left much to be desired. One of the main corridors was congested with departing guests. Suddenly Miss Topham felt herself being jostled, then flung against the bemedalled breast of a high dignitary.

A few of the older men and court officials [wrote Miss Topham] did their best to protect the ladies but the young officers hustled and thrust regardless of consequences and seemed to have quite lost any sense of decent behaviour ... The ladies' veils and dresses were torn and jerked, they were flung backwards and forwards, and shouts and screams of remonstrance could be heard, adding obviously to the joy of the 'hooligans' of the crowd.[18]

However, when the various royalties, who were trying to pass through the room to their apartments, began to be jostled matters were felt to be serious. The officials remonstrated angrily in stentorian tones, and the Master of Ceremonies, the Prince Fürstenburg, who half an hour before had been leading the pages in the Torch Dance with a stately tread, seized his wand of office and struck it on the floor, finally restoring order. It developed that the Mistress of the Robes was distributing garter souvenirs and everyone was determined to get one. When the Kaiser learned next day what had happened he decreed that in the future those entitled to souvenirs would receive them by the impersonal but methodical hand of the post.

Berlin had scarcely recovered from the wedding before the streets were beflagged again for the two-day celebration in the middle of June in honour of the Kaiser's Jubilee. The occasion aroused deep emotion, and the capital was more densely populated than ever before in its history. The avenues were decorated with eagles and flowers, and slogans with excerpts from the Kaiser's speeches such as 'Our future lies on the water'. A massive military parade moved down the Linden to the stirring music of regimental bands. Field-Marshal General von Haeseler presented William II with a jewelled baton 'from the German Army to the German Emperor', while Admiral von Tirpitz presented a silver eagle to go on the bow of the new yacht *Hohenzollern*. The Kaiser, accompanied by his six sons, marched across the square outside the Castle to the Zenghaus for the ceremony of giving the pass-word which was 'Berlin: 1871'. The American steel king, Mr Andrew Carnegie, who had given ten million dollars to launch the Carnegie Endowment for International Peace, was one of the Jubilee guests, representing the American Peace Society. The Kaiser singled him out saying: 'I have given my people twenty-five years of peace.' Carnegie beamed and replied: 'Your Majesty is our best ally.'

On the 17th, ten thousand people marched through the city representing the trades of Berlin – fishmongers, shoe-makers, butchers, bakers, stone-masons, etc. – in all two hundred guilds. At high noon the rulers and reigning princes of the twenty-five independent states, which composed the German Federation, paid homage to the Kaiser; and that night attended a banquet of mediaeval splendour in the White Hall. The room blazed with diamonds and decorations, gold epaulettes and polished boots, reflecting the German Empire – 'an eternal union for the protection of the realm' – at the height of its glory.

Apart from the Kaiser, the German royal princes consisted of three kings with three kingdoms; six grand dukes with six grand duchies; five dukes with five duchies; seven princes with seven principalities. However, as the Kaiser was King of Prussia, and Prussia had a population of forty million out of Germany's sixty million, there was not a great deal left for them. Prince Frederick of Waldeck, for instance, only had 2,793 subjects, and the Prince Adolphus of Schaumburg-Lippe only 5,745. Even some of the Grand Dukes were badly off for people. The Grand Duke William Ernest of Saxe-Weimar had thirty-four thousand, the Grand Duke Frederick Francis IV of Mecklenburg-Schwerin forty-two thousand; the Grand Duke Ernest Louis of Hesse eighty-seven thousand.

Nevertheless, no matter how small the domain, they were royal; and as such were suitable matches for the royalty of other lands. Their sisters, brothers, aunts, uncles and cousins were intermarried with every reigning family, indeed with every royal household in the western world. The Kings of Greece and Roumania were married to Hohenzollern princesses; the Czar of Russia to a Princess of Hesse; the King of Denmark to a Princess of Mecklenburg-Schwerin; the King of Spain to a Princess of Battenburg; the King of Sweden to the daughter of the Grand Duke of Baden; the Queen of Holland to a Mecklenburg prince. Almost all the Russian Grand Dukes and Duchesses, and scores of English princes and princesses, were interwoven into the same pattern.

The Kaiser, therefore, was the head of an international family; and the glittering assembly he addressed on the night of the banquet represented the very life-blood of the monarchical tradition. Yet there was no feeling of elation in his heart, for he could not rid himself of the dire foreboding that the curtain was falling on all he held dear. When Bishop Boyd-Carpenter, the English cleric, who had travelled to Berlin to offer the respect of the British Council of Churches, talked to William II he sensed the despair. 'He was quite cordial,' wrote the Bishop, 'but he spoke with a note that was new to me . . . He seemed apprehensive; he spoke of the dangerous position in which Germany was placed between two powers which understood one another and might prove hostile. When I left him, I felt that he was under the influence of a great fear.' [19]

The cheering died away during the second half of the year. From August onwards there seemed to be nothing but annoyance. Such names as Krupp, Diesel, Zeppelin, Crown Prince William figured in the news in a disobliging context. It began with the trial in August of several young army officers in Berlin who were accused of revealing secrets to the Krupp armament firm. The trial was something of a farce because everyone knew that the Krupp firm worked hand in glove with the Government. The case arose because the fiery socialist member, Karl Liebknecht (who after the war tried to establish communism in Germany), told parliament that he had received seventeen documents through the post, from a source that he could not disclose, proving that the Krupp firm had been bribing junior officials to feed them information about projects under consideration by the War Office and tenders put forward by rival firms. Liebknecht sent his documents to the Prussian Minister of War, who was obliged to order an investigation.

The trial revealed nothing but petty detail; despite the huge orders put through the Krupp firm by the Government – armour-plating for battleships, cannons, anti-aircraft guns, gun carriages – the relations between Krupps and the Field Artillery Department at the War Office were not good. Consequently another firm had got the order to supply steel barrels in the event of mobilization. In order to improve the firm's position, Herr Brandt, an ex-artillery officer, was sent to Berlin as the Krupp representative. Brandt was on close terms with many of the junior officials. He treated them to dinners, sent them Christmas presents and everyone freely talked shop. But his total expenditure was not more than sixty pounds. 'Krupps could, must and ought to hear anything,' wrote Maximilian Harden in *Zukunft*. 'What they didn't know today they were bound to know tomorrow . . . Is that what all the fuss has been about?' Nevertheless Herr Brandt and several junior officers were sent to prison for a token few weeks and two young men were dismissed from their jobs.

What puzzled the public was the mystery. Who had sent the documents to Karl Liebknecht? Was it the Krupp employee whom Brandt had displaced at the War Office, or someone else? Soon people were whispering that the villain of the piece was none other than seventy-five-year-old August Thyssen, the Steel King, who had got the order for the steel barrels and meant to keep it.

Scarcely had the talk about Krupp died down before newspaper headlines announced that Dr Rudolph Diesel, inventor of the famous engine, had disappeared mysteriously from the steamer in which he was travelling from Antwerp to London. Diesel was fifty-four years old, a slight, fair-haired man with gold-rimmed spectacles. He was on his way to the Annual General Meeting of the Consolidated Diesel Engine Manufacturers in London. He had no financial worries, the press said, as he had amassed five hundred thousand pounds from world patent rights. He was in excellent spirits when he said good-night to his travelling companions, two business associates, promising to meet them for an early breakfast.

Tongues began to wag in London. Whispers went around that Diesel had been murdered by the German Secret Service in order to prevent him from giving his know-how to the British. In Berlin they said the opposite. The British Secret Service had shoved him overboard to deprive Germany of a great inventor and to pin the act on the Germans at the same time.

Talk did not die down until 14 October when the Bavarian Auditing Company called a meeting in Munich and disclosed the fact that Diesel was on the verge of bankruptcy. He had lost all his money in reckless land speculation in Munich and Hamburg. He had raised mortgages on his property to the tune of thirty thousand pounds and was a further twenty-five thousand pounds in debt. His family had known nothing of his financial difficulties and were now penniless. Friends were in the process of raising money for them.

The name of Diesel, however, was swept away by the appalling news of a Zeppelin disaster, the third crash of the year and the second in six weeks. In September the naval dirigible L1 had been wrecked by a gale during a flight at sea, near Heligoland, while returning from army manoeuvres in Silesia; fourteen men out of twenty had been killed. But the catastrophe of October was even worse, for the L2 was Germany's newest naval Zeppelin – the largest in the world – and had been carrying twenty-eight passengers, many of them eminent engineers and scientists, all of whom perished except for one survivor. The Zeppelin had begun its journey from Johannisthal Airfield near Berlin. Three minutes after take-off, when it had reached a height of six hundred and fifty feet, there was a sudden burst of flame in the forward engine car accompanied by a loud explosion. The eighteen gas bags ignited and the ship began to fall. At one hundred and thirty feet another explosion took place and, when the ship hit the ground, causing a third explosion, nothing was left but a scrap heap of aluminium and metal.

The Kaiser was deeply disturbed as the accident marked the tenth Zeppelin disaster in seven years. He had consistently backed the 'lighter than air' school against heavy aircraft, and frequently referred to Count Zeppelin as 'the greatest man of the century'. Only two months earlier, on the Count's seventy-fifth birthday, William had sent him a telegram: 'The Emperor and the Empire are proud of their gallant conqueror of the air.' [20] All the countries of Europe sent messages of condolence to the Kaiser and praised Germany's courageous and tenacious pioneering; but the English *Times* remarked what everyone was thinking: the accident would raise new discussion on 'the relative merits of the Zeppelin and other types of aircraft.'

The Kaiser continued to lament the loss. A few weeks later the German press announced that His Majesty had drawn a sketch to commemorate the tragedy, which would be finished in colour by Professor Bohrat. The picture showed a naval airship lighthouse on a rocky coast and a shining cross in the sky. On the left was a figure of Germania holding the imperial shield, and in the centre Christ wearing a crown of thorns.

The Kaiser not only took national tragedies to heart. As the father of his people, he felt deep concern for the morals and good names of individuals, particularly princes. That autumn he had plenty to worry about for people were whispering that Prince Leopold of Lippe was augmenting the family coffers by selling titles and decorations. Even worse, in September Captain von Westhagen, a reserve army officer stationed in Berlin, was so angered by malicious whispers accusing him of having bought from the Lippe court his title 'Kammerherr' that he challenged one of his calumniators, the portrait painter Professor Heinrich Maass, to a duel. The case was placed before a Court of Honour and the two men summoned to court at different times. Unfortunately they met accidentally in the corridor. The Captain struck the professor and drew his sword, whereupon the professor pulled a revolver out of his pocket and shot the captain dead. The professor was acquitted on the grounds of self-defence.

The selling of titles was not new, for in the past both Prince Gunther of Schwarzburg-Sonderhausen and Prince Frederick of Waldeck had been accused of doing the same thing. Some people blamed the Kaiser for setting a bad example, for he frequently solicited money from big business for his pet museums, laboratories and excavation projects, and usually rewarded the donors with decorations. The small states were following suit, but operating for personal gain. In October the *Frankfurter Zeitung* published documents showing how widespread the practice had become; thirty thousand marks for a Kommerzienrat, lesser sums for titles of Hofrat, Baurat and Professor, with skilful agents handling the cash and drafting the petitions. [21]

Prince Leopold of Lippe charged from two thousand pounds to five thousand pounds for the title of baron or count. German business firms received a letter from the so-called 'English' firm saying: 'Everyone knows that titles are only granted by reigning monarchs; but naturally the monarchs do not know all the recipients. It is my good fortune to know persons who can induce monarchs to sign letters of nobility. The recipient is, of course, expected to donate money to a public institution.' [22] A relation of Prince Leopold, Prince Adolphus of Schaumburg-Lippe, settled his monetary affairs with more circumspection. In order to meet mounting costs, in November he disbanded his ancient sailing fleet which for a hundred and fifty years had plied the island lake of Steinhuder Meer. The fleet consisted of small sailing boats and eighteen seamen in eighteenth-century uniforms who were paid as officials of the state.

There was also trouble, much worse trouble, at the court of Saxe-Weimar. In September news came that the beautiful twenty-five-year-old Princess Sophie of Saxe-Weimar had shot herself in the palace of her father, Prince William of Saxe-Weimar, brother of the reigning Grand Duke, at Heidelberg. She had killed herself because she was deeply in love with Baron Hans von Bleichröder, son of the Jewish banker whose house had helped to finance Bismarck's wars, and neither the Grand Duke nor her father would give their consent to the marriage.

At the funeral Prince William was so overcome with grief that he threw himself sobbing across his daughter's lily-covered coffin. Yet the tragedy did not soften his heart, for although Baron von Bleichröder called at the house, Prince William put out the following statement a few days later: 'Baron Hans von Bleichröder, like all acquaintances of the House of Saxe-Weimar, had a farewell view of the departed but was expressly forbidden to participate in the funeral or attend the cremation. As for the stories set in circulation in regard to a marriage between Princess Sophie and von Bleichröder, all the money in the world would never have sufficed to bridge the gulf between a Princess of Saxe-Weimar and Baron von Bleichröder.'[23]

Another aristocratic scandal concerned a member of the Reichstag, a Polish nobleman, Count Matthias Mielzynski. One night in December, at his home

Castle Dakowymokre near Graetz, the count thought he heard burglars. Armed with a revolver he searched the house. When he flung open one of the doors he found his wife in bed with his nephew. He shot them both dead and went back to bed. In the morning he rang the Public Prosecutor and reported what he had done. At his trial some months later he was acquitted.

The Bavarian court offered light relief to these tragedies by carrying on a feud with the ladies of the aristocracy. Pressure from the Catholic Church had wrung support from the King for the banning of the tango and hobble skirts that revealed part of the leg. The ladies of Munich, however, refused to accept this last decree. They persuaded the secretary of the Archbishop of Munich to instruct priests to refuse mass to men in shorts with bare knees. Tempers flew; the Tyrolean Society for the Preservation of the Costumes of Bavaria leapt into the fray; and in the end the authorities conceded the point and allowed the ladies to attend receptions in the new skirts.

In Berlin the Kaiser had more to worry about than hobble skirts. He was perturbed by the deterioration of morals. While Court society was stuffy and provincial the society of the cafés and night clubs was wild and uncontrolled. That winter people were shocked by the trial of the Countess von Treuburg, an admitted morphine addict, who was found guilty of extortion, usury and blackmail. Drinking was increasing, and although gambling was against the law, more clandestine gaming rooms flourished in Berlin than ever before. The suicide rate (due to gambling, people said) was the highest in the capital's history. In November the Kaiser ordered his Minister of the Interior, Herr von Delbrück, to investigate the figures and send him a report; if the laws were not stringent enough he proposed to introduce new legislation. The Kaiser believed that the root-cause of the evil was drink. He was disappointed that the example set by himself in September had not reaped better results: he had gone 'teetotal'. This news was announced by the palace, accompanied by statistics showing that drink was responsible for one thousand six hundred suicides; one thousand five hundred accidents; thirty thousand cases of delirium tremens; two hundred thousand crimes. The Kaiser gave permission for his health in the future to be drunk in water. The newspapers commented adversely on the innovation because of the large number of beer advertisements in their pages.

Meanwhile the Kaiser was having difficulties with the Crown Prince. It was not surprising that father and son had never got on well, for one was a puritan, the other a playboy. For years William II had been fuming about his son's partiality for horses and women. The Crown Prince was a goodnatured young man with protruding blue eyes, a receding chin and a vacuous expression. He fell for every pretty face he saw and wrote impulsive letters signed 'Yours forever'. The Kaiser hoped that his marriage to Princess Cecilie, the daughter of the Grand Duke Francis III of Mecklenburg, would quiet him down, but the prince's habits did not alter. He led the agreeable life of an officer of cavalry in the Prussian Army, with plenty of spare time for enjoyment.

This was bad enough; but it became far worse in 1911 when the Prince suddenly began to interfere in politics. The first occasion was the Moroccan crisis which brought Germany to the brink of war with France and England. The Kaiser saw the red light flashing and shrank back. He instructed his Foreign Secretary to alter Germany's tone and to come to terms with France. German nationalists were angry and humiliated, while some of the army officers went so far as to insist that the honour of the Fatherland had been stained. The Berlin *Post* cried hysterically: 'Are we a race of women?' while Maximilian Harden's paper, *Zukunft*, launched an attack on 'William the Peaceable' concluding with the words:

> Here ends, O Zollern, thine historic glory,
> And here, but not in battle, fell a king.

The Crown Prince added fuel to the fire by leaving his regiment without permission and attending a debate in the Reichstag, where he applauded the war-like speech of the Conservative leader, Herr Heydebrand. When the latter attacked the Imperial Chancellor, Bethmann-Hollweg, for shameful timidity, the Crown Prince struck the pommel of his sword on the railing of the *loge* and nodded enthusiastic approval. From then on he was the darling of the militarists. The Kaiser was worried by the wild outbursts of applause he began to receive when he appeared in public, and sent him to Danzig to keep him away from the capital.

But the Prince was flattered by people who told him that his features resembled those of Frederick the Great, and now saw himself as the leader of the militarists. 1913 offered him plenty of scope for bellicose gestures. In May a book entitled *Germany in Arms* was published in commemoration of the War of Liberation. The Prince contributed a chapter glorifying war. 'Diplomacy can postpone a conflict but will not settle it,' he wrote. 'The sword will always remain the final settlement.' He went on to describe the thrill of the cavalry charge which always marked the end of the annual army manoeuvres, adding that only one thing could be more exhilarating: war itself. 'How often', he wrote, 'has my ear caught the longing cry from some companion, "*Donnerwetter* if this were only the real thing!"'

The Kaiser was not one to shrink from the provocative remark; but with the Balkan wars raging, and the powers of Europe so delicately poised, he found the Prince's outbursts unpardonably irresponsible. By this time, however, the Kaiser was being lampooned by Maximilian Harden as *Guillaume le Timide*, and the Prince was being hailed by the war party as the great deliverer. This was heady wine, and the young man was in no mood to listen to anyone. He was patron of the Breslau Centenary celebrations which opened with a play written by Gerhart Hauptmann, Germany's leading dramatist. The play contained a verse put in the mouth of Scharnhorst which criticized the Hohenzollern king, Frederick William III of Prussia. But coming at a time when a large section of the militant press was attacking the Kaiser, it was widely interpreted as a shaft at the latter's incapacity:

> If only a new old Fritz might grace
> To delight our hearts the leader's place!
> But a man we lack to match the mood
> Of the hour, the monarch of Germanhood
> Of Prince and People to bow the knee
> And show them the path to liberty.[24]

The Crown Prince attended the opening night, and laughed loudly at the verse, but a few days later, much chastened, he ordered the withdrawal of the play.

This did not end the conflict between father and son. The Crown Prince was as irrepressible as a champagne bubble. He suddenly sent a telegram to the Imperial Chancellor demanding that the Duke of Cumberland, who had married his sister only four months previously, should not be allowed to assume the title of Duke of Brunswick until he officially had surrendered all claims to the throne of Hanover for himself and his descendants. The Kaiser had considered the matter closed, as his son-in-law had taken an oath of loyalty to the throne upon entering the Army. The Crown Prince's attempt to stir up fresh mischief enraged him. A quarrel took place; the Crown Prince left without permission the festival of Leipzig, where the federated princes had gathered to commemorate the War of Liberation, and went to Munich. His father sent General von Gontard to fetch him back.

And now, in November 1913, came the celebrated Zabern affair, which not only deepened the quarrel between Kaiser and Prince, but attracted world comment; set the Prussian Minister of War at the Imperial Chancellor's throat; excited the Reichstag; underlined the deep tensions between French and Germans in the province of Alsace; and brought the German Army into ridicule. It began in the Alsatian town of Zabern, population ten thousand. A twenty-year-old officer, Lieutenant von Forstner, told his recruits: 'If you are insulted by a *Wackes* (a derogatory name for a native of Alsace) and you stab him, you will not be punished but I will give you ten marks.'

This was an indiscreet pronouncement to say the least, for Forstner's regiment contained a number of Alsatian soldiers who reported the remark to a local newspaper which printed it. In the evening a noisy demonstration took place before the Officers' Mess; and that night, when Forstner was visiting a friend's house, a crowd of a thousand gathered outside, obliging him to summon an armed escort before he could go home.

The townspeople continued to torment the lieutenant and his brother officers, barracking and jeering at them. Forstner could not even go shopping without a guard of four soldiers with fixed bayonets. Then came an afternoon when even the pupils of the secondary school, on their way home, began to make offensive remarks. Colonel von Reuter, the colonel of Forstner's regiment, decided to teach them a lesson. He ordered sixty of his men to load rifles and to form two lines. He then announced that he would arrest any civilian who did not immediately retire. The scene that followed was pure comedy. A fireman who left his supper when he heard the roll of the regimental drums was arrested at his door; the judge and prosecutor of the civil court, which had just risen, were arrested when they left the court. The judge was allowed to go home but all the others (twenty-seven in number) spent the night in the cellars of the barracks and were not liberated until the next day when they were brought before the judge for trial.

The German public was furious with the military for making the country a laughing stock. But the Crown Prince took the side of the army. He chose this moment to intervene, wiring 'Bravo' to the General commanding the Army Corps in Strasbourg, and sending Colonel von Reuter a telegram saying '*Immer feste druff*' (Keep right on . . .).

This was not the end of the affair. A few days later Lieutenant von Forstner was marching a platoon through the village of Dettweiler when onlookers made disparaging remarks. Whereupon Forstner ordered their arrest. A lame cobbler cried excitedly as a soldier approached him: 'If you touch me I will punch you on the nose.' Forstner drew his sword and struck the man. Blood trickled down the cobbler's face and there were cries of angry indignation from the villagers. Luckily the cobbler had little more than a scratch. Forstner defended his action by insisting that 'German officers were required to act energetically against every sort of abuse and insult on the part of the civilian population.'

The Imperial Chancellor, Herr von Bethmann-Hollweg, took a poor view of von Forstner's activities, and rebuked him in a public speech. This stung the Prussian Minister of War, General von Falkenhayn, into replying that the 'civilian officials talked lightly about the youth and inexperience of the officers who had been insulted, but unless the authorities could suppress the civil agitation, life for a German soldier at Zabern would be far less safe than in the Congo.'

Colonel von Reuter and Lieutenant von Forstner were sent before a military tribunal who ordered Reuter to appear before a court martial and sentenced Forstner to forty-three days' detention. By now the affair had become a *cause célèbre*, a fierce battle between civilian law and army rule. Although a Centre Party deputy reflected the mood of the Reichstag by shouting: 'If we abandon the civilian population to the military, then finis Germaniae!' Forstner appealed against his sentence and won. A higher court declared it null and void on the grounds of 'putative necessity'. Colonel von Reuter not only was acquitted at his court martial, but on the recommendation of the War Office received the Order of the Red Eagle, third class, with ribbon.

Meanwhile the Kaiser was so angered by the Crown Prince's intervention in the affair that he relieved him of his command of the Death's Head Hussars Regiment in Danzig and had him transferred to Berlin where he could keep an eye on him. 'His Majesty', wrote the Prince in his memoirs, 'took my dear regiment away from me and ordered me to Berlin, so that my overgrown independence might be curtailed and my doings better watched.' [25]

However, the move did not appear to impair the Prince's *joie de vivre*. Just before Christmas he spent a few days with the Princess of Pless, at the Pless Castle in Silesia. 'I spoke of old times to the Crown Prince', she wrote in her diary. 'His letters of affection used to disturb me, wondering who might get them and read them before they were posted. I told him many home-truths, one being that he must never ask a lady, as he had just asked me [to ask another lady], to stay in her house to meet him. He wanted Lady X and unfortunately wrote and told her so – thinking he would find me *complaisant*!' [26]

In December the German Emperor could look back on twelve months of tireless effort. He had received the Russian Czar, the King of England, the

Berlin

The 1913 style for
riding in the
Tiergarten.

The Zeppelin L2 at Johannisthal airfield near Berlin, before its last flight.
Three minutes after take-off it crashed, leaving only one survivor.

The L1 over the Grand Fleet at Kiel on its last flight. Fourteen people
perished when it crashed off Heligoland in a gale, less than a month before the
L2 disaster.

A group of advertisements, for Opel and Benz motor cars, for Burgeff Sekt (German Champagne), and for beds—showing 'Europa', well-armed, at rest on one of M. Steiner's 'Paradise beds'.

The 'Zabern Affair' hit
international headlines at the end
of 1913, after a young infantry
lieutenant, von Forstner, had
enraged the local population at
Zabern in Alsace, where his
regiment was stationed. The
illustrations show (*right*) Forstner
crossing a street escorted by an
armed guard, to protect him from
the fury of the townspeople, and
(*above*) the return of the 99th
Infantry Regiment to Zabern, led
by its new colonel, in December.

Above. Gustav and Bertha Krupp von Bohlen und Halbach at the Gelsenkirchen air show. Bertha Krupp's fortune was said to amount to 280 million marks (about £14,000,000), double that of the Emperor.

Left. In majorem Kruppi gloriam. The army were again implicated in the two Krupp trials in August and October. In the first, Brandt, who had bribed military officials to obtain details of tenders of rival firms, was chief witness for the prosecution; in the second, he was the defendant and was sent to prison. The cartoonist suggests Krupp's would have preferred to deal more drastically with witnesses for the prosecution.

'Hunting the Schiebetanz dancers'. The Schiebetanz was a poor man's tango and was forbidden durin[g] the Carnival season by the Munich police, who took vigorous measures to enforce their regulation.

A hotel reception desk: illustration to an article on the modern hotel, which stated, rather optimistically, that 'nowadays a woman travelling on her own is not unusual; and it is possible for a young girl to go alone into a hotel without her reputation suffering.'

The afternoon *Thé Tango* in Berlin. Although the Kaiser forbade uniformed men to be present when the tango was danced, it had become socially quite acceptable in 1913.

Die Wiesenthals by Arthur Grunenberg, typical of traditional art in a year better remembered now for the work of Futurists, Duchamp, Matisse and Picasso.

'Every smart woman should ask for LL's Tango-Corset, obtainable from all good stores. . . .'

CORSET TANGO

LL
Marke
Training

King of Italy, the King of Greece and the King of the Belgians. Apart from innumerable speeches commemorating the War of Liberation, he had talked on agricultural development, German yachting, German trade, military training, music, archeology, aeronautics and town planning. And he had travelled thousands of miles. Earlier in his reign a German editor had estimated that William had spent a hundred and ninety of the year's three hundred and sixty-five days in motion. 1913 did not surpass this record but it compared favourably. In February he had visited Karlsruhe, in April Hamburg. In June he had attended the Regatta at Kiel, in July taken his annual cruise on the *Hohenzollern*. In August he had visited Rostock, Lübeck and Posen, in September attended the army manoeuvres at Breslau. In October he had visited Bonn and Leipzig, the Archduke Franz Ferdinand at Konopischt and the Emperor Franz Joseph at Vienna. In November he had visited Stuttgart, Baden-Baden and Munich, and in December been the guest of Prince Fürstenberg at Donaueschingen in the Black Forest. The Kaiser made all his trips on the Imperial train, and frequently was angered to see railway employees turning their backs on the train. Consequently on 7 December the Prussian Minister of Railways issued the order that when the royal train passed, switchmen and gate-keepers at the crossings must face the train and adopt a military attitude of attention with eyes to the front, holding a covered signal flag on the right arm.

Throughout 1913 the Kaiser had also kept a strict eye on foreign affairs and could rightfully claim to be more responsible than any other single person for preserving peace. Not only had he written many personal letters to Austria urging non-intervention in the Balkan conflict, but in July had instructed his Chancellor to deliver a sharp warning to the Viennese Foreign Office about the folly of trying to 'gobble up Serbia'. 'A European war,' declared the 1913 British *Annual Register* 'would in all probability have broken out if the Emperor William had not plainly declared . . . to Austria-Hungary that he would not support her should she be involved in a war with Russia . . . and to Russia that if she attacked Austria-Hungary . . . he would fight by the side of his Austrian ally.' [27]

Nevertheless, William II did not share the optimism that emanated from the English capital at the close of the year, and from some of his own advisers. Once again he was having trouble with Russia. In December the Turkish Government asked Germany to send them a military adviser to try and piece together their shattered army which had been crushed and routed by the joint attacks of the small Balkan states. The Kaiser sent General Liman von Sanders, which threw St Petersburg into a state of anger and excitement. M. Sazonov, the Russian Foreign Minister, saw the move as an effort to thwart Russia's historic mission of obtaining control of the Straits and raised a violent protest. The German Government pointed out that General von Sanders' position was no more dominant than that enjoyed by Admiral Limpus, the English instructor to the Turkish navy. Although this argument was unanswerable, M. Sazonov tried to make the appointment an international issue, and told the British that 'this question must be the test of the value of the Triple Entente'. But the British refused to play; and the Kaiser made an effort to pacify Russian feeling by transferring von Sanders from his command of the First Corps, an operational position, to that of General-Inspector of the Turkish Army.

In December the Imperial Chancellor told the Reichstag of 'the improvement of our relations with England' and held out hope 'of a permanent *rapprochement* between nations of the same stock'. The Kaiser refused to be assuaged. He was still depressed and apprehensive. When the flash-point came England would go with France and Russia. And Russia would ignite the flame. 'As a soldier,' he had written some months earlier, 'I feel, from all the information received, not the slightest doubt that Russia is systematically preparing war against us and I shape my policy accordingly.' [28]

The Kaiser's friend, the Jewish intellectual Walter Rathenau, who had inherited his father's great electrical industry, the *Allgemeine Electrizitäts Gesellschaft*, watched the darkening scene with desperation. The cult of nationalism was to blame; the only solution was a European Common Market.

There is one possibility left [he wrote on Christmas Day 1913]: an industrial customs union, of which sooner or later, for better or for worse, the states of Western Europe would become members . . . Fuse the industries of Europe into one . . . and political interests will fuse too. This is not world peace or disarmament, nor is it general debility; but it is an alleviation of conflicts, an economy of power and the solidarity of civilization.[29]

Unfortunately Rathenau was forty years before his time.

THREE

ST PETERSBURG

In January 1913, scandal and speculation concerning the imperial family swept the drawing rooms of St Petersburg. The year opened gloomily with the announcement that the Grand Duke Michael, the Czar's only surviving brother and next in line of succession after the Czar's only son Alexei, had been dismissed from his position as Presumptive Regent because of having contracted a morganatic marriage. His bride was a twice-divorced commoner, the ex-wife of Captain Wulfert, a Russian Army officer. Everyone knew that the Grand Duke Michael had been in love with Mrs Wulfert for years, but he had promised the Czar not to marry her. The news came as a thunderbolt to the whole family.

I have just got a letter from Misha in which he announces his marriage [wrote the Dowager Empress Marie to her son Nicholas II]. It is unbelievable – I can hardly understand *what* I am writing – it is so appalling in every way that it *nearly kills* me! I beg only this one thing of you: that it be kept *absolutely secret* to avoid *another scandal*! There have been secret marriages in the past which one *pretended to know nothing about*. I think this is the only way out – otherwise I won't be able to show my face *anywhere* for the *shame and disgrace of it all*! May God forgive him – I can only pity him ...[1]

Nicholas replied to his mother in a calmer vein.

I am sending you Misha's letter which I got on the way in the train. Read it and then say if, after all he says, he can possibly remain in the Service and comand your Chevalier Guards ... Between him and me everything is now, alas, at an end: because he has broken his pledged word. How many times he promised of his own free will, not because I pressed him, not to marry her! What revolts me more than anything else is his reference to poor Alexei's illness, which, he says, made him speed things up. And then the disappointment and sorrow it brings to you and to all of us and the scandal of it all over Russia mean absolutely nothing to him! At a time, too, when everyone is expecting war, and when the tercentenary of the Romanovs is due in a few months! ... At first I had an idea of keeping it all secret, but having gone over his letter two or three times I see clearly that *now* he must not return to Russia – sooner or later everybody here will know the truth, and begin to wonder why nothing has been done to him when others have been so severely dealt with . . . [2]

The news that the Grand Duke Michael had surrendered his position as Regent Presumptive and had been banished from Russia heightened the gossip surrounding the Czar's eight-year-old son and heir. Three months earlier the boy had been so gravely ill that daily bulletins had been issued. The tone was guarded; the Czarevich had injured his leg and a haemorrhage had occurred. People began to whisper that Alexei was too often ill. What was wrong with the child? Some said that he had been born with too few layers of skin, others that he had an incurable bone disease. The speculation was so wide-spread that on the 4 February 1913, General Dumbadze, the Governor of Yalta, issued a letter to the St Petersburg press 'repudiating alarmist reports'. The General said that he had seen the Czar's son within the last month and was much impressed by the boy's robust appearance and healthy colour. His left leg was certainly somewhat bent at the knee, but the trouble was quickly disappearing, and the doctors anticipated a complete cure. The boy chattered with the General about how 'awfully bad' he had been at Spala, but now nearly all the pain had disappeared.

The following day the *Berliner Tageblatt* announced that Professor Enderlen, an eminent surgeon at the University of Würzburg, and his assistant Dr Hotz, had gone to St Petersburg at the request of the Czar and Czarina. Readers were reminded that Professor Enderlen had performed a remarkably successful operation on a Russian actress whose life he had saved by a blood transfusion from her husband's veins. The London *Daily Mail* [3] was even more imaginative, asserting that a medical council at Tsarskoe Selo had recommended for the Czar's son a mud-bath cure at Helouan near Cairo.

These reports were so baffling that, far from quietening people, they loosed a fresh crop of rumours and whispers. There was plenty to whisper about, for the Empress herself was shrouded in almost as much mystery as her son. For ten years there had been no balls in the Winter Palace. Indeed, the Empress had scarcely spent a night in the capital in all that time. She had persuaded the Czar to live at the Alexander Palace at Tsarskoe Selo, fourteen miles away. She rarely appeared in public, and when she did was always cold and unsmiling. [Was it true that she had come under the influence of a peasant who claimed to have spiritual powers?] People whispered that she was infatuated with him, and had written indiscreet letters which had fallen into unscrupulous hands. [His name was Rasputin, which meant 'the disreputable one'.]

This was the talk in St Petersburg as 1913 opened. It had been hoped that the year would be one of rejoicing in which the great families would pledge afresh their fealty to the throne, for [1913 marked the three hundredth anniversary of the House of Romanov.] A special stamp bearing the Czar's head had been issued, but soon protests were made both by the Church and the Post Office. The Church regarded it as *lèse-majesté* to put a cancellation mark over the Czar's features, and junior postal officials were so frightened by the disrespect that they were only blacking a corner of the stamp, allowing many to be used again. The Government pronounced that it was impossible to withdraw the stamps which were in wide circulation, but that no more would be issued.

Early in the morning of 6 March a salute of thirty-one guns from the Fortress of St Peter and St Paul announced the opening of the [Tercentenary ceremonies.] Soon the city was astir with people gathering in the streets to watch the royal procession, scheduled for high noon, when the Czar and his family would drive from the Palace to Kazan Cathedral. At the Cathedral itself swarms of officials were making last minute preparations. The huge, three-hundred-pound President of the Duma, M. Michael Rodzianko, was remonstrating with the Master of Ceremonies insisting that members of the Duma should not be relegated to the back of the church but given seats at the front.

Having achieved my object [wrote Rodzianko], I walked out into the Cathedral porch for rest, as there was still plenty of time before the arrival of the members of the Duma. I must add that in order to 'fortify' our newly occupied 'positions' I surrounded them by a cordon of the available Duma sergeants-at-arms. I had not been in the porch ten minutes when Baron Fersen, the senior sergeant-at-arms, rushed out of the Cathedral, looking very excited, and told me that an unknown man, in peasants' dress and wearing a pectoral cross, had placed himself in front of the space reserved for the Imperial Duma and refused to move. I guessed at once who it was, and hastening to our places found there the individual described by Baron Ferson. Sure enough, it was Rasputin. He was dressed in a magnificent Russian tunic of crimson silk, patent-leather top boots, black cloth full trousers and peasant's overcoat. Over his dress he wore a pectoral cross on a finely-wrought gold chain.

I drew quite close to him and said in an impressive whisper: 'What are you doing here?'

He shot an insolent look at me and replied: 'What's that got to do with you?'

'If you address me as "thou", I will drag you from the Cathedral by the beard. Don't you know I am the President of the Duma?'

Rasputin faced me, and seemed to run me over with his eyes; first my face, then in the region of the heart, then again he stared me in the eyes. This lasted for several moments.

Personally I had never yielded to hypnotic suggestion, of which I had had frequent experience. Yet here I felt myself confronted by an unknown power of tremendous force. I suddenly became possessed of an almost animal fury, the blood rushed to my heart, and I realized I was working myself into a state of absolute frenzy.

I, too, stared straight into Rasputin's eyes, and speaking literally I felt my own starting out of my head. Probably I must have looked rather formidable, for Rasputin suddenly began to squirm and asked: 'What do you want with me?'

'Clear out at once, you vile heretic, there is no place for you in this sacred house!'

'I was invited here at the wish of persons more highly placed than you,' Rasputin answered insolently, and pulled out an invitation card.

'You are a notorious swindler,' I replied. 'No one can believe your words. Clear out at once, this is no place for you.'

Rasputin shot a sidelong glance at me, fell heavily on his knees and began to pray, bowing to the ground. Outraged by such insolence, I nudged him in the side and said: 'Enough of this tomfoolery. If you don't clear out at once, I'll order my sergeants-at-arms to carry you out.'

With a heavy groan and a murmured: 'O Lord, forgive him such sin!' Rasputin rose slowly to his feet and, shooting a parting look of anger at me, slunk away. I followed him to the Western doors of the Cathedral. There a Court Cossack helped him on with his magnificent sable-lined coat and placed him in a car, and Rasputin drove away. [4]

Meanwhile troops in red, green and blue uniforms, some with helmets and breast plates, had taken their places on the route which ran through the Morskaya along the Nevski Prospect. It was raining hard and the crowds were embarrassingly thin. The bunting on the lamp posts, and the flags on the key buildings, hung disconsolate in the downpour. Even the standards of the famous regiments – Household Cavalry, Lancers, Chevaux Légers, Dragoons and Grenadiers – failed to arouse much enthusiasm. Just before twelve the soldiers came to the salute, the bands struck up the Russian National Anthem and faces turned to the lofty archway of the General Staff Building which spanned the entrance to the Morskaya. First came the trumpeters riding milk-white horses, then a *sotnia* of scarlet-coated Cossacks of the Guard. 'Picked men these,' wrote *The Times* correspondent, 'superb riders and all reputed sharpshooters. They carried their carbines unslung, the butt resting on the right thigh and the muzzle pointing upwards. They rode in double line and formed a screen for the Imperial cortège across the entire breadth of the roadway.' Immediately behind them came an open victoria drawn by two horses, in which sat the Czar and the eight-year-old Czarevich. This was followed by two state coaches, one carrying the Empress and her mother-in-law, and Dowager Empress Marie (a sister of Queen Alexandra of England), and the other the Czar's four young daughters.

The cathedral was filled with the highest dignitaries of the state. The huge interior glowed with icons and candles while the Patriarch Antiochus, a fine old man in a mitre flashing with jewels, stood waiting to conduct the service. A hush fell over the assembly when the Imperial family entered. The Czarevich, looking painfully thin and drawn, was carried by a Cossack of the Guards, and the beautiful German-born Empress Alexandra Feodorovna, a princess of Hesse-Darmstadt and a grand-daughter of Queen Victoria, appeared as remote and disdainful as ever. It was a fairy-story setting, yet there was no feeling of warmth in the vast assembly, only cold curiosity.

The St Petersburg nobility had hoped that the Empress would make a real effort in this tercentenary year to win over the people in the capital, that the Winter Palace once more would resound to music and laughter, and that the Czar would seize the occasion to grant long overdue concessions to the Duma. None of these things happened. Indeed, Nicholas II seemed deliberately to lean the other way. He allowed a ninety-year-old village elder to present the felicitations of a peasant delegation in words carefully prepared by his ministers, so feudal and archaic that it was obvious no reforms would be forthcoming.

Thou lord [said the old man] art our protection against all enemies. In thee is truth, in thee is mercy. Thou hast granted us peasants many tokens of thy favour ... God give thee long life and bless thee! May thy exalted son, our Lord the Czarevich and the Heir to the Throne, grow up to be a joy to thee, little mother Tsaritsa, and to all thy lieges. Be sure that our lives belong to thee. Be sure that at the first call we shall place ourselves before thee like a wall and sacrifice ourselves, like Ivan Susanin for thy dear life, thy House, and the glory of our country. Rule Czar of the true faith to our glory and the terror of our foes.

The only gesture made by Nicholas II was to grant a general amnesty to prisoners – except for political offenders. Murderers, thieves, blackmailers, rogues of all descriptions poured out of the gaols.

If the Emperor lived in another century, the Empress moved on another plane. She not only failed to give a ball in the Winter Palace, but did not even turn up at the two receptions held by the Czar. Her mother-in-law, the Dowager Empress Marie, deputized for her. The only ball that took place was the one given by the St Petersburg nobility in the *Salle de la Noblesse*. The Empress performed the first dance with the Czar, then disappeared for the rest of the evening. The only real glimpse the public had of her was at the Gala Performance at the Maryinsky Opera House where Glinka's *Life for the Czar* was sung.

She was very pale when she came in [wrote the daughter of the British Ambassador, Miss Meriel Buchanan], the pale blue ribbon of St Andrew that crossed her breast matching the turquoises in her magnificent tiara and parure, the soft folds of her white velvet dress setting off her stately figure. But her lovely tragic face was expressionless, almost austere as she stood by her husband's side during the playing of the National Anthem, her eyes, enigmatical in their dark gravity, seeming fixed on some secret inward thought that was certainly far removed from the crowded theatre and the people who acclaimed her. Not once did a smile break the immobile sombreness of her expression when, the Anthem over, she bent her head in acknowledgement of the cheers that greeted its conclusion and sank down in the gold-backed arm-chair that had been provided for her.

The Diplomatic Body had been given places all along the first tier and our box happened to be next to the Imperial one, and, sitting so close, we could see that the fan of white eagles' feathers the Empress was holding was trembling convulsively, we could see how a dull, unbecoming flush was stealing over her pallor, could almost hear the laboured breathing which made the diamonds which covered the bodice of her gown rise and fall, flashing and trembling with a thousand uneasy sparks of light. Presently it seemed that this emotion or distress mastered her completely, and with a few whispered words to the Emperor she rose and withdrew to the back of the box, to be no more seen that evening.

A little wave of resentment rippled over the theatre, women glanced at each other and raised their shoulders expressively, men uttered despairingly below their breath. Was it not always the same story? The Empress hated St Petersburg, disliked its society, its people, anything to do with it; she refused to take her proper place by the Emperor's side, would not put her own personal feeling in the background and make herself pleasant. Later on I remember my mother and father asserted that whatever the reason for the Empress's sudden withdrawal had been, it was certainly a very real torment or affliction and no whim or fancy, but the disagreeable impression remained in people's minds and would not be conjured away by any argument or discussion. [5]

No one except the immediate family of the imperial couple knew the truth. The press speculated wildly most of the year. It was not until the autumn when a book appeared, written by Princess Catherine Radziwill under the pseudonym of Count Vassili, that people grasped the facts. The Czar's son suffered from haemophilia, an incurable malady stemming from the weakness of the finer blood vessels, which was carried by the female but only transmitted to males. Queen Victoria was the carrier. Her son, Prince Leopold, was afflicted by the disease; three of her daughters transmitted it to their sons; and two of her grand-daughters, Princess Henry of Prussia and the Czarina, transmitted it in turn to their sons.

The Heir Apparent had nearly died at the Emperor's shooting lodge at Spala in the autumn of 1912. He had bumped his leg climbing out of a boat. Internal bleeding began, and a tumour developed in the groin, causing excruciating pain and the risk of blood poisoning. The swelling pressed on all the inflamed nerves of his leg and his temperature rose alarmingly. For eleven days the Empress never undressed, never went to bed, never lay down for more than an hour at a time. She sat soothing the brow of the child who lay huddled on one side, moaning with pain, his left leg drawn up so sharply that for nearly a year afterwards he could not straighten it out. No one thought the boy could live.

After dinner when we were sitting very quietly in the Empress' boudoir [wrote the Czarina's companion, Madame Anna Virubova], Princess Henry of Prussia, who had come to be with her sister in her trouble, appeared in the doorway very white and agitated and begged members of the suite to retire as the child's condition was desperate. At eleven o'clock the Emperor and Empress entered the room, despair written on their faces. Still the Empress declared that she could not believe that God had abandoned them and she asked me to telegraph Rasputin for his prayers. His reply came quickly. 'The little one will not die.' it said. 'Do not allow the doctors to bother him too much.' As a matter of fact the turning point came a few days later, the pain subsided, and the boy lay wasted and utterly spent, but alive. [6]

It is not surprising that the Empress felt Rasputin to be indispensable. This was not the first time that his prayers appeared to save the life of her child. She believed utterly that he was a man of God; and his presence not only seemed to relieve the Czarevich of pain but gave the Empress herself bodily strength and new hope. Ever since she had learned of her child's incurable disease, shortly after his birth, she had suffered from dizziness and palpitations of the heart, which today probably would be diagnosed as hysteria. That was why she rarely attended large functions; why she often looked so pale and seemed to be having difficulty in breathing. 'At the great ball in the *Salle de la Noblesse*,' wrote her lady in waiting, Baroness Buxhoeveden, 'she felt so ill that she could scarcely keep her feet. She underwent tortures from the feeling of faintness that overwhelmed her, before she was able to attract the attention of the Emperor who was talking at the other end of the room. When he came up it was only just in time to lead her away and prevent her from fainting in public.' [7]

The politicians and courtiers surrounding the Czar scarcely could be expected to view Rasputin in the same light as the Empress. They saw him as a charlatan – an illiterate, lascivious peasant who had managed to get a hold over the Imperial couple by perpetrating a gigantic hoax. Although the President of the Duma had persuaded the Czar to banish Rasputin from the capital early in 1912, the 'miracle of Spala' had restored him to favour and in 1913 he was firmly installed once more in a flat in St Petersburg. His brush with M. Rodzianko in Kazan Cathedral had not discouraged him and he appeared at other tercentenary celebrations in remote parts of the country. These gatherings were no more successful, as far as the Imperial couple were concerned, than the fêtes in St Petersburg. After attending the wedding of the Kaiser's daughter in Berlin in May, the Czar and Czarina travelled to Moscow, Vladimir, Bogoliubov and Nijni Novgorod. The trip was made on the Imperial train. There were two Imperial trains, exactly alike, with an engine and eight carriages painted blue and decorated with coats of arms and monograms. The Czar and his entourage always travelled together in one, while the other went off empty as a form of camouflage, either before or after the royal train. Not even the heads of the passenger department knew which was conveying the Imperial family. The first coach contained the escort. The moment the train stopped, sentinels ran to take up position at the doors of Their Majesties' carriage. The second coach contained the kitchen; the third a dining room for sixteen, and a heavily curtained drawing room with a grand piano; the fourth coach the bedrooms and sitting rooms of Their Majesties; the fifth a nursery upholstered in bright cretonne with white painted furniture; the sixth the Czar's suite; the seventh luggage; the eighth the Inspector of the Imperial trains, a dispensary, physicians and domestics.

At Nijni Novgorod the Czar and Czarina embarked on a boat and sailed up the Volga. The Prime Minister, M. Kokovtzov, accompanied the Emperor, and hoped to see enthusiastic demonstrations all the way down the Volga. 'There was nothing in the feeling of the crowd,' he wrote dejectedly, 'but shallow curiosity.' [8]

The Czar did not help to improve matters. He did not seem in the least interested in winning over his people, but became increasingly withdrawn each day. 'Down the Volga from Nijni there was a biting cold wind,' wrote

Kokovtzov, 'and the Czar did not once show himself where stop-overs had been arranged. There were handsomely ornamented descents from the shore to the water where small groups of peasants were gathered apparently waiting to see their Czar; but in vain, for the steamship went steadily on till it reached Kostroma, where it stopped for the night . . .' [9]

Although the Empress did not dare to scandalize her court officials by having Rasputin on the boat with her, she secretly arranged for him to follow the route, and saw that he received the necessary permits. 'At Kostroma Rasputin was seen in one of the churches,' wrote the Prime Minister. 'I asked General Dzhunkovsky . . . what the *starets* was doing there. He said he didn't know; that he had nothing to do with the issue of permits.'

Not many tourists visited Russia in 1913. St Petersburg was fifty hours from London, forty from Paris, thirty from Berlin. Apart from the tedium of the long journey, the language presented difficulties. 'I had imagined that all Russians were linguists,' wrote the English actor, Sir Herbert Beerbohm Tree, who visited Moscow in January 1913, 'but it was soon borne in on me that there is one language in Russia and that is Russian . . . it is almost impossible to make one's self understood either on a railway platform, in restaurants or hotels . . .' [10] There were other hurdles as well. Russia was the only country in Europe that insisted on passports, and demanded visas both for entering and leaving. The suspicions of the customs officials were so notorious that travellers were advised not to wrap articles in newspapers or anything that carried the printed word. Holy Russia was a country of furs and sleigh bells and bombs, of gypsy music, jewels, beggars, bureaucracy and a secret police that numbered more than twenty thousand. The officials and the police had a tendency to compete with one another in sudden bursts of vigilance, invariably at the expense of tourists. In October Captain Wavell, a member of the British General Staff, attended manoeuvres at the Czar's invitation. But on the way home he was arrested at the frontier. Despite his frantic protestations, his luggage was confiscated and he was returned to Warsaw under police guard. After long hours of detention he was allowed to get in touch with the British Embassy who secured his release.

Foreigners, however, were not the only people who suffered inconvenience. A far worse misfortune fell upon M. Petrov, a Russian diplomat who had been appointed to the embassy at Bucharest as Councillor. In November 1913, Petrov was on his way to St Petersburg to receive final instructions. When the train stopped at Klin, between Moscow and Tver, he jumped off to buy a paper. Before he could return, the train started and he had to climb on the baggage van. A guard tried to push him off but he managed to get into a third class compartment. Three guards then came up and asked him to pay a fine for jumping on a moving train. Petrov showed his diplomatic papers but the guards threw them on the floor. When the train reached Tver, Petrov was arrested. After protesting vehemently, he was allowed to send a dispatch to the Foreign Office in St Petersburg. But he made the mistake of observing protocol and wrote the telegram in French. This aroused the suspicions of the police, who decided that he must be mad. Other officials agreed, and Petrov was bundled off to a lunatic asylum, where he was detained for several days. Finally the doctors pronounced him sane, and allowed him to proceed to St Petersburg. No one apologized to him, but the Foreign Secretary, M. Sazonov, sent a huffy letter to the Minister of Railways protesting that Petrov's diplomatic papers had not been respected.

Apart from hazards such as these, many tourists were intimidated by the sheer magnitude of the country and the time required to travel about it. Stretching from the Baltic to the Pacific, the Empire covered nearly a sixth of the earth's surface. Although Czar Nicholas II was an autocratic ruler, Russia claimed to be 'a constitutional monarchy', for since 1905 she had possessed an elected Parliament – or Duma – which exercised the right of free speech. While the Duma had no authority over the Czar's ministers, and could be dissolved at the wish of the sovereign, by 1913 it had established itself so firmly that Nicholas no longer dared to abolish it. The Russian press had considerable freedom. Over three hundred daily, weekly and monthly periodicals were published in St Petersburg alone, but editors had to be careful what they printed, for if the authorities decided that the material was 'subversive' the paper might be suspended or permanently suppressed. This usually did not happen until after three warnings.

The total population of European and Asiatic Russia, including the dependencies of Khiva and Bokhara, numbered a hundred and sixty-six million, yet there were only thirty-three cities in the vast Empire with more than a hundred thousand people. The most important of these were: St Petersburg, Moscow, Warsaw, Kiev, Riga and Lodz. Eighty per cent of the population consisted of peasants and factory workers, the majority of whom were illiterate. The middle classes – shop keepers, business managers and professional people – numbered only a few hundred thousand. The nobility, on the other hand, which was not aristocratic in the western sense (although aristocrats were included in it), was reckoned to number anywhere from one to two million people. The ranks were composed mainly of bureaucrats and military officials who, as soon as they reached a certain grade in the civil service hierarchy, were endowed with 'hereditary nobility', which sometimes carried a title, and always carried such privileges as the right to attend Court, to own land, to educate children at special schools, and to take precedence on all sorts of occasions over ordinary mortals. The church was visible everywhere; not only because Holy Russia was steeped in superstition but because people had a sense of theatre and liked to act and sing.

In pacing up and down the station . . . in the first frontier town at which our train stopped [wrote Sir Herbert Beerbohm Tree], my attention was attracted by the sound of music. I entered the great waiting room and found that in it a Divine Service was being held, with all the impressive ceremony of the Greek Church. There was the gorgeously robed priest in front of an altar; there was the icon with burning candles and incense. At this Saturday night service I listened with wonder to the hymn sung by the peasants in their clear trebles and rich basses with a beauty and solemnity I do not remember to have heard elsewhere . . . [11]

Most foreigners revelled in St Petersburg. Although it lacked the oriental magnificence of Moscow, which blazed with Byzantium domes, it had a melancholy beauty of its own. Built by Peter the Great on the marshes of the Neva to give him 'a window on Europe', it had sprung to life in the short space of ten years, costing the lives of thousands of workmen. It was Russia's only western city and the avenues and great squares had the unmistakable look of Paris; yet the Slav stamp was apparent in the pink granity quays lining the river, in the dark red buildings and the gilded spires.

In January there were only five hours of daylight and the sky was low and grey. Nevertheless, the unseen sun frequently managed to search out the gilded domes of St Isaac's and the spire of the Fortress Cathedral, causing them to flash and glitter through the murky haze, in a blaze of eerie splendour. Because of the cold the streets were less animated than in other European capitals, but they rang to the sound of sleigh bells for there were few motor cars in 1913. The coachmen were immense figures. They dressed in padded greatcoats under which they placed successive layers of newspapers to add further warmth. By the end of the winter they reached gargantuan proportions. They drove at breakneck speed, often using the sleigh road across the frozen Neva which was marked by lamp posts and sawn-off fir trees. Tramcar lines were also laid across the river, and every year tea houses and a little wooden tavern were set up. In former days a colony of Lapps came each year and camped on the ice with their reindeer, for the temperature of St Petersburg rarely fell lower than ten degrees below zero, which they regarded as a temperate climate; but in 1913 they had disappeared.

Almost every man in the street was in uniform: not only army officers who, just as in Berlin, were not allowed to wear mufti, but civilians of all professions. The colour and variety of the uniforms seemed to transform the ice-bound city into a huge stage set. Every great house, for instance, had its special livery, usually in a bright shade, except for scarlet which was reserved for royalty. The Horse Guards wore spotless tunics and gleaming brass helmets; the Cossacks flowing robes and furry busbies. The policemen were dressed in black with orange or green facings and astrakhan caps; students in green or grey with peaked caps; concierges in long blue overcoats with gold lace; and house attendants or *dvorniks*, whose job was to sweep the front steps and clear the paths, scarlet blouses and caps with a brass plate giving the address of the house to which they were attached. Even the wet-nurses had a uniform of their own. They wore blue for boys, pink for girls, with a diadem of false pearls on their heads, draped with a white mantle.

This was not all. A reminder that Russia stretched to the Orient was given by immense Turcomans in shaggy hats of white sheepskin, and dark-haired Caucasians in long skirted kaftans of white or brown, with double rows of cartridge belts across the breast, a dagger of classical silver stuck in the belt and a sugar-loaf hat of astrakhan. But perhaps the door porter of the Astoria Hotel outdid them all. 'In his long black blouse and twisted pink sash, and his black astrakhan cap with an upstanding row of peacock feathers, he might have stepped out of the ranks of the Russian ballet,' wrote the correspondent of the *Daily Mail*. [12]

The most famous shops were on the Morskaya and the Nevski Prospect. Just before the New Year, Fabergé, with its huge granite pillars and air of breathless opulence, was thronged with people buying gifts. Once the season was under way, however, the most crowded rendezvous was the hairdresser on the Morskaya, where guests sat in gold and blue chairs and caught up with the gossip. Afterwards the ladies often went to Eliseiv's to buy sweets and cream tarts, or to the Ural Stone shop to examine the wonderful animals carved in jade and amethyst, chalcedony and topaz.

There were plenty of parties in St Petersburg that winter to make up for the darkened windows of the Winter Palace. The social season opened a fortnight before the New Year with the Grand Duchess Vladimir's Christmas Bazaar, held in the Hall of the Nobles. All the leading members of society had smaller stalls grouped around the large royal stall; crowds poured in to buy expensive knick-knacks; and ladies exchanged gossip while making a mental note of each other's clothes.

All the great houses of St Petersburg had their own ballrooms, and for the next two months the fashionable area of the capital resounded all night to the strains of dance music and the jingle of sleigh bells. Fancy dress parties and amateur theatricals were much in vogue and hostesses vied with one another for original ideas. One lady gave a black and white ball; another a party where everyone was asked to come in ordinary evening dress but to wear a wig. Miss Meriel Buchanan arranged a series of tableaux for the British Embassy party, ranging from Bluebeard to Jack the Ripper. The Princess Obolensky gave a Greek mythology party, and wrote the music for a ballet which her friends performed. A more serious effort was made by the Grand Duke Constantin Constantinovich, President of the Imperial Academy of Science, who had translated Hamlet into Russian and was a poet of considerable repute. He spent most of the year writing a play entitled *King of the Jews* which contained two thousand verses. By the autumn the play was being rehearsed in the Hermitage Theatre, and the Grand Duke was playing the leading role of Joseph of Arimathea.

The *bals blancs* given for unmarried girls were tepid affairs compared to the *bals roses*. Heavy-lidded chaperones sat in gilt chairs around the room; there was no orchestra, only a very old piano player known as a *tappeur*, who had played at debutante parties for fifty years. There were very few waltzes; the two-step was considered vulgar; and the Czar had gone one better than the Kaiser by banning the one-step as well as the tango. The evening, therefore, consisted mainly of quadrilles organized by a red-faced Master of Ceremonies whose orders rang through the room with the bark of a sergeant major: 'Advance! Retreat! Join Hands! Form a Circle! Chassé!'

Apart from the Grand Duchess Vladimir, St Petersburg society was led by the highly rouged, sharp-tongued Countess of Kleinmichel, who ran the most entertaining *salon*; the Countess Betsy Shuvalov, who had a huge palace on the Fontanka canal with a wonderful string of reception rooms, and a private theatre as well as a ballroom; and the slim, elegant, forgetful Princess Olga Orlov, whose husband, Prince Vladimir Orlov, was the head of the Czar's military Cabinet. The Orlovs lived in a white palace on the Moika and their hospitality was famous. When the Prince invited Mr Frederick Cripps, a son of Lord Parmoor (and a brother of Sir Stafford Cripps), to dinner, the Englishman asked what time he was expected. 'It starts next Wednesday at nine o'clock,' Prince Orlov replied, 'and it goes on for two weeks. You will always find people there, in one of the dining rooms, or playing cards.' [13]

The houses were very hot and often filled with palm trees dispatched from the Crimea, or flowers sent by special train from the south of France. Dinner was a meal that required strong powers of gastronomical endurance. It always began with Zakhuska – hors d'oeuvres – which were served in a special room and eaten standing up. While guests helped themselves to caviare, smoked salmon, salted cucumbers, hot mushrooms in a special cream sauce, gangfish from the Volga, and hundreds of other delicacies, footmen moved about refilling the glasses of vodka. After this the dinner proper began. The menu might be borsch with thick cream and hot pastries, then sturgeon or sterlets, venison or tree partridge, ending with a wonderfully elaborate sweet. 'Between every course little yellow cigarettes would be handed round,' wrote the daughter of the British Ambassador, 'and through the blue haze of smoke the jewels on women's fingers would flash with some quick movement or the light would catch a thousand sparks in some decoration, or gleam on the golden aiguillettes swinging from the shoulder of some young Grand Duke.' [14]

Frequently, after one of these dinners, people would decide to visit the gypsy quarter, Novaia Derevnia, on the outskirts of the capital. This district was known as 'The Islands' for the canals of the Neva had turned it into an archipelago. The journey was always made in troikas, the fastest type of transport. The centre horse trotted in a shaft while the outside horses, loose save for long traces, galloped. Driving a troika was a special art, for the driver had to stand. He wore a special badge, peacock feathers set in a round cap, he had a special name, *yamshchik*, and he charged a very special price. As the last houses of the suburb gave way to forest and frozen land, the driver would let his horses go; the two loose horses would break into a furious gallop while the centre horse, in shafts, trotted at breakneck speed.

The wild pace through the bitter-cold forest, under a starlight sky, was an excitement in itself. Then the troika would draw up before a low building hidden among a clump of fir trees; everyone would jump out and bang loudly on the doors; and a few minutes later a sleepy-eyed Tartar would appear. Soon the bare white-washed room was alive with waiters lighting candles, bringing champagne bottles, arranging seats and adjusting the samovar. The gypsy troupe usually numbered twenty to thirty. They sang in a curious metallic voice, 'with a ring in it of something Eastern, barbaric and utterly strange to European ears, to the thrum of the guitars', wrote Lord

St Petersburg

The Czar and Czarina leaving the Kazan Cathedral in St Petersburg after the service of thanksgiving for the third centenary of the Romanov dynasty.

One of the first pictures of the Czarevich taken in January 1913 after his recovery from the 'mysterious' illness that intrigued Europe.

A rare informal picture of the Czar and Czarina on a hunting expedition, photographed by a lady of the court.

Grand Duke Nicholas' famous pack of borzois, about to set out wolf-coursing at Gachina, near St Petersburg.

A river-boat on the Shilka in Siberia, still a typical means of transport in Russia in 1913.

A party of French and English skiing at Yuki, near St Petersburg.

Russian caddies with Miss Everth at Murino, a nine-hole golf course fifteen miles from St Petersburg that was a great attraction to English residents.

The pupils of the State Smolny
Institute for noble girls. The girls
were kept there for seven years in
almost total seclusion, sometimes
even from their families. Once a year
they were served at a ceremonial meal
by the Czarina.

The Grand Duchess Vladimir
(grandmother of Princess Marina),
who dominated St Petersburg society,
while the Czarina kept herself in
seclusion.

Grand Duke Michael on the golf-links at
Cannes with the Countess Zia Torby.
His morganatic marriage created a great
disturbance in the Imperial family.

Rasputin, the dissolute monk, who
gained ascendancy over the Imperial
family by convincing them of his
healing powers.

Grand Duke Alexander and Grand Duchess Xenia (the Czar's sister) with five of
their children, photographed on their estate in the Crimea.

Mendel Beilis, the defendant in the notorious 'ritual murder' case at Kiev, who was released in November after a trial that had lasted weeks.

Lenin addressing the Russian Socialist Democratic Labour Party Conference in Cracow, from where he controlled Bolshevik revolutionary activities throughout 1913.

In 1913 Maxim Gorky was furthering the Bolshevik cause with his school for
revolutionaries on Capri. Five years previously Lenin had visited him there, and is
here seen (on the left) playing chess, while Gorky, head in hand, looks on.

Frederick Hamilton. 'A tempest of wild, nasal melody arose, in the most perfect harmony . . . The un-European *timbre* of the voices conduced doubtless to the effect, but . . . it had about it something so novel and fresh – or was it something so immemorially old? – that the listeners felt absolutely intoxicated. On the Russians it acted like hypnotism.' [15]

Prince Felix Yusupov loved the music and often played gypsy tunes on his guitar. The first time he visited 'The Islands' he was a boy of fifteen. As his school uniform was unsuitable, his elder brother dressed him up like a woman. 'The peculiar atmosphere created by the singing and dancing', he wrote, 'and by the beautiful primitive women stirred the soul as well as the senses. Everyone fell a victim of their spell. Some visitors who came for a few hours stayed for days and spent fabulous sums of money in the place.' [16] Indeed, so much money was lost by the sons of the aristocracy the Czar put 'The Islands' out of bounds for anyone who had attended the *Corps des Pages*, the most exclusive boys' academy in St Petersburg.

A less costly midnight sport than 'visiting the gypsies' was introduced by the toboggan-mad English, and enjoyed great popularity. Every winter the British Embassy staff erected two ice hills, forty feet high, facing each other. This scenic railway run was navigated on two-foot sleds with steel runners. The great sport was to take a lady passenger. The man would sit with his companion kneeling behind him, her arms entwined around his neck. The intimacy was even more exciting than the speed or the danger of over-turning.

The German-born Grand Duchess Vladimir ran what was often described as 'a substitute court' for the absent Empress. As the widow of the Czar's uncle, Marie Pavlovna was the third lady of the land, preceded only by the Czar's wife and mother. Tall, handsome and politically ambitious, the Grand Duchess always filled her rooms with the prettiest women and the most distinguished men in the capital. It was no secret that she regarded the Empress with a mixture of contempt and derision, and that much scandalous gossip originated in her house. Once, when she travelled to Bulgaria for an official engagement, and talked to guests for three hours, remembering names without a single mistake, one of the officials congratulated her. 'One ought to know one's job,' she replied. 'You may pass that on to the Grand Court.' [17]

The sharpest clash between the Imperial family and the Grand Duchess had come in 1905 when the latter's eldest son, the Grand Duke Cyril, married his first cousin, the divorced wife of the Grand Duke of Hesse. This was contrary to the laws of Russia and the laws of the church. No member of the

Imperial family could marry without the Czar's consent, and marriage between first cousins was expressly forbidden. Furthermore, the Grand Duke of Hesse was the Empress's brother, and she took a poor view of the woman who had abandoned him. When the newly married couple arrived in St Petersburg, Nicholas II's Court Minister called upon them and conveyed the Czar's instructions; they must leave Russia at once and never again set foot on the soil of the country. Grand Duke Vladimir and his wife were outraged by the edict. Although some years later the ban was withdrawn, the Grand Duchess blamed the Empress for the severity of the punishment and never forgave her.

This did not mean that she cut herself off from the Imperial Court, merely that her sharp tongue was more indefatigable than ever in tearing the Empress to shreds. In 1913 she was particularly spiteful as only a few months earlier she had written to the Czar asking him to consider her second son, the Grand Duke Boris, as a suitor for the hand of his eldest daughter, the sixteen-year-old Grand Duchess Olga. As Boris was a stupid dissipated young man the request was curtly refused, which did not improve matters between the two families.

The Grand Duchess had succeeded her husband as President of the Academy of Fine Arts and often took guests to the Imperial Theatre on Sundays to watch the ballet. Like the rest of fashionable St Petersburg she had a permanent box at the Maryinsky. Indeed, it was almost impossible for outsiders to gain admission unless they were taken by a subscriber, as all the seats were booked for the season. In the winter of 1913 St Petersburg gossiped about the Grand Duchess' youngest son, Prince Andrew, who was rumoured to be infatuated with the prima ballerina, Madame Kshesinskaia. They said he had given her fabulous jewels and was begging his mother to persuade the Czar to allow him to marry her. When Kshesinskaia was dancing people often turned their opera glasses on the Grand Duchess' box to fathom her thoughts, but her expression was always impervious. The rumours were true, however, and after the war the Prince married the ballerina, for then there was no one left to object.

Although the Imperial ballet possessed great dancers the theatre was under the direction of a man named Teliakovsky, a former officer in the Guards whose talents were more conspicuous as a courtier than an artist. The new ballets produced in St Petersburg between 1907 and 1913 – *Chopiniana*, *Nuits d'Egypte*, *Le Pavillon d'Armide*, *Prince Igor*, *Carnaval* – followed the rigid pattern that had not changed for a century. The only really exciting ballet was the 'travelling branch' of the Imperial Theatre, composed of artists scooped up when the theatres closed between May and September, and taken to Paris and London by the great Russian impresario, Serge Diaghilev. Although the Grand Duke Vladimir had been Diaghilev's prime backer, the Grand Duchess showed little interest in his revolutionary ideas.

For four years Diaghilev had thrilled the capitals of the west by blending music, poetry, painting and dancing in a way that had never been done before. Sometimes he created new ballets; sometimes he took the Maryinsky's staid productions – *Le Pavillon*, *Prince Igor*, *Carnaval* – and cast his magic over them. He employed great artists such as Benois and Bakst to design his sets; encouraged great choreographers such as Fokine to strike out on new lines; and finally commissioned such great composers as Stravinsky to write music for ballet rather than adapting ballet to music.

Although Diaghilev employed the same dancers as the Marynsky, they blossomed under his inspiration and displayed talents that the Russians themselves never saw, for Diaghilev's ballets were not shown in St Petersburg until after the First War. '*Swan Lake*, *Aurora and the Prince*, *Giselle*, even with Karsavina, Pavlova and Nijinsky were a bore,' wrote Richard Capell in the London *Daily Mail* on 4 February 1913, 'yet this is the sort of ballet still supreme in Russia. The advanced pieces such as *Scheherazade* or *The Firebird* or *Thamar* are never shown. . .' The truth was that the Grand Duchess Vladimir – and other Russians who travelled abroad – found many of the impresario's ideas distasteful. Nor did she like Nijinsky who on one occasion had deeply shocked the Maryinsky by appearing in form-fitting tights without wearing the customary strap to conceal the contours of his body. The Grand Duchess certainly was not alone in preferring the classical pattern to the two revolutionary ballets being shown in the spring of 1913. 'Praxiteles was wrong; Hogarth completely at sea; while the dancer who obeys the famous "Code of Terpsichore" is the worst of all,' scathingly wrote the London *Daily Express* on 12 July. 'We suspected something was wrong when we saw *L'Après-Midi d'un Faune*, suspicion became stronger when the movements of *Jeux* met our astonished eyes, and now after seeing *Le Sacre du Printemps*, the new ballet produced at the Drury Lane last night, we must surely be convinced of the error of our ways.' The writer went on to describe hissing in the audience; referred to Nijinsky's steps as 'comic' and Stravinsky's music as sheer anarchy. Two days later Nijinsky, who had choreographed *Jeux* and *Le Sacre du Printemps*, replied in the *Daily Mail*: 'People who say that the piece was hissed cannot know what real hissing is . . . I am accused of a "crime against grace" . . . Really I begin to have a horror of the very word. "Grace" and "charm" make me feel sea-sick. . . I detest conventional "nightingale-and-rose" poetry; my own inclinations are "primitive". I eat my meat without Sauce Béarnaise.'

The Grand Duchess adored bridge, which was the craze of 1913, and filled her house with people who played at all hours of the day and night. People accused her of lowering the tone of society because she liked rich business men who would play for high stakes. Although all Russians had a penchant for gambling, the most serious card players preferred their clubs, free from female distraction. The three most exclusive clubs in St Petersburg were the Imperial Yacht Club on the Morskaya (which had nothing to do with yachting), the English Club and the New Club. The Yacht Club was dominated by the Grand Dukes, of whom there were twenty-two, and its membership was limited to a hundred and fifty people. The Club possessed the best French chef in the capital; its members had direct access to the Court, and within its precincts the best administrative jobs in the Empire were parcelled out.

The Russian weakness for gambling led to many dramatic incidents, particularly among army officers. Although the Russian army was patterned on the German, with the same 'courts of honour', duelling was far more prevalent in St Petersburg than Berlin. If an officer could not pay his debts, social ostracism or suicide were his only alternatives. However, in order to prevent disgrace falling upon the regiment, brother officers occasionally ruined themselves to pay up for him.

Mr Frederick Cripps, who was joint managing director of the newly formed Russian and English Bank in 1913, had first hand experience of what 'honour' meant to a Russian officer. One night he was invited to a bachelor party by Count Leiders, who worked in the Russian Foreign Office. Other guests were 'Peps' Nekhludov and Prince Pavlik Urusov, a young officer in the Guards. They played poker and when Cripps lost his counters Urusov offered him a hundred pounds from his own pile. Later Cripps was more fortunate and when he had retrieved most of his losses he handed back the counters to Urusov. The latter jumped up from the table and complained to the host that Cripps had insulted him as he had not asked for the counters to be returned. Cripps apologised deeply but worse was to come. At the end of the evening Nekhludov suggested to Cripps that the hundred-pound counters be given to him as he saw Urusov daily, and that he would return them on demand. This caused a fearful outburst and Urusov promptly challenged

Nekhludov to a duel, which was duly arranged for six in the morning. By this time both men were shut up in separate rooms with their seconds. Cripps was so horrified that he went first into one room and begged Urusov to have a late supper with him on the grounds that he might never see him again. Then he did the same with Nekhludov. Both men agreed to meet him at a restaurant. They kept their word and when they were confronted with each other, wrote Cripps,

there was a kind of hysterical outbreak of good fellowship; we all kissed each other. I was overjoyed that the duel was off; but if I had not worked so desperately hard to keep the peace, someone would probably have been killed.

While I was in St Petersburg an officer in the Guards, who was marching with his men to change the guard at the Winter Palace, was spat upon by a peasant in the street. The officer did nothing at the time, but after completing his duties, he committed suicide that night, as someone had spat upon the Czar's uniform which he was wearing. Since he was on duty when the uniform was insulted, he could not apparently punish the offender, so his only resource was to destroy himself. I found that his brother officers all thought he had behaved correctly and could not have done otherwise.

Another occasion I can recall which has a bearing on this touchiness was when I was at the Medvet, or Bear Restaurant, on Christmas Eve. When the National Anthem was played, some civilian did not stand up, whereupon an officer killed him on the spot. The body was removed, and subsequently the officer was temporarily transferred to a regiment elsewhere. [18]

Duelling and fencing satisfied the urge for excitement that in England and America was met by competitive sport. Although the Imperial Alexander Lyceum, the fashionable boys' school in St Petersburg, always employed English instructors, the reverse of the English public school spirit was encouraged. Solitary confinement in a cell was preferred to corporal punishment; no games were played, and schoolboys were encouraged to 'split' on their fellow pupils by reporting each other's faults, which were discussed in full assembly. One of the gravest short-comings a pupil could have was a desire for privacy.

However, in 1913 there were signs of a change. The English had introduced polo and horse-racing, and the young were showing considerable interest in the Olympic Games scheduled to be held in Berlin in 1916. Athletics, particularly among the girls at state school, were becoming increasingly popular. In September a 'Russian Olympic' was held at Kiev in which the female sex carried off most of the honours. Mlle Popova beat the Russian women's record for the standing long jump by jumping 6 feet $9\frac{1}{2}$ inches; she also set up a new record for the long jump by accomplishing 13 feet 6 inches. Mlle Ratkova broke the record for putting the weight; and a record time of one minute four seconds was set in the women's 437-yard relay race.

As far as the older generation was concerned, shooting was the most popular diversion. The most famous hunting establishment in Russia was Pershimo, in the province of Talsi, an eleven-thousand-acre estate which originally had been given to the banker Lazarev by Catherine the Great. The Sovereign had bestowed it in gratitude for the huge diamond which Lazarev had presented to her – a diamond so beautiful that it was placed in the centre of the Czar's crown. The estate had been bought in the nineties by the Grand Duke Nicholas Nikolaievich who, when war broke out in 1914, became Commander-in-Chief of the Russian Army.

The Grand Duke's speciality was 'wolf coursing', and he boasted the finest breed of borzois in the land. These dogs were very fast and very fragile. They pursued the wolf at breakneck speed, but if they collided with one another, or took a false step, they were apt to break their backs or legs and had to be destroyed. The dogs were trained to overturn the wolf and pin it to the ground. By 1913 the Grand Duke's borzois had destroyed 635 cubs and yearlings but only fifty-six full-grown male wolves, for the latter invariably proved too strong for the dogs.

The killing of most animals in Russia was not a sport but a business. Over thirteen million squirrels were trapped annually; and seven million other fur animals, chief of which were ermine, fitch, foxes, kolinsky, mink, bears, badgers, musquash, otters and lynx. By 1913 the number of sables, formerly a hundred thousand a year, had fallen to ten thousand. This was because the best pelts could fetch as much as a hundred pounds and the animals were being hunted to extinction. One small district in the region of Amur was known to contain 172,000 traps. Consequently, in 1913, the Russian Government announced a closed season for sables until 1916.

Throughout the spring of 1913 Russia was in the grip of a fierce surge of Pan-Slav sentiment which nearly propelled the country into war. Russia had two dreams: one was the conquest of Constantinople, which would mean the domination of the Straits; the other was the formation of a Greater Serbia embracing millions of Slavs, now the nationals of other countries. Both these aspirations were blocked by the presence of Austria-Hungary.

Nevertheless Russia persisted. She engineered a pact between Bulgaria and Serbia which laid the foundation of the Balkan League. 'The Treaty contains the germ not only of war against Turkey but a war against Austria,' wrote the Prime Minister of France, M. Raymond Poincaré. 'It establishes further the hegemony of Russia over the Slav Kingdoms, because Russia is made the arbiter of all things.' [19] Poincaré's assessment was correct, for the Balkan League launched a joint attack on Turkey in the last months of 1912, while Russia watched with excited attention. No one expected the Little Allies to achieve very much; therefore, when they scored one victory after another, Russian interest increased to fever pitch. In March 1913, only a few weeks after the Czar's tercentenary celebrations in St Petersburg, the Bulgarian general and national hero, Radko Dmitriev, visited St Petersburg. The day after his arrival news came that Adrianople had fallen to a joint assault of Bulgarian and Serbian troops, and the Russian capital went wild. A Te Deum was celebrated in the Church of the Resurrection, and when the General came out on to the streets he was carried shoulder high by the crowds, who broke into the national anthems of the two countries. 'I have come on a secret mission to lay Constantinople at His Majesty's feet,' the General told the President of the Duma. [20]

Rodzianko was a passionate Pan-Slav himself and did everything in his power to embroil Russia in the war. He even sought an interview with the Czar and urged his opinions on Nicholas: 'Your Majesty,' he said, 'there is still time. We must take advantage of the popular enthusiasm. The Straits must become ours. A war will be joyfully welcomed, and will raise the Government's prestige.' [21]

However, Rodzianko tells us that Nicholas II maintained a stony silence. The truth was that the Czar had toyed with the idea of intervening a few months earlier. He had even called together his Prime Minister, Foreign Secretary and War Minister and announced flatly that he was planning to mobilize troops on the Austrian frontier. Prime Minister Kokovtzov was horrified. Russia, he pointed out, was totally unprepared for a world war, and a world war it was bound to be for Austria could not ignore such a provocation, and she, too, would be compelled to intervene. 'I ended,' wrote Kokovtzov, 'by an impassioned appeal to the Czar not to permit the fatal error, the consequences of which were immeasurable, since we were not ready for a war and our adversaries knew it well, and added that only by closing one's eyes to the sad actuality could one bring oneself to play into their hands.' In the end the Czar acquiesced in his usual tame, charming way. 'Of course,' he smiled, 'the mobilization orders would not be sent.' [22]

Instead, the Czar and his Foreign Secretary, M. Sazonov, contented themselves by encouraging the Serbs to increase their subversive activities in Bosnia and Herzegovina. In a long interview with M. Pashitch in January 1913, Nicholas II talked of the day when these Austrian provinces would be part of the Serbian kingdom. Although he conversed in his usual dreamy way, by May this line of argument suddenly became vested with political urgency. Bulgaria and Serbia, the victorious allies, were now at each other's throats arguing about the spoils. Partly to dissuade Serbia from doing anything rash, partly because he believed it, M. Sazonov wrote to the Russian Minister in Belgrade, 'Serbia's Promised Land lies in the territory of the present Austria-Hungary, and not where she is now making efforts and where the Bulgarians stand in her way . . . Time works on the side of Serbia and for the ruin of her enemies, who already show evident signs of decay. Explain all this to the Serbians!' [23]

However, in June the Bulgarians attacked Serbia, once again setting Europe on tenterhooks. 'What an abomination is this war in the Balkans,' wrote Nicholas II to his mother. Aggressive Bulgaria came out the loser. Much of the territory which she had won in the First Balkan War was wrested away from her by Serbia, while Turkey, who also entered the fray, managed to re-take Adrianople. Indeed, Serbia was the victor in every sense of the word, for the two wars doubled her territory and increased her population from three to four and a half million. Even more significant, she was now fired with a new self-confidence which boded ill for 1914.

Meanwhile, the nationalists were still complaining angrily that the Czar had missed a golden opportunity by not intervening in the war. Rumours were sweeping St Petersburg that the real culprit was Rasputin, whose influence for peace had been decisive. 'Fear, fear war,' he had told the Empress. This gossip later proved true, for in a letter which the Empress wrote to her husband in 1916 she reminds him that Rasputin 'always said the Balkans were not worth fighting over.'

In December 1913, the official Holy Synod newspaper the *Kolokol* (The Bell) came out with the statement: 'That we escaped a war last year is due to the influence of the holy *startsy* who direct our foreign policy, for which we should be profoundly grateful . . .' [24] Very few people in St Petersburg were in doubt as to whom was meant by the 'holy *startsy*'. It is ironical that Rasputin's role as preserver of the peace should have been another factor in alienating the upper classes from the throne in 1913.

There were others, besides the nationalists, who were deeply disappointed that peace had been maintained. 'A war between Austria and Russia,' wrote Lenin in the spring of 1913 to his friend Maxim Gorky, who ran a school for revolutionaries on the unlikely island of Capri, 'would be a very useful thing for the revolution but it is not likely that Franz Joseph [the Austrian Emperor] or Nikolasha [the Czar] will oblige.'

Things were not going well for the Bolshevik revolutionaries in 1913 and more than once Lenin toyed with the idea of giving up his subversive activities, and getting a job that paid a regular salary. He had moved from Paris with his wife, Krupskaya, in the summer of 1912 and taken up residence in the Austrian section of Poland, in Cracow. 'You ask me why I am in Austria,' he had written to Maxim Gorky. 'Between ourselves the Central Committee has established its Bureau here; it's near the frontier, which we make use of; nearer to Petersburg – we get papers from there on the third day; it's ever so much easier to write for the Petersburg press, and collaboration is better arranged . . .' [25]

Lenin's man in St Petersburg was Joseph Stalin. Stalin supervised the newspaper *Pravda*, launched in 1912 as the Bolsheviks' official organ. He was Lenin's organizer par excellence, plotting ways (mostly illegal) of getting his hands on much-needed money, fomenting strikes, inciting violence. 1913 found him busy preparing a great demonstration scheduled for 9 January. Thousands of leaflets were distributed calling for a republic; an eight-hour day; and the confiscation of the landowners' estates. Special emphasis was laid on the three-hundred-year 'shame' of the Romanovs' rule.

Yet events did not seem to be moving Lenin's way. He had split his party, the Social Democrats, because he refused to entertain any ideas but his own. He led the Bolshevik wing, while Plekhanov and Trotsky led the Mensheviks. And in 1913 the Mensheviks, much to Lenin's disgust, were beginning to advocate 'legal' rather than 'subversive' methods to achieve their goal.

Often Lenin had written mournfully, 'I do not expect to live to see the revolution'; and in 1913 had no reason to change his opinion. The truth was that both economic and political conditions were lessening the attractions of the violence he preached. As far as Russian industry was concerned, 1913 was a boom year. Production was increasing, foreign trade was expanding and the gold reserves swelling. Strikes were also increasing (most of them incited by paid revolutionary agents) but, as the stoppages were not serious, the employers regarded them as normal growing pains.

'Russia was rapidly moving ahead along the capitalist lines of development, catching up with the older capitalist countries which had gone ahead,' a Soviet historian tells us in *Outlines of the History of the October Revolution*. 'The gross output of industry increased by 44.9 per cent between the years 1900 and 1905, and by 1913 it had increased by 219 per cent.' There was a similar expansion in agriculture. From 1905 to 1913 the area of land cultivated increased by sixteen per cent, the yield by forty-one per cent. This was partly due to the change in government policy. Formerly the government had tried by all kinds of artificial means to preserve the landlords' holdings. Now it had seriously begun to encourage the transfer of these lands into the hands of the peasants. Between 1906 and 1913 the State Peasant Land Bank had bought up from the landlords and resold to the peasants over twenty million acres of land. Indeed, by 1916 nearly ninety per cent of all arable land was being cultivated by the working peasant farmer and only a little more than ten per cent remained in capitalist cultivation. Even Trotsky admits that the pre-war years saw giant strides. 'Agriculture entered upon a state of indubitable capitalistic boom', he wrote. 'The export of agricultural products from Russia rose between 1908 and 1912 from one billion roubles to one and a half billion roubles.' [26]

Russian expansion, and with it the first feeble glimmer of prosperity on a national scale, increased the desire of the educated people for a truly representative government. The right and centre parties of the new Duma supported the monarchy but were no longer content that the Emperor's power should be absolute. They urged that the Duma should appoint the Czar's ministers, and the ministers should in turn be responsible to the Duma. While almost all the left-wing members were Republicans, they were also democrats; nor did they wish to see a republic established by bloodshed. Even the handful of Marxists in the new Parliament were divided on the subject of violence. The Mensheviks were beginning to look with favour on the weapon of 'persuasion'. Only Lenin and the Bolsheviks still insisted that violence and subversion must continue.

Alexander Kerensky, a republican and a newly elected Labour deputy in the Fourth Duma, claims that by 1913 there was no longer any need of secretive underground activity.

The public was now accustomed to a free press, to political meetings, to political parties and clubs [he declared]. Trade unions, professional unions and co-operative societies were firmly rooted as part of the daily life. There were endless meetings during the election campaign, at which the government policy was criticized from every possible angle. With the weighted 'electoral college' system of suffrage – actually involving three-stage elections in the case of the peasants – the Duma could not give a fair representation of the political forces in the country. What it could do, however, was to give expression to the feeling of every class, since freedom of speech for the deputies was absolute . . . To me the two years in the Duma before the war were years of the most strenuous political, organizing and revolutionary work. The old, secretive, underground, conspirative methods of revolutionary activity had passed to the limbo of history . . . [27]

The Fourth Duma, which was elected in 1912, contained only a handful of Marxist extremists – eight Mensheviks and six Bolsheviks directed by Lenin. Throughout 1913 Lenin's supporters slipped over the Russian-Polish frontier to consult their leader and work out conspiratorial plans. Yet the year was not an encouraging one. Lenin's battles with the Mensheviks, who were no longer the minority but in the majority, were both bitter and tedious; and he was so poor he found it hard to survive. 'His chief means of livelihood was the meagre salary the party was able to pay him, which at times was far from sufficient, so that in 1913 he even considered having to give up his work in Austria, emigrate to England, and find there some means to earn a living.' 'There were terrible moments,' one of the Duma Deputies records. 'What if the party cannot find any means? Then Ilyich will have to leave the movement, for he never gets his work into either bourgeois journals or newspapers.' [28]

Lenin clung on. The highlight of 1913, as far as he was concerned, was news that his most trusted deputy, Malinovsky, had succeeded in wresting control of the St Petersburg Metal Workers Union from the Mensheviks. This news was relayed to Lenin, on the day that Stalin was celebrating the the first anniversary of *Pravda* – the '*Pravda* which,' says one of Lenin's biographers, 'somehow survived both censorship and police prosecution in an almost miraculous manner and reached a circulation of forty thousand.' [29]

The fact becomes less miraculous when we examine Lenin's protegé, the brilliant, loquacious, thrusting Malinovsky. 'For the first time among our people in the Duma there is an outstanding worker leader,' declared Lenin enthusiastically. But the truth was that Malinovsky was a 'double agent' working for the Okhrana, the Czarist police. Lenin wrote many of Malinovsky's Duma speeches, but the police always vetted them first. Through Malinovsky the police knew every Bolshevik plot, every plan, every assignation.

Malinovsky astounded his fellow deputies by openly calling for the overthrow of the Czar. Because of him *Pravda* was allowed to function untouched. In the end he betrayed Joseph Stalin, who was whisked off to Siberia in 1914;

and that same year, on orders from the police, he gave up his seat in the Duma and fled to Austria. When war came he was imprisoned by the Germans, returned to Russia in 1917 and was shot.

The purpose of the police in employing Malinovsky was to keep the Marxist forces split in two. But it is still a matter of controversy which side he helped or for that matter on which side his sympathies really lay. Lenin thought that, on the whole, he had served the revolutionaries best, for he had sustained *Pravda*, the life-blood of the movement.

Malinovsky was far from unique. Several thousands of Russians in 1913 were playing the same double game. Was it due to the oriental trait which finds excitement in deceit or merely a desire to be on the winning side no matter what turn events took? In 1913 the Okhrana was said to number well over twenty thousand agents, who swarmed everywhere, not only inside Russia, but in all the capitals of Europe where conspirators gathered. And at least two thousand of them were members of revolutionary parties. To complicate matters even further, rival revolutionary organizations were set up within the Okhrana itself, each one trying to do down the other.

How far the pre-war revolutionaries corrupted the police, or the police the revolutionaries, no one will ever know; only that in 1913 very few people were what they appeared to be. Indeed, even the millionaires were playing a curious game. Many of them subsidized the revolutionaries as a sort of insurance policy. Nicholas Paramonov, one of the richest men in the country, had been sentenced to two years in prison for financing Bolshevik pamphlets, but had succeeded in getting his sentence revoked by contributing a large sum of money to the Czar's tercentenary celebrations; while Morozov, the textile king of Moscow, sent money to Maxim Gorky for his school of revolutionaries.

In the autumn St Petersburg talked about the trip that Prince Felix Yusupov had taken with the Grand Duchess Elizabeth, a sister of the Empress, who had renounced the worldly life and become a nun. They had travelled to Solovetzky monastery on an island in the White Sea. On the return journey they had stopped at Archangel, and while the Grand Duchess was visiting churches, the Prince strolled about the town. A notice about a bear being sold at auction caught his eye. He tracked down the owner, bought the bear and had it put in a cattle truck and attached to the Grand Duchess' special train. 'We spent a very bad night,' wrote Yusupov, 'being awakened at each stop by blood-curdling snarls. A large number of people, including court officials, awaited the Grand Duchess at St Petersburg. One can imagine their stupefaction when they saw her return from a pilgrimage with a huge white bear!' [30]

People also talked about the Prince Dadiani, the son of the old reigning family of Mingrelia who had been arrested at Sukhum-Kaleh on the charge of being the leader of an armed band of robbers who had been terrorizing towns on the Black Sea coast. The name of Dadiani had a familiar ring in St Petersburg society, for a few years earlier the Prince, who was in the Cossack Guards, had called on the Grand Duchess Olga, the Czar's sister, and showed her some paintings by famous artists. The Prince said they were family possessions, he was desolate at having to part with them but he needed the money. Could she not interest Nicholas II in buying them for the Hermitage? The Grand Duchess liked the pictures and persuaded the Czar to buy them. However, the police intervened in the nick of time and informed her that the 'heirlooms' had been stolen from a neighbour's art gallery. 'I am thankful to say that the man was dismissed the service,' the Grand Duchess told her biographer. 'All the same the scandal was terrific.' [31] But not fatal, for apparently Prince Dadiani lived to rob another day.

Most of the events, however, that found their way into the world press in the last months of the year had a gruesome flavour. In September the Minister of Railways ran special trains to the suburbs of St Petersburg to allow thousands to watch the revolting scenes that always took place on St Paraskeva's Day. Priests drove the devil out of miserable semi-naked men and women by pouring muddy water and unclarified oil down their throats. The absence of clothes was essential as the devil had a way of hiding in knots and bows and fastenings. When the poor wretches seeking salvation screamed that they were being drowned the crowd roared its approval. 'Oh, so the devil is being drowned, is he? Quick. Quick. More oil. More water!' The sufferers were returned to their relations more dead than alive.

Even more macabre was the story of the fifty criminals, known as 'The Demons of the Steppes', who were captured in December and put in a prison at Ekaterinoslav. Eleven were sentenced to death and thirty-nine to long terms of imprisonment. For months they had operated as a gang, attacking lonely peasant houses and robbing and killing the inhabitants. They were so cruel that the doctors who examined them decided they must be mad. At first they killed their victims by hanging in order to avoid the charge of 'spilling blood'. However, when they learned that occasionally a peasant survived the hanging and came back to life, they decided it was better to make sure of killing them by using an axe. Some of the gang evolved other methods, such as placing dynamite cartridges between the victims' teeth. 'The bandits might still be at work', reported the New York *Tribune* on 21 December, 'if one of the leaders had not quarrelled with other chiefs. The police always failed to detect them, but the reason was very simple, for money buys anything in Russia and the bandits paid large sums to very high police officials in the Kuban district.'

The event that caused the greatest sensation, however, was the murder trial at Kiev in October of a young Jew named Beilis. Beilis was accused of committing a 'ritual murder' on a twelve-year-old boy, near a factory where he worked, and draining the body of blood. The proceedings aroused passionate feelings as the Crown Prosecutor launched his case upon the flimsiest evidence. People, not only in Russia, but all over the world, declared that the trial was nothing but an attempt to stir up fresh anti-Jewish feeling.

The Crown Prosecutor called a bizarre assortment of witnesses in an attempt to get a conviction. First, there was a Roman Catholic priest dressed in a cassock with a large golden cross suspended from his waist, who declared that all Rabbis fomented hatred against Gentiles; that ritual murder was part of their creed as it was believed to hasten the coming of the Messiah. Then there was a man who, after claiming to have seen Beilis chasing the murder victim, broke down and said he had seen nobody, but had been instructed by detectives to name Beilis; and a young girl who burst into tears and said that the secret police had told her she would die unless she named Beilis.

The Kiev newspaper *Kievlianin* attacked the Procurator of the Holy Synod as the person responsible for trying to give the crime a ritual appearance, and prophesied that the day might come when 'instead of a Procurator seeking out ritual murders a man would stand at the head of the Court seeking out those who incited pogroms.' At almost the same time, another Kiev paper, the bitterly anti-Semitic *Double-Headed Eagle*, came out with a verse that translated, roughly, into the following:

> Lord God, the Martyrs' guiltless blood
> Appeals to thee on high.
> It cannot be our Justice should
> In Jewish hell-power lie.

As the trial progressed it was increasingly obvious that Beilis was innocent. Evidence pointed towards a band of common criminals, and particularly a family named Cheberyah. A seamstress, a former friend of Vera Cheberyah, testified that she had spent a night with the family, and felt a corpse at the foot of her bed. Although Beilis was acquitted, it was impossible to convict the Cheberyahs as the evidence was only circumstantial. Apparently the boy had been killed because he was witness to a previous crime. Medical evidence tended to reject the theory that the boy had been deliberately drained of blood as it seemed more likely that he had bled to death because of his wounds.

As the year closed, St Petersburg was caught up in a fever of stock market speculation. The names of three millionaires were on everyone's lips; Putilov, a member of a well-known St Petersburg family who had learned banking in France and London; Batolin, who had started life as a messenger boy in a wheat firm and risen to the top; Yaroshinsky, who amassed a fortune in a sugar business somewhere in the south of Russia and was said to be the nephew of an Italian cardinal. These men sometimes were referred to as 'The Big Three of St Petersburg', sometimes as 'the Unholy Three of the Empire'. They formed a combine and began to buy up the shares of the banks. Usually fifteen per cent was sufficient to give them control of a bank, and to allow them to appoint their own board of directors. Once adequate finance was in their hands they systematically set about acquiring private businesses – tobacco firms, plantations, mills, iron and steel plants, etc. The pattern was always the same. They paid the owner a price that would give him an income larger than the profit he was making. Then they turned the business into a public company and floated the shares on the market in a blaze of publicity. As long as they were successful in persuading the public to buy, the shares rose automatically, enabling them not only to pay off the owner, but to make a large profit themselves. They repeated this formula successfully with dozens of businesses and set the whole city alight. In a census taken in 1913, forty thousand people registered themselves as 'stock market speculators'.

The provinces joined in the gambling orgies of the capital [wrote the Grand Duke Alexander] and by the fall of 1913 the Russia of idle landlords and under-nourished peasants was seemingly ready for a long jump over the obstacles of the economic laws into the domain of its own Wall Street . . .

The haughty leaders of society included stockbrokers in their visiting lists. The aristocratic officers of the Imperial Guards, though unable to distinguish stocks from bonds, began to discuss the imminent rise in the prices on 'broad' steel. Smart men-about-town nearly petrified unsuspecting book-dealers by demanding a supply of all the available manuals dedicated to the mysteries of high finance and to the art of understanding the annual corporation reports. Fashionable hostesses acquired a habit of featuring the presence of 'that marvellous genius from Odessa who has made a terrific killing in tobacco'. The holy men of the church subscribed to the financial publications, and the velvet-upholstered carriages of the archbishops were often observed in the neighbourhood of the Stock Exchange.' [32]

British businessmen flowed into St Petersburg as well; the interest shown by financial circles in London was so great that *The Times* ran four special supplements on Russia during the course of the year.

Meanwhile, the Russian Government had completed its negotiations with the French Government for a huge loan to be spent building strategic railways necessary in the event of war. The news was hailed joyfully by the Pan-Slavs and militarists. Chauvinism and belligerence began to spread. In the last week of 1913, army officers in St Petersburg were echoing sentiments which found their way into the official army paper and caused a sensation in the capitals of Europe. 'We all know we are preparing for a war in the West. Not only the troops, but the whole nation must accustom itself to the idea that we arm ourselves for a war of annihilation against the Germans . . .' Although the Imperial Russian army was short of guns and shells, and even uniforms, the article ended on a triumphant note: 'We are ready.'

FOUR

VIENNA

The dawn of 1913 found Vienna vibrant with the talk of war. The fact that her arch-enemy, Serbia, had scored unexpected victories in the Balkans against Turkey had raised the question of intervention and turned it into a red-hot issue. Everybody knew that the Serb leaders, encouraged by the Russians, dreamed of a Greater Serbia composed of territories and peoples under the rule of the Dual Monarchy; if Vienna did not crush Serbia at once, the great ramshackle Austro-Hungarian Empire, presided over by the eighty-two-year-old Emperor Franz Joseph, might disintegrate and collapse without a blow being struck.

Austria had partially mobilized; so had Russia; and 1913 found the two countries glaring at each other across the Galician frontier. The argument for dismantling Serbia, regardless of whether it brought Russia to the aid of her sister Slavs and precipitated a world war, was referred to as 'The Forward Policy' and dominated the conversation at the fashionable Jockey Club. It was supported by such powerful families as the Schwarzenbergs and the Czernins, by Nostitz, Clam-Martinitz and Latour. It was also discussed by businessmen at Sacher's and the Hotel Bristol, and received the backing of Schoeller, Urban and Kestranek, three of the most powerful industrialists in the Empire.

On 31 January, the British Ambassador, Sir Fairfax Cartwright, wrote to the London Foreign Office:

Serbia will some day set Europe by the ears, and bring about a universal war on the Continent. I cannot tell you how exasperated people are getting here at the continual worry which that little country causes to Austria under encouragement from Russia. It will be lucky if Europe succeeds in avoiding war as a result of the present crisis. The next time a Serbian crisis arises I feel sure that Austria-Hungary will refuse to admit any Russian interference in the dispute and that she will proceed to settle her difference with her little neighbour *coûte que coûte.* [1]

The most influential figure in favour of immediate war was the newly appointed Chief of the General Staff, Baron Conrad von Hötzendorf. He believed that he had an ally in the Heir Presumptive, Archduke Franz Ferdinand, a nephew of the Emperor. Two days before 1913 was ushered in he wrote to the Archduke: 'The moment is critical, and calls for decisive action. Serbia must be defeated in war.' And on 20 January he did his best to persuade the old Emperor to take the plunge, declaring that the root of the evil was Russia, and once Russia was defeated all would be well.

The stumbling block was Germany. The German Kaiser, William II, was doing everything in his power to prevent war. In February he wrote to Archduke Franz Ferdinand about the 'intolerable tension which has been bearing so heavily on Europe for the past six months' and said: 'To lift it would be a truly epoch-making act of peace, worthy of an *energetic* man who has *moral* courage to speak the redeeming word . . .' [2] The Archduke, torn between the bellicose Chief of Staff and the pacific German Kaiser, finally came down on the side of the Kaiser. He interceded strongly, Emperor Franz Joseph heeded his words and peace was maintained, much to the disgust of the aristocracy and the most sophisticated army officers. 'The ancient man on the throne,' wrote Josef Redlich, a member of the Lower Chamber, 'and the weaklings around him, do not see that only the sword can still save Austria. Insurrection is lying in ambush in Dalmatia, Croatia and Bosnia! Sometimes I blame myself for not speaking for war energetically . . .' [3]

When the Balkan wars finally ended in July 1913, Serbia was twice its original size, strong and aggressive. The Archduke Franz Ferdinand was held responsible for missing the opportunity to smash the little troublemaker. He was not a popular figure. Although he was the most powerful personality in the land after the Emperor, the public saw him as a mean, miserly, quick-tempered autocrat, entirely divorced from the affairs of ordinary people. Yet he was much else as well. Politically he was imaginative and brave, and domestically a model of tender devotion.

Indeed, Franz Ferdinand's marriage was proof that the charmless, wooden exterior hid a romantic nature. When gossip spread that he was courting the daughter of the Archduchess Isabella, people were delighted, for this lady was a member of the Croy family, one of the most illustrious names in Europe. The Duke of Croy was both a Belgian and an Austrian, and in his palace in Brussels he had a cartoon which reflected the apogee of family pride. It represented the Madonna and Child with the current Duke of Croy kneeling in adoration. The Virgin was saying: 'But please put on your hat, dear cousin.'

The Archduchess Isabella had several daughters and, although she was not certain which one of them the Archduke was interested in, she relished the prospect of becoming mother-in-law to the future Emperor. She pressed Franz Ferdinand with invitations to her house at Pressburg, not far from Vienna. He was an ardent tennis player and one day when he had departed for Vienna after a strenuous game it was discovered that he had left his watch in the dressing room. A servant took it to the Archduchess. The watch chain contained a number of trinkets which Franz Ferdinand had collected over the years, one of which was a locket. Hoping to discover which daughter the Archduke fancied, Isabella opened the locket and to her amazement – and anger – saw a picture of her lady-in-waiting, Countess Sophie Chotek. She rushed from the room and discharged Sophie on the spot.

Although Sophie came from a noble family, she was not royal and, therefore, not eligible to marry the Archduke. Franz Ferdinand, however, begged the Emperor to allow him to marry the Baroness morganatically. The Emperor refused flatly, and Franz Ferdinand threatened to kill himself. Finally, after Pope Leo XIII, Emperor William II of Germany and Czar Nicholas II of Russia all had interceded on behalf of the Archduke, Franz Joseph relented. The Countess Sophie, of course, could not assume her husband's rank, and Franz Ferdinand had to take an oath renouncing the throne for all his descendants. The Emperor conferred the title Duchess of Hohenberg upon Sophie, but no Hapsburg, apart from Franz Ferdinand's step-mother and two daughters, attended the ceremony.

Viennese society went out of its way to remind Sophie of her humble rank. At every royal function, although her husband might lead the procession, she was forced to enter the room after the youngest archduchess. She was not allowed to ride with her husband in the carriage, nor sit by his side in the Court box at the opera. The Archduke minded these slights more than Sophie; gradually he began to curtail his appearances at Court and turned away from society. Yet he never regretted the step he had taken. 'The *most* intelligent thing I've ever done in my life', he wrote to his step-mother four years later, 'has been the marriage to my Soph . . . we love each other as on our first year of marriage, and our happiness has not been marred for a single second . . . And our children. They are my whole delight and pride. I sit with them and admire them the whole day because I love them so . . .' [4]

One of the reasons why the Archduke got on so well with the Kaiser was because William II went out of his way to treat the Duchess of Hohenberg as though she were an Empress. When the couple visited Berlin the banqueting table was moved out of the dining room and small tables put in its place. The Archduke and his wife dined at a table *à quatre* with the Kaiser and Kaiserin; thus no royal princess could complain of her placement *vis-à-vis* the Duchess.

Despite the ever-present possibility of war throughout 1913, Viennese life on the surface was gay and feckless. No capital in Europe seemed to have the same intimate charm as Vienna, with its baroque buildings and leafy avenues, its agreeable inefficiency, its mixture of races, its strains of waltz music and its seven hundred street cafés, crowded with laughing, talking people, no matter what the time of day. Whipped cream melting into black coffee seemed to reflect the capital's air of froth and impermanency.

The Viennese were passionately attached to their city. The Ringstrasse, a broad street planted with four rows of trees in the manner of a Paris boulevard, and the Kai which ran along the Danube were the glories of the capital with their succession of palaces, monuments and public buildings intermingled with parks and gardens. The Prater, a huge wooded common to the east of the town, was the playground for people from all walks of life. The aristocrats took early morning canters or drove their carriages along the Hauptallee, and drank their morning coffee at Konstantinhügel and Krieau; while the lower classes flocked to the Würstelprater, which was a permanent village fair with merry-go-rounds, Punch and Judy shows, moving pictures and sensational sideshows. But what gave Vienna its most distinctive charm was its environs. Ringed by mountains less than three hours away by rail, it offered its inhabitants hill resorts of majestic beauty, which were particularly popular in the summer months.

Yet despite its outward appearance of friendly intimacy, Vienna was not a capital that many foreign diplomats enjoyed. It was a place to visit, they said, not to live. The truth was that Viennese society was so haughty and exclusive that it had turned itself into the most parochial society in Europe. It took its cue from the Court, which operated an archaic Spanish etiquette. Everything depended on pedigree. No one could go to Court unless he possessed sixteen quarterings. It did not matter how brilliant or charming or rich a man, unless every one of his ancestors, on both sides of his family, was impeccably well-born for the required number of generations, the doors were irrevocably closed to him. 'An Austrian might be Shakespeare, Galileo, Nelson, and Raphael in one person,' wrote the American Minister, 'but he would not be received in good society if he did not possess the sixteen quarterings of nobility which birth alone can give him.' [5]

And there were no short cuts. A lady, for instance, was not entitled to her husband's rank. The beautiful Countess Karolyi, wife of a great Hungarian landowner, and ambassadress in Berlin, was excluded from Court because of faults in her pedigree, while her husband was summoned without her. The whole nation lived on the traditions of the sixteenth century when the proud Hapsburgs ruled the whole of Europe with the exception of France, England, Russia and Scandinavian countries.

To a non-Austrian mind [wrote Lord Frederick Hamilton], it seems illogical that the lovely lady representing Austria in Berlin should have been thought un-fitted for an invitation from her own sovereign. The immense deference paid to the Austrian Archdukes and Archduchesses was very striking after the compara-tively unceremonious fashion in which minor German royalties were treated in Berlin. The Archduchesses especially were very tenacious of their privileges. They never could forget that they were Hapsburgs, and exacted all the traditional signs of respect. [6]

The only people allowed to attend Court without the proper genealogical requirements were officers in the Austro-Hungarian army; but only once a year and under conditions so humiliating that foreigners wondered how they could be induced to come at all. Two balls were given at Court. One was a very small, chic affair known as a 'Ball at the Court' (*Ball bei Hof*); the other a large crowded gathering known as the Court Ball (*Hof Ball*). All those on the Palace list, including several hundred officers, were received – or rather tolerated – at the *Hof Ball*. But they were made to feel their inferior rank.

A scarlet cord divided the lower end of the ball-room from the upper [wrote the wife of a British diplomat], and behind this cord they had to stand herded together the whole evening watching the dancing they were forbidden to share, and never honoured by so much as a look or a nod from any member of the Imperial family or the 'smart' society . . . When supper-time came the officers' refreshments were served in a great hall reserved for them. I commented sharply on the way they were treated, and the man I was talking to said: 'Let me show you something, and you will see that it would be impossible to let them mix with us – they are wild beasts.' So he led me to their deserted supper-room – and though I could not give up my contention, the sight convinced me that, at any rate, the despised guests had taken their revenge. The long tables were absolutely stripped. Whatever could not be eaten on the spot, or stuffed into pockets or caps to take home, was strewn on the floor. It looked as if a horde of savages had just swept through the place. But – à qui la faute? The gulf which separates the commoner from the noble all over the

Empire is even more insolently marked in the army than elsewhere. There is no brotherhood of arms, no tie of any kind between the two classes there. [7]

The exclusive *Ball bei Hof* drew the cream of Viennese society, which through intermarriage literally was one large family.

There are few belonging to it [wrote Lady Paget, wife of the British Minister] who are not related to nearly all the others. Putting official rank on one side their respective positions would come in this order: the Liechtensteins, being a still reigning family, come first. After them the mediatized Princes, i.e. those who at one time exercised sovereign rights directly under the Holy Roman Empire. These have the privilege of intermarrying with the Royal houses on an equal footing. The next in rank are the Austrian Princes created after 1806. Then there are mediatized Counts and also Counts of the Holy Roman Empire. The title of baron is almost unknown in this society; it is reserved for the *haute finance* and is considered specially Semitic . . . [8]

The exaggerated emphasis on pedigree made the Viennese aristocracy slightly ridiculous, for society continually was swept by scandals arising from impossible marriages. In 1913 three Archduchesses were in the news. In January the daughter of the Archduchess Isabella (who had expelled the Countess Sophie Chotek from her house) announced that she was seeking an annulment of her eleven-month-old marriage to Prince George of Bavaria; in March the Archduchess Marie Dorothea Amalia, a daughter of the Emperor's cousin, the Archduke Joseph, announced that she was suing her estranged husband, Prince Phillipe of Orleans for three thousand five hundred pounds a year maintenance; and in the summer the Archduchess Louisa, daughter of the Grand Duke of Tuscany, and the divorced wife of the King of Saxony, announced that she had written a musical comedy revealing the secrets of the Dresden Court to be performed in Rome in the autumn.

Princess Louisa of Tuscany, as the Archduchess was known, had scandalized society for many years. When she first married she had shocked Dresden by taking bicycle rides with her dentist. In a book of memoirs published in 1911 she informed the world that her marriage had been ruined by jealous courtiers; that she had fled from Dresden in the middle of the night, abandoning her three children, because she learned that her father-in-law had decided to commit her to a lunatic asylum. Her son's tutor followed her to Switzerland; so did her brother, the Archduke Leopold Ferdinand (who preferred to be known as Herr Wulfing) and his actress lady friend. The Emperor Franz Joseph issued an edict forbidding Princess Louisa to use her Austrian titles and depriving her of her royal status. Some time later the Princess married a twenty-four-year-old Italian pianist, Signor Toselli, to show the world, she said, that she had finished with her former life. Although in 1913 she was estranged from Toselli, she had collaborated with him in writing the musical comedy entitled *La Principessa Bizarra*. The opening night took place in Rome in October. Although the theatre was packed out, the 'scenes' from the Dresden Court were described by the press as 'farcical' and the play as 'a calamitous failure'. The curtain had to be lowered in the third act because of the boos and cat-calls. It was not performed again.

Although the Emperor Franz Joseph cared nothing for society, and himself led a Spartan existence, he was a stickler for the haughty etiquette which stifled the Viennese Court. He would not allow a single rule to be relaxed, a single exception to be made. The etiquette was part of the Hapsburg tradition and he was the guardian of it.

Franz Joseph was not a sympathetic character, yet many people warmed to him because of the tragedies in his life. His brother had been killed in Mexico; his only son had committed suicide; his beautiful wife, Elizabeth, had died at the hand of an assassin in Switzerland. Despite these appalling shocks the Emperor's routine had never altered. He lived in two simply furnished rooms, slept on an iron bed, and rose each morning at four o'clock. His courtiers had to begin their work at six, for he expected a sheet of paper with the programme for the day brought to him at seven.

Although his long reign saw the carriage give way to the motor car, the pen to the typewriter, the telegraph to the telephone, Franz Joseph refused to change his habits. He never set eyes on a typewriter and refused to have a telephone installed in his study. Only once, when Edward VII visited him at Ischl, did he ride in a motor car. He never read a book, cared nothing for music and art. His tastes were wholly middle-class. He ate his lunch on a small table in his study. Despite the magnificent chefs in his service, it usually consisted of soup, meat and a glass of beer. Like the Austrian bourgeoisie he dined at five o'clock. He never touched the magnificent French wine in the Hapsburg cellars, but occasionally drank Austrian wines supplied by the Schottenkloster.

The sole irregularity of his life – if it can be so described – was his friendship with the Burgtheater actress, Katharina Schratt, which had ended some thirteen years earlier. Gossip declared that the Empress Elizabeth had brought Frau Schratt into her husband's life to keep him company while she travelled abroad. Although he relied heavily on Katharina he was neither an ardent nor a generous lover. He never did anything to ease her path, either by assisting her career or giving her money. In 1899 she left him through sheer boredom.

Indeed the relationship between the Emperor and the actress, which lasted for fourteen years, was so ordinary that countless stories were invented to give it colour. Once, people said, when the Emperor left Ischl in the early hours of the morning the cook came out of her room and began to scream, thinking he was a burglar. 'Don't you see that I'm the Emperor, you silly woman?' Whereupon the cook dropped to her knees and began to sing: *Gott erhalte Franz den Kaiser.*

At eighty-two the Emperor's only companions were his daughters. He still worked conscientiously, reading the official papers each day and keeping in close touch with his ministers. But he was a sly old fox. When he received a friend on 5 March 1913, he was sitting in the garden, cigar in hand, holding a portrait of the newly inaugurated President Woodrow Wilson. 'He is a very great man,' said the Emperor. 'A very fortunate man, too. It is much to know that you have really been chosen as most fit to govern by such a vast number of people.' It is not surprising that this homely little scene found its way into the New York *Tribune.* [9]

Despite the strictness of Viennese society, the unmarried girls of the aristocracy had a unique position. Whether Princesses or Duchesses they were all referred to as the *Comtessen*. And the *Comtessen* had a much freer, more amusing life than unmarried girls anywhere else in Europe.

In the first place they were allowed to smoke. After every dinner party the guests, ladies included, always retired to a smoking room.

One's aesthetic sense is rather shocked [wrote Lady Paget], by seeing a beautiful young woman, with bare shoulders and a blazing tiara, lighting a big cigar over a lamp. The first thing a man does when he gets engaged is to request leave from his future mother-in-law for his *fiancée* to smoke. Many girls, however, do not wait for this moment and anticipate; and there are evening parties with nothing but *Comtessen* where the fumes of havanas have been seen hovering in the air. The *Comtessen* have an enchanting time of it before they marry. They dance, they ride, they shoot, they go to the races, they have expensive hats and frocks, they eat as many sweetmeats as they like every afternoon at Demel's shop; in fact, there is nothing that they wish for which is refused to them . . . It strikes strangers as very curious that girls brought up in severely religious and strictly moral households should be allowed to go to every race for weeks together. Such, however, is the case. In freshest dresses of latest fashion the *Comtessen* crowd together in the passages and on the steps of the grandstand or walk about in bevies in the enclosure. [10]

Vienna

The Emperor Franz Joseph at a state occasion in September.

Count Zeppelin welcomed by Archduke Eugene and Archduchess Maria Josepha, after arriving in Vienna in his airship.

Archduke Franz Ferdinand skiing at St Moritz with his family.

The Emperor and Archduke Franz
Ferdinand taking the salute in the
Schwarzenbergplatz during the
centenary celebrations of the
Battle of Leipzig on October 16.

The Emperor arriving for the
dedication of the Imperial Jubilee
church with Archduchess Maria
Theresa.

General Conrad von
Hötzendorf, the militaristic
Austrian Chief of Staff,
studying a map of the Balkans.

Count Stephen Tisza, who
became Prime Minister of
Hungary in June. He was the
most experienced duellist in
Europe.

Captain Redl, former head of Austrian Intelligence, who shot himself on May 25 after being unmasked as a Russian agent.

Below. A German cartoonist envisaged a horned Redl as a double agent between Heaven and Hell.

'*To His Holiness the Pope, Rome. The undersigned is in a position to reveal certain important secrets of Hell's plans of action at a reasonable price . . . Please reply by return. Redl.*'

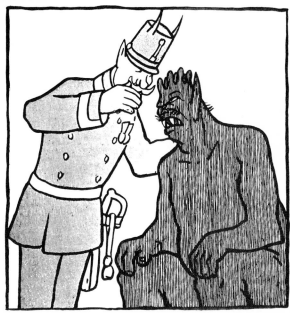

'*My ecclesiastical connections enable me to betray to your Hellish Majesty important secret documents of the Heavenly Host.*'

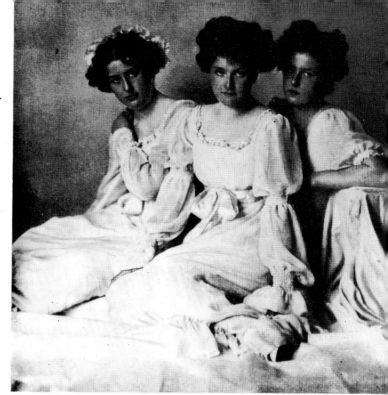

Opposite. Countess Esterházy, one of the beautiful *Comtessen* of Vienna.

Right. Countess Gabriele Bellegardt, Princess Weikersheim-Czernin, and Countess Willy Czernin-Kinsky; a group portrait by Fräulein d'Ora, the most fashionable photographer in Vienna.

Georgina Countess Karoly, a member of one of the most distinguished families in the Austro-Hungarian Empire.

Frau Anna Sacher, proprietress of Vienna's most famous hotel, photographed in 1913.

Interior of the Café Griensteidl, the best-known 'literary' café in Vienna.

Even at balls the *Comtessen* had an enviable position. A room was always set aside for them, known as the *Comtessen-Zimmer*, into which no married lady or gentleman was allowed to penetrate. After every dance the girls retired to this room. Young men seeking partners had to brave the den, but the less popular could at least chat with each other and were spared the embarrassment endured by girls of other lands. At a Court Ball the *Comtessen* stood in a group half way down the huge Hofburg hall, exercising their privilege to be in the sovereign's presence.

Whereas the *Comtessen* boasted many pretty girls, few foreigners found the male members of the Austrian aristocracy either attractive or interesting. Interbreeding had weakened their physiques and not quickened their brains. They seemed to have the same profiles, the same mannerisms, even the same gait – they walked with long strides, heads bowed forward and shoulders slightly bent like the Emperor's. Cut off by snobbishness from intellectual stimulus, they had few aims or interests apart from the pursuit of pleasure. They had three passions; shooting, gambling and women.

Shooting came first and took up eight months of the year. It began with the chamois in August, followed by stag and roe-deer, the partridge and the pheasant. Then came the wild boar season, and in February, amongst the mountains of snow, the arduous shooting of the hinds. When this was over the stalking of the capercailzies began. There was no lack of terrain to shoot over for almost all the noble families of Austria and Hungary were immensely rich. Prince Liechtenstein kept over one thousand one hundred gamekeepers in Bohemia alone, and drew a rent roll in Moravia said to exceed one hundred thousand. In the same province, Prince Schwarzenberg had vast interests including ninety-five castles; and in Galicia the Potocki estate exceeded half a million acres. Among the great Hungarian landowners were Prince Esterhazy, Marquis Pallavicini, the Karolyis, the Andrassys and the Zichys.

The only time the male members of the aristocracy were certain to be in Vienna was from the beginning of April to the end of June, when the gambling season was at its height and the racing was on. In 1913 the Derby was run on 8 June. Baron Oppenheim's *Czardas* came first; Prince Lubomirski's *Moscze Kiaze* second; and Count Festetic's *Fatalist* third.

Most of the female spectators, however, regarded the race as of secondary importance compared with the fashion parade; for Derby Day was the most important social event in the spring calendar. The smart set travelled to the race track, on the edge of the Prater, by carriage or motor car. The total number of private vehicles was 2,660 compared with 2,150 the previous year. The crowds numbered over thirty thousand, most people arriving by electric train.

The show of clothes was spectacular.

One should sing an ecstatic song of praise to modern fashion [wrote the Vienna *Neue Freie Presse*]. Each individual outfit, each fabric, each colour is worthy of such a song. It was not the conventional costumes but the fantasy outfits that triumphed today. One saw pictorial clothes of sweet-smelling flowers on white backgrounds; one saw costly works of art in the realms of hats; and extremely imaginative accessories particularly where shoes and blazing parasols were concerned. It was an orgy of colour in which the men provided a sombre background; for the men, as if by agreement, remembered the requirements of Derby Day dress and were conventionally attired in frock coats and top hats.

The writer goes on to tell us that the Princess Karl Windischgraetz wore a rose-point dress and a yellow straw hat covered with tulle and net; Princess Liechtenstein a silk crêpe dress adorned with 'bobbles' and a large black picture hat; Princess Fürstenberg a white crêpe dress and a white silk hat with blue ribbons and red roses; Princess Gottfried Hohenlohe a black and white printed silk dress and a black hat with white feathers.

In 1913 the return from the races was no longer the great sight of former days. Even five years earlier the long Prater Avenue was filled with carriages, three or four abreast, most of them horsed with very fast Hungarian *yukkers*, racing along at breakneck speed. The coachmen always held the reins in two hands at arms' length, laughing and shouting despite the fact that they were splashed with mud from head to foot. Indeed the mud was regarded as very chic, for mud meant expensive horseflesh, speed and *panache*. Only the Viennese, commented a diplomat sarcastically, could manage to make mud 'chic'.

If it was fashionable to race and to gamble, it was even more fashionable to have a mistress; two or three mistresses if possible. The titled youth usually formed liaisons with actresses and dancers. It was a recognized custom that stars of the first rank should have noble lovers and some of them were protected by a curious agency. The *corps de ballet* of the Hofoper, for example, was organized into a league, known as the *Tugendbund*, 'the League of Virtue'. This association systematized the relations between the dancers and their aristocratic lovers. When a cavalier selected a mistress, the association stipulated a contract on her behalf which established beforehand the indemnity which he must pay her, as having been well served, when he took a wife or left her.

The Viennese aristocracy showed little interest in literature, the arts or sciences. When Lord Lytton was an attaché at Vienna he ventured one evening at Prince Schwarzenberg's house to suggest to a young lady the fitness of attracting a small pinch of intellectual salt within the charmed circle of society. He only, however, earned the frigid rejoinder, 'Mais, mon cher Lord, where would you have us draw the line – we would end by landing ourselves in the gutter.'

Some Austrian noblemen went into the diplomatic service, others into politics; many, however, did nothing but enjoy their leisure. Although Austrians were musical by nature the upper classes only attended the opera on gala occasions and seldom went to a concert. This was due to a curious custom which the upper classes lamented but seemed powerless to alter. Every house in Vienna had a hall porter; and every hall porter had the right to levy a toll of threepence on each person going in or out after 10.15 p.m. Consequently, the life of the bourgeoisie was regulated in an effort to escape this *Schlüsselgeld*. As a result the theatre started at 6.0 or 6.30, and people dined at 5.30. The Viennese aristocracy preferred to forego musical entertainment and retain more civilized hours.

Music, therefore, was patronized almost exclusively by the bourgeoisie, and the Jewish bourgeoisie at that. 'They were the real audience', wrote Stefan Zweig. 'They filled the theatres and the concerts, they bought the books and the pictures, they visited the exhibitions . . . they were the exponents and champions of all that was new . . .' [11]

But the Jews of Vienna were far from passive. Although many of their names glowed through Europe, it was curious that they did not succeed in infusing Vienna with their vitality. Vienna seemed to belong to a world that was decaying; they to an age that was flowering. Many of them no longer resided in the imperial capital. In 1913, Max Reinhardt lived in Berlin; Stefan Zweig in Paris; while Oscar Strauss, Franz Lehar and Leo Fall were spending much of their time in New York where their operettas were meeting with tumultuous applause. That same year the poet Hugo von Hofmannsthal was collaborating with the musician Richard Strauss in creating *La Légende de Joseph* for Diaghilev. Sigmund Freud's book on dreams was being published in English for the first time; and Arthur Schnitzler's plays were being read by New York impresarios. Vienna was not growing as a literary and artistic centre, but fertilizing other capitals with her talent.

The intellectuals were not the only ones to seek outlets abroad. In 1913 thousands of Austro-Hungarian subjects, mostly Czechs, Slovaks, Poles and

Magyars, tried to escape the war they saw approaching by emigrating to the New World. In October, an American, Mr Samuel Altman, the manager of the Canadian Pacific Steamship Company in Vienna, was arrested on a charge of arranging the illegal emigration to Canada of Austrians from Galicia, liable for military service. Regular sailings of the company's vessels took place from Trieste. However, Altman was able to prove that the Company's steamers had only carried four thousand Austrian passengers between January and September, whereas North German liners had carried 172,000. Nevertheless, an Austrian commissioner and two sub-governors accused of supplying passports and visas were arrested, for it was estimated that a hundred thousand men had avoided military service and left the country illegally.

Meanwhile Vienna had been shaken to the core by revelations of treachery in her highest military circles. In May Captain Redl, a member of the Austrian General Staff and a former Chief of Intelligence, a courtly gentleman of impeccable background and a friend of the Archduke Franz Ferdinand, was unmasked as a paid Russian spy. The revelation, coming at such a moment of tension, had the same impact as the Alger Hiss or the Burgess and Maclean cases two generations later.

The first evidence that something was wrong came in January 1913, when Austrian agents in Russia reported that the Austrian Plan of March, to be put into operation in the event of war, had been sold to the Russians. As the plan revealed every tactical move on the part of the Austrian army, and as the traitor could only be one of a very few men at the top, the news threw the General Staff into a panic. Redl was assigned the task of uncovering the traitor. The Foreign Office, however, was not convinced that the military were competent enough to solve the mystery, and without informing the General Staff, started an investigation of its own. It instructed the police to open every letter from abroad addressed to General Delivery, regardless of the inviolability of the mails.

One day a letter arrived at a post office from the Russian border station Podvolochiska with only a code address 'Opera Ball'. It contained nothing but money – seven or eight new Austrian thousand-crown notes. A detective was detailed to arrest whoever came to claim the envelope. Some days later, at noon, a man appeared at the desk and asked for the letter but the detective apparently had grown bored with his fruitless task and had gone out for lunch. By the time he returned the stranger had disappeared, letter in pocket, in a horse-drawn cab. Now everyone was in a flap. Luckily a small boy whose job it was to wash the cabs and feed the horses outside the post office had noticed the number of the stranger's carriage.

The police were notified and within an hour cab and driver were located outside the Café Kaiserhof. The driver described the man who had ridden in his carriage and said that he had deposited him at the Hotel Klomser. He handed the police a pen-knife which, he said, the gentleman must have dropped, for he had found it on the seat of the cab. The detectives hurried to the Klomser and interrogated the waiters who cheerfully assured them that the man they were after could be none other than Captain Redl. Apparently the detectives stood rooted to the spot for now it was clear why all the Austrian spies who had been sent to Russia in the past year had been captured and condemned. A wild round of telephoning began until finally the Chief of the General Staff, Conrad von Hötzendorf, was reached. 'An eye-witness of this scene told me that at the very first words the Chief of Staff turned white as a sheet,' wrote Stefan Zweig.

A telephone conversation with the Imperial Palace ensued, and conference followed upon conference. What was to be done? In the meantime, the police had taken precautions to prevent Captain Redl's escape. When he again left the Hotel Klomser, and while he was talking to the porter, a detective approached him unobtrusively, held out the pocket knife, and asked politely: 'Did not the Captain forget the knife in the cab?' In that second Redl knew that all was lost. Wherever he went he saw the familiar faces of the secret police who were watching him, and when he returned to the hotel, two officers followed him into his room and laid down a pistol. It had been decided upon in the palace that this affair, with its scandalous implications for the Austrian army, was to be terminated as quietly as possible. Until two in the morning the two officers walked up and down outside Redl's room in the Hotel Klomser. Then they heard the pistol shot. [12]

The next day the newspapers carried a short obituary of the highly respected Captain Redl who had died suddenly in his sleep. But too many people were involved to keep the story quiet and rumours spread like wildfire. Before long it became known that Captain Redl had been a homosexual, and for years had been at the mercy of Russian blackmailers who finally drove him to this last desperate act.

Light relief to the chilling story of Captain Redl was offered by fifty-two-year-old Count Stephen Tisza, who was in the news repeatedly throughout 1913 because of his pugnacity. Tisza began the year as Speaker of the Hungarian Parliament, and sprang on to the front page early in January when he fought a duel against thirty-four-year-old Michael Karolyi, leader of one of the opposition parties and a member of an ancient and famous family. The cause of the conflict had occurred a few weeks earlier when Tisza's party had demanded an increase in armaments and opposition members had opposed it by obstructive and disorderly tactics. Tisza had settled the argument by concentrating twenty thousand troops in Budapest; surrounding the Parliament Building with soldiers; posting cannon in the street; and then having opposition Deputies thrown out by a specially organized 'Parliamentary Guard'.

After this parliamentary coup [wrote Michael Karolyi], I was pacing up and down in suppressed rage in the rooms of our club, the National Casino, when Tisza entered and, as if nothing had happened, came up to me with outstretched hand. 'How are you?' I put mine behind my back and walked on. 'Don't you hear?' he asked turning pale. 'Yes, but after what has happened I do not care to know you,' I answered. The same day Tisza's seconds called and the next day, at five in the afternoon, the duel took place. [13]

Tisza was Hungary's champion duellist. He had fought more duels than any man in Europe and had never once been seriously wounded. He had learned the art from the best masters in Germany, France and Italy and was equally good with sword or pistol. Even the fact that he had had a cataract operation on one of his eyes, and wore thick horn-rimmed spectacles, did not seem to impair him. In the duel with Karolyi thirty-four bouts were fought with cavalry sabres, lasting an hour. Then he cut Karolyi's arm and the seconds stopped the fight. A week later Tisza challenged Count Aladir Széchenyi to a duel; like Karolyi the latter had refused to shake hands with him. This time the duel lasted for only one bout, for Tisza gave his opponent a long cut across the head and the seconds declared Széchenyi *hors de combat*.

In June Tisza became Prime Minister of Hungary as the result of a scandal which had gripped the country for several months. Three Opposition leaders accused the Premier, Dr Lukacs, of having received 4,150,000 kronen (£166,000) from the Hungarian Bank, which had never been paid into the Exchequer. The Opposition parties, which had absented themselves from Parliament ever since Tisza had ordered the police to eject them in December, now began to fill the Chamber in strength. Every time the Prime Minister's name was mentioned they booed and cat-called. On 8 June, Tisza again called in the Parliamentary police to maintain order. One of the deputies, who was loud in his abuse of Lukacs, was struck by the police with a sabre. The deputy was not hurt but the incident created fresh pandemonium. Order was not restored until Lukacs and his Cabinet offered their resignation. Oddly enough,

Tisza, who not only was Lukacs' champion, but a member of the same party, was appointed Premier in the latter's place. The fact that the money received by Lukacs from the Hungarian Bank had been paid into the funds of his party seemed to make no difference. It was also revealed that the party had found other means of swelling its coffers. It had received a large sum from a finance company in exchange for a state gambling concession on the Island of St Margaret near Budapest.

Some people, however, were critical of Tisza's behaviour. One of them was the Marquis Pallavicini, son-in-law and supporter of the Opposition leader Count Julius Andrássy. Pallavicini accused Tisza of trying to influence witnesses appearing in a law suit connected with the Lukacs case, and Tisza followed his usual procedure of challenging his critic to a duel.

The combat took place at a fencing school in Budapest, and apparently afforded a fine exhibition in the art of the sabre. Conditions under which the duel was fought were severe; only slight protection of the body was allowed, and heavy cavalry sabres were used. The contest, it was decided, would last until one of the antagonists was declared *hors de combat*. The duel, in fact, lasted eleven minutes. At the end of the ninth bout both men had cuts on their foreheads and blood was streaming down their faces. The seconds declared that neither could see well enough to continue. The contest ended happily. The two men shook hands, then embraced, kissing each other on both cheeks, and declared themselves reconciled.

That autumn, when Tisza's escapades began to pall, people talked about the active part that Franz Ferdinand was playing in political affairs. In October the Archduke entertained the German Kaiser at Konopischt; and in November he travelled to London, accompanied by his wife, for a state visit. King George v got on well with the Archduke, no doubt because they both shared an enthusiasm for shooting. The Prince of Wales, who was summoned to Windsor Castle by his father, was a spectator at the duck shoot in the Great Park laid on for the benefit of the visitor. 'There I watched the Archduke, who could match my father as a wing shot, pull two hundred and seventy-three birds down out of the air.' Sir Arthur Nicolson, the head of the British Foreign Office, did not share the King's admiration for the Archduke. 'I met the Austrian Heir Apparent at Windsor,' he wrote to his son. 'A sly and stupid man. I tried to draw him but without success.' [14]

Sir Arthur was wrong, and the King was right; for the Archduke, despite his lack of charm, was neither stupid nor reactionary. He knew that the Hapsburg Empire would not survive unless drastic changes took place, and gave deep thought to the causes of unrest. The problems were not easy to solve for the Dual Monarchy, designed as a partnership between Germans and Magyars, with the twin capitals of Vienna and Budapest, was a strange make-shift affair. 'Not a state,' a wit remarked, 'but a Government.' Apart from Germans and Magyars, it contained Poles, Czechs, Roumanians, Italians, Jews, Croats, Slovaks and Serbs – 'A broken pot held together with a piece of wire. It might do duty as long as it was treated with due care, but woe if it were exposed to too many hard knocks or got some kick or other. Then it would be liable to fall to pieces.' [15]

In 1913 many of the nationalities ruled by the Hapsburgs were becoming restless. A multiracial empire seemed out of keeping with the modern age, which demanded that each nationality form its own nation. Many Magyars demanded an independent Hungary; the Poles campaigned for a new Polish state; and most troublesome of all, the Serbs, Croats and Slovenes, encouraged by Russia, talked of a great Slav state formed around Serbia.

The Archduke Franz Ferdinand recognized the importance of the new movements and toyed with two ideas; one was to create a federal system based on Switzerland or the United States, the other to transform the Dual Monarchy into a Triple Monarchy, giving the Slavs the same recognition and autonomy as the Magyars enjoyed. This enlightened approach worried Belgrade for, if such a policy were put into effect, it probably would end the dreams of a Greater Serbia.

Serbian firebrands went even further; they decided that Franz Ferdinand must die. When they learned of his intention to attend manoeuvres in Bosnia in June – a decision that was taken in the autumn of 1913 – they began to make their dark plans.

In December, the eighty-three-year-old Emperor Franz Joseph observed the sixty-fifth anniversary of his succession. He shrank from the limelight and appeared in public as little as possible. He requested that the anniversary should not be celebrated officially, for he preferred to spend the day quietly with his family. He had already sat on the throne a year longer than Queen Victoria, and he was very old and very tired.

FIVE

ROME

In 1913 Italy was caught, uncharacteristically, in an ecstasy of nationalist sentiment. On 19 January all Rome turned out to welcome home the ten thousand Italian soldiers who had recently returned from a victorious sixteen months' campaign in North Africa where, with almost no resistance, they had wrung from the dying Turkish Empire the provinces of Tripoli and Cyrenaica. Flags hung from every building and the crowds were dense. The forty-four-year-old King Victor Emmanuel III (Italy's third king and, as fate would have it, almost her last) led the procession on horseback, accompanied by the Prince of Udine, the Count of Turin and the Dukes of Aosta, Abruzzi and Genoa. A review was held in the parade ground of Castra Pretoria; later medals were conferred in front of the Victor Emmanuel monument, a recently constructed and massive tribute to the sovereign's grandfather.

This patriotic demonstration confounded foreign observers who were fond of dismissing Italian unification as a mirage, insisting that the anarchistic temperament of the people would never permit Italy to become a nation in the real sense of the word. It was true that in 1913 most Italians still thought of themselves as Neapolitans, Genoese, Venetians, Florentines, etc. Yet on this day in January a flame of pride – and acquisition – touched the Italian spirit, animating such widely different personalities as the writer D'Annunzio and the Socialist leader Mussolini. The fire was destined to spread, re-forging Mussolini's Socialism and twisting it into a new creed of boundless ambition.

Italy was the Cinderella of Europe. Although her beauty inspired admiration, her poverty condemned her to servility. Rich foreigners wooed and patronized her at one and the same time. Envious of the affluence and prestige of other great powers, she tried to model herself on England, for England seemed to have the secret of eternal success. Like the English sovereign, her

King was a constitutional monarch presiding over a two-chamber Parliament, the lower house of which was democratically elected.

But here the resemblance ended. The Italian aristocracy, which might have brought wisdom and detachment to the country's service, was too pleasure-loving to bother with politics. (Only in Rome did such historic names as Gaetani and de Medici appear on election posters.) Consequently most of the deputies were lawyers and professional men who entered the arena for monetary gain. The difficulties that faced them were prodigious, for half Italy's thirty-two million people were illiterate. Three-quarters of the wage-earning population were peasants living in miserable conditions. Industrialization was the answer, yet in 1913 Italy possessed only two major industries: silk and cotton. Although in the north the Pirelli works had sprung up near Turin, although a steel foundry was in operation, electrical plants were opening, ship-building was expanding, the promise lay in the future.

Meanwhile King Victor Emmanuel III traversed his Kingdom tirelessly in an effort to induce cohesion. A short, stocky, forthright man, he had married the tall dark-skinned daughter of a mountain chieftain, the King of Montenegro. The Queen had spent much of her youth in St Petersburg, for her two sisters were married to Russian Grand Dukes. These ladies were known in society as 'the black pearls'. They were very superstitious and spent much of their time table-tapping. In 1908 they had become fascinated by a holy man who, they believed, possessed supernatural powers. They had introduced him to the deeply religious Empress. His name was Rasputin.

Many people admired Queen Elena's raven-black hair and huge dark eyes and thought her immensely beautiful.

At ten minutes before eleven the notes of the Royal march were sounded and, to its accompaniment, Their Majesties entered the ballroom [wrote an American lady who attended a Court Ball at the Quirinal Palace]. The King wore the uniform of a General of the Italian Army, with the 'Collar of the Annunziata' and entered the room with the Queen on his arm . . . I thought her the most beautiful woman I had ever seen . . . She was simply *éblouissante*, and even that expressive French word is insufficient. She wore a beautiful gown of white satin, embroidered effectively with opalescent spangles. About her neck was the wonderful emerald necklace (it is beyond all words really) worn with many diamonds and a pearl dog-collar, while in her hair she wore the great diadem which completes this world-renowned set . . . [1]

The Court did not dominate the social life of Rome as it did in Vienna. Indeed, many old families would not go to Court as they regarded the King as an upstart and only recognized the authority of the Pope. Consequently,

Italian society was fluid and made its own rules. It was the most cosmopolitan and the least exclusive society in Europe.

Rich foreigners – mainly English and American – flooded into all the most agreeable cities – Rome, Venice, Florence – buying up or renting the best villas and organizing a social life, which seemed to fill a vacuum, and in which most Italians were pleased to participate. Some of the English, however, did not want to be bothered with Italians. They had come to Italy for sun, scenery and the low cost of living. 'The English colony in every Italian city,' wrote Mr Richard Bagot, 'is a little – a very little – England. It has its English life, its English habits, even its English food, and that not only material but spiritual.' Most Englishmen spent their time visiting other Englishmen; calling on the English chaplains, dining with the English Consul, playing lawn tennis at the English club, dancing at the hotels frequented by English visitors. 'Except for the satisfaction of being able to print Palazzo this or Villa that on his note-paper and his visiting cards, he might quite as well be in South Kensington . . .' [2]

However, in sophisticated Roman circles Latins and Anglo-Saxons mixed with pleasure and mutual benefit. Scores of rich American mothers were looking for titled husbands for their daughters, while scores of Italian nobles were looking for hard cash. By 1913 the business of marrying American heiresses had almost become an obsession. Half the most prominent hostesses in Rome came from the far side of the Atlantic; among them were the Marchesa di Vita de Marco, Marchesa di Sorbello, Countess Gianotti, Countess della Salla, Countess Cora Brazza, Countess Leonardi, Countess Sanminiatelli, Princess Poggio Suasa, etc.

Considering the proliferation of Italian titles it is curious what value Americans attached to them. As most titles were passed to all the sons of a family, and to their sons after them, they multiplied with frightening rapidity. Apart from this, it was not difficult for a self-made man to acquire a coronet on his own initiative. As both the Vatican and the Quirinal had the authority to create titles, the aspirant merely had to make up his mind whether he wished to donate money to the Church or to the State.

An original way of obtaining the coveted distinction [wrote Signor Villari] is by adoption. There are a great many titled people, especially in the South, who have gone down in the world and exercise the humblest professions to earn their bread. The aspirant to nobility . . . discovers one of these *nobili decaduti* and persuades him, for a consideration, to adopt him as his son. At the death of the chimney-sweeping prince or the cabman earl, the parvenu adopted son inherits the title, and plain Signor Eugenio Donatini blossoms forth into the Principe di Torre San Gennaro, with coat-of-arms, coronet, family portraits and liveries all complete. [3]

The Roman season began at Christmas and ended in June. Dinner parties were rarely given, for most hostesses preferred the flexibility of an 'At Home' where people dropped in at 11 p.m. and stayed as long as they liked. Most of the great Roman *palazzi* were converted into flats with a separate family occupying each floor. However, the rooms were so vast that many of the flats had their own ballrooms and a dozen other rooms as well.

The rage for fancy-dress parties had spread from England, and the ball of the year was given on 9 April by the British Ambassador and his wife, Sir Rennell and Lady Rodd. Over a thousand guests were invited. Many of them took part in elaborate 'tableaux', which spanned the centuries and encircled the globe, ranging from Olympus to Renaissance Italy; from Arabia to the France of Louis xv.

Lady Rodd appeared as Juno accompanied by the heroes of Homeric legend, while Sir Rennell was attired as an Elizabethan Ambassador.

My wife in a classic dress of blue and gold with a crown of turquoise took her seat on a throne composed of two peacocks [wrote Sir Rennell], while the other divinities grouped themselves around her ... There was, I believe, some misgiving among the Ambassadors as to whether their dignity might not be compromised by appearing in fancy dress. But the diffident adjusted their scruples by putting on dominoes. I could not well take part in my wife's classical group as an Olympian deity, but I had no hesitation in assuming the part of an Elizabethan Ambassador, and my costume was a copy, made at home, of the famous Court suit of Sir Walter Raleigh, only that the real pearls with which its white silk was studded were replaced by the beads which a well-known Roman industry supplies. Dering, the Counsellor, supported me as Sir Francis Drake, and we received the guests in the ballroom, conversing with Count San Martino, gorgeously attired as the envoy of Ivan the Terrible. After the guests had assembled in the ballroom, in the centre of which a space was kept clear, the various processions entered successively. [4]

One of the most magnificent groups depicted scenes from *The Arabian Nights*. It was headed by Prince Liechtenstein, the naval attaché of the Austro-Hungarian Embassy, and included some of the most beautiful women in Rome. They danced a languorous Eastern dance which was considered very daring. Another group, in the costumes of Louis xv, provided an anti-climax by performing a stately minuet.

The Duke Lorenzo Sforza played the part of the Milanese tyrant, Ludovico il Moro, while the Princess of Paliano depicted Beatrice and the Countess

Virginia della Somaglia the beautiful Isabella d'Este. Somaglia himself followed his patrons as Leonardo da Vinci. The Duchess of Sermoneta, who until her marriage had been Vittoria Colonna, played her ancestor of the same name. She was dressed in dark grey velvet embroidered with gold and walked with the famous book of sonnets in her hand. She was accompanied by her uncle Don Prospero, in the guise of Ascanio Colonna, and his three sons wearing the old Colonna armour. Don Domenico Orsini was dressed as Napoleon Orsini; the Marchese Vitelleschi as Michelangelo; Count Giuseppe Primoli as Bernardo Castiglione. 'We little imagined then that a year later they were to be divided in the fiercest struggle in human annals. For me personally that historic ball, which was one of the last great social events before the breaking up of the old order, has therefore always seemed to have a certain analogy with the famous ball at Brussels on the eve of Waterloo.' [5]

The most spectacular figure at the Rodd Ball was the bizarre and fascinating Marchesa Casati, 'a strange shimmering golden figure, attended by satellites with gilded faces – a sun-goddess as conceived by Bakst.'

Luisa Casati was the brightest star in the Italian social firmament. Born the daughter of a rich Milanese industrialist, she had married the equally rich Marchese Casati. In 1913 she was thirty-two years old. She was not classically beautiful, but her tall, almost pencil-like figure, her exquisite hands and feet, her wonderful eyes, and perhaps above all her wildly extravagant, exotic clothes, had made her a legend from one end of Europe to the other. Diaghilev sought her advice; Augustus John and Boldini painted her; Bakst designed clothes for her; Epstein sculpted her; D'Annunzio wrote to her. She wandered wherever the fancy took her, rented palaces on impulse and spent a fortune giving parties. The money not only went on food and drink but on creating a fantastic background, sometimes as elaborate as a stage decor, to provide the right atmosphere for the party. Once, at Capri, when the heavens were uncouth enough to cloud over on the evening of her dinner party, she managed to have an artificial moon strung up which actually moved across the sky.

The fabled Luisa Casati [wrote Lady Diana Cooper, describing a trip to Venice] lived in the half-built Palazzo Vanier dei Leoni. I saw her drifting down the Grand Canal under a parasol of peacock's feathers, but this surprise was nothing to the succession of glorious shocks that were to come. At the first of her parties she received us in her roofless palace by the light of a brazier on to which a nakedish slave for each new arrival flung a fuel that flared up into a white flame. Another slave struck a reverberating gong announcing every guest while she, the Casati, tall and elegant in a lampshade shirt, seemingly growing out of a wide bowl of tube-roses, presented each of us with a waxen flower. I remember thinking with what grace the foreigners received the flower and how clumsy we poor English were, saying 'Doesn't it smell good!' when another said '*Quelle émotion, Madame!*'

At the next party 'the Casati' wore the trousered Bakst-designed dress of an animal-tamer. On her shoulder was a macaw, on her arm an ape. She was followed closely by an attendant keeper leading a restive leopard, or puma it may have been . . . [6]

The Marchesa probably was the most extravagant woman in Europe. Whereas other women travelled with twenty trunks of clothes, she travelled with forty. Her luggage often matched her clothes; she had a set made of black velvet, another of leopard skin, the two fabrics she wore most often. Her animals were no passing phase; she loved her menagerie of whippets and pumas, and soon began to collect snakes. She refused to move without her reptilian companions, and ordered satin-lined boxes from her jewellers so that the snakes would find the journey comfortable. 'She was the D'Annunzian Muse incarnate', wrote Harold Acton. 'Wisely she seldom uttered; ordinary sentiments from the lips of so chimerical a creature were inconceivable; they would have struck a discord. The companions of her choice were albino blackbirds, mauve monkeys, a leopard, a boa-constrictor, and, among Englishmen, Lord Berners.' [7]

If the Marchesa talked little, she had a sly sense of humour. And when she did make an observation, it was to the point. Once when she was living in the Pavillon Rose near Paris – one of the many houses she took on impulse – an Englishwoman, Mrs Hwfa Williams, called on her.

She said she wanted to show me her pet python [wrote Mrs Williams]. I was by no means eager for the privilege as I am not a lover of snakes. However, I could not very gracefully refuse, so off we went to the python's lair. Repressing my emotion as best I could, I gazed at the lustrous black-and-yellow coils, only half-reassured by the Marchesa's information that the python was not a venomous snake, but merely crushes its victims to death. I looked with some apprehension at the motionless knot. Was it waiting to spring? Did pythons spring? Did they give one long squeeze or a sharp jerk?

'He is very still,' I said after a minute.

'Yes, he is, isn't he,' replied the Marchesa. 'He's been dead quite a long time now.' [8]

The Marchesa was half a century ahead of her day as far as make-up went. She achieved the 1968 look after hours of labour. For instance, she wore false eye-lashes which meant she had to glue every hair on separately. Her face was dead white, and her eyes outlined in black. She dyed her hair auburn, back-combed it and wore it so high that Jean Cocteau remarked that there was scarcely a closed vehicle in Paris that could accommodate her.

At every costume ball 'the Casati' always outshone all the other ladies. Once, she went to a party as Lady Macbeth, dressed in black velvet; at her throat was a perfect wax replica of a hand, blood-stained and clasping a dagger. On another occasion she anticipated Goldfinger by arriving as an Oriental princess followed by a boy gilded from head to toe.

Her passion for snakes upset many people. She frequently wore a wonderful necklace made of gold, with the head of the snake clasping the tail. People often asked her if it was Egyptian, but she always shook her head and smiled enigmatically. When the necklace began to move, they knew the answer.

One of the most distinctive features of Italian social life was the reluctance on the part of the upper class to engage in work. Managing an estate was the only occupation deemed worthy of a gentleman. Young men of good families, no matter how poor, felt it more dignified to loaf about the streets, gossiping and ogling pretty girls, than to take a job.

Mercifully the tango craze, which swept across Europe in 1913, gave these youths a new interest in life. Some of them turned professional, others merely surrendered to an agreeable occupation. At tea rooms in Rome and Venice and Florence tango-partners, looking like Rudolph Valentinos, set the pace. 'It was diverting to watch them,' wrote Harold Acton, 'so conscious of their mastery of adventurous side-steps, twining and twisting in and out of those gliding, dragging measures with a sharp click at the end, as when a peacock clicks open the fan of its tail, their impassive virility contrasting piquantly with a flashing wrist-watch, a sparkle of rings and a silk handkerchief reeking of Coty . . .'

In Florence these young men haunted the Via Tornabuoni, the social hub of the town. By mid-day the famous tea rooms of Doney and Giacosa on either side of the street were crowded with males exuding an air of infinite leisure – 'super lounge-lizards,' wrote Acton, 'button-holed, brilliantined and bespatted, all their goods in the shop window, they spilled on to the pavement to inspect each passing ankle and compare notes in a voice loud enough to be overheard . . . It was from these unemployed Narcissi that Mussolini was to draw his most rabid supporters . . . The prime attraction was the uniform, the right to cut a dashing figure without entailing risks.' [9]

The Pope joined the Kaiser and the Czar in trying to outlaw the tango, but it was as much use as trying to stop a tidal wave. His attention was called to the new phenomenon by one of his Cardinals, who reported that Signorina Adele Pertici, a star pupil of Taglioni, who ran one of the most famous dancing schools in Rome, had danced the tango at a soirée at the Sale del Municipio di Nettuno. The cardinal advised the Pope to ban the dance before it got out of hand. The Pope nodded but said it was best first to find a substitute. What about the Furlana, the peasant dance of his boyhood? The Cardinal looked puzzled so the Pope demonstrated how it was done. Apparently the Cardinal was impressed, for Adele Pertici received instructions from Taglioni that she was to dance the Furlana at the next big public ball. Despite her efforts the popularity of the tango continued to grow.

The Pope was not against all innovations. In July he allowed an American, Mr Charles Urban, to give a 'Kinemacolor' entertainment at the Vatican. It was shown in one of the throne rooms of the Papal suite. Among the spectators were the Pope's two sisters, his niece, and about twenty relatives of his household. Pope Pius apparently was fascinated by moving pictures; according to the London *Times* of 11 July he gave permission to a film unit to photograph the daily life of the Vatican.

Later that month the Pope was in the news again when the world learned with astonishment that the famous Swiss Guards, formed in 1506 to protect the Vatican, and familiar to millions of tourists for their sphinx-like faces and resplendent red, black and yellow uniforms designed by Michelangelo, had revolted against their commanding officer because of 'excessive military drill'. The trouble was caused by an item in the Vatican newspaper the *Osservatore Romano* on 19 July, which talked of 'insubordination'. Indignant soldiers of the Swiss Guard believed that Captain Répond had deliberately leaked the story in order to present them in an unfavourable light. A group of them assailed the captain so vigorously that, he claimed, he was compelled to draw his revolver to force them to retire. The Pope's secretary, Cardinal Merry del Val, intervened and took charge of the situation. The Swiss Guard was disarmed, relieved of all military duty and placed under house detention. The men, it transpired, were making the following demands: the dismissal of Captain Répond; the increase of their number of eighty to a hundred; the selection of officers from among themselves; the abolition of the prohibition against wine shops; the suppression of 'useless' military exercises such as gymnastics, bayonet drill, target shooting and climbing on to the roofs to protect the Vatican against imaginary attacks.

On 24 July Cardinal Merry del Val read a letter to the assembled Swiss

Guard expressing the Pope's surprise and displeasure at their behaviour. His Holiness invited those not willing to accept discipline to take their free discharge and not to place him under the painful necessity of dismissing them. Three ring-leaders were named in an Order of the Day. They had already left the Vatican, departing in trucks, singing the *Marseillaise* and *Viva Garibaldi*. Nevertheless the revolt proved worth while, for before the year was over Captain Répond was transferred and concessions were made almost wholly meeting the demands made by the men.

Fashionable Rome was never short of gossip. In January people talked about the ball given by the Skating Club at the Hotel Excelsior where the Princess Radziwill, emulating the Casati, rode through the ballroom in a small cart flanked by a leopard and a lion; in February about the success of a musical comedy based on the story of Lady Godiva, written by Pietro Mascagni; in March about the tragic death of Prince Vincent Windischgraetz, an attaché at the Austrian Embassy who shot himself because of a hopeless passion for an unsuitable Italian girl.

The middle classes, on the other hand, talked about the repeal of the law forbidding women telephone operators to marry; about the visit of the dancer Isadora Duncan to La Duse, who was living in semi-retirement near Venice; about the discovery by the Roman archeologist, Signor Adolfo Cozza, of a port at Pompeii buried beneath twenty-three feet of earth and lava and situated seven hundred feet from the ruined city.

And for a few days in August everyone talked about the Countess Tarnowska, who in 1910 had been sentenced to eight years' imprisonment near Venice for the murder of Count Kamorowski. A newspaper story declared that she had been found dead in a railway carriage between St Petersburg and Kiev. How had she escaped from prison? And how had she died? Was it murder or suicide? The Countess was a very beautiful, very wicked *femme fatale*. Born Marie O'Rourke, a Russian subject of Irish extraction, she had eloped at the age of eighteen with Count Tarnowska. The marriage was not a success, and she soon engaged a lawyer, M. Prilukov, to initiate divorce proceedings. Unfortunately this gentleman became so infatuated with her that he deserted his wife and began to rob his clients in order to shower gifts upon her.

Although the Countess Marie tired of M. Prilukov when his money ran out, she kept him dancing attention in order that he might assist in her nefarious schemes. She bewitched an old gentleman, Count Kamorowski;

then commanded Prilukov to persuade the old man to take out a life insurance policy for twenty-five thousand pounds in her favour. For the third act she employed another lover, M. Naumov. She worked upon the jealousy of Naumov until he became so demented that he consented to kill Count Kamorowski.

The Countess Marie's hope of collecting the twenty-five thousand pounds and continuing her exciting career abroad was dashed by the investigations of the insurance company which finally led to her arrest. Although the infatuated Naumov was the *de facto* murderer the judge sentenced him only to three years' imprisonment, while his evil genius, Marie, was put away for eight years.

The story of the Countess' death in the Russian railway carriage was printed in every newspaper in Europe. But two days later it was announced from St Petersburg that the dead woman was another Countess Tarnowska, a cousin of the adventuress. Countess Marie Tarnowska was still doing time in Trani Prison near Venice.

Meanwhile everyone was talking about the 'building scandal'. The new Palace of Justice which was in the process of construction was costing twice its original estimate. An investigation was held in the spring and letters came to light pointing to malpractice involving business contractors, civil servants and politicians. However, the Rome correspondent of the London *Times* declared that the real scandal was not corruption but ugliness.

The inartistic vulgar love of mere size combined with an unchastened taste in ornament is more responsible for the waste of public money than the reprehensible profits made by the contracts . . . If it had been an artistic success commanding the admiration and not the derision of critics there would have been much less outcry against statesmen who have made political capital out of giving contracts . . .

The scandal at least provided ammunition for the General Election which took place in November. Candidates of all parties fulminated against corruption and promised honest government. The election was the first to be based on universal suffrage. As a large proportion of the population could not read or write, particularly in the south, candidates used symbols. For instance, the name of Signor Tamburini was flanked by a drum; that of Signor Gallo by a cock crowing.

Although there were a few stormy meetings, where knives and pistols were brandished, the election was fairly orderly. In Rome the campaign organized by Don Leone Gaetani, who stood for the anti-clerical party, provided much amusement. His supporters managed to plant colossal posters bearing his name on the towering façade of the Gesù Church. How they achieved it, no one knew; and how the Jesuit fathers would succeed in removing the name of the anti-clerical candidate was a matter of hilarious speculation.

When the election, with its many ballots, finally was over, the Party led by the Prime Minister, Signor Giolitti – the Constitutional *Ministerialists* – had two hundred and nineteen seats, a clear majority over the nine opposing parties, who together mustered only two hundred and seventeen seats. Thus the mixture was very much as before.

The election excitement had scarcely subsided before the name of a thirty-two-year-old Italian, Vincenzio Perugio, was plastered across the front page of almost every newspaper in the world. The *Mona Lisa*, which had been stolen from the Louvre in August 1911, had been found in his possession. Perugio had been employed as a keeper in the Louvre. While walking the galleries every day he had become depressed to see how many masterpieces had been pilfered from Italy by Napoleon. So he decided to put matters right. When no one was looking he took the picture from the wall and hid it under his coat.

For two years he kept it in a chest which he built himself. In November 1913, he decided that the sensation caused by the disappearance of the painting had been forgotten. So he wrote to an antique dealer in Italy, Signor Geri, and offered to sell him the picture for half a million lire. Signor Geri visited Perugio to make sure that the picture was not a fake. When he was satisfied he notified the police.

When Perugio was interrogated he said: 'I stole the *Mona Lisa* because I wanted to do a good turn for my country, giving back to her a picture that is rightfully hers.'

Perugio was sent to a hospital for observation.

Throughout 1913 Italy's eyes were fixed on Albania. Indirectly Italy was responsible for the Balkan wars which did not end until the summer of 1913. Her attack in 1911 on Turkey, in North Africa, had prompted Bulgaria and Serbia to strike at the same enemy while the iron was hot.

Although Italy was committed to Germany and Austria, through membership of the Triple Alliance, her two partners regarded her as a dubious ally. She was always having 'an extra little dance' on the side. Her relations with Austria had been notoriously bad for the past few years, but in 1913 the two countries jointly backed the ruling of the London Conference in favour of creating an independent Albania. However, for months parts of that unfortunate country were occupied by Montenegro and Serbia, who refused to move out of the territory that was to form part of the newly born country. It was not until Austria shattered the nerves of Europe by presenting Serbia with an ultimatum that the latter finally complied with the verdict of the Great Powers.

Austria's reason for championing Albania, of course, was to prevent her arch-enemy, Serbia, from reaching the sea; while Italy's motive was a secret desire to control Albania herself and to become the undisputed mistress of the Adriatic. Consequently Italy twisted and turned, sometimes supporting Austria, sometimes undermining her, with eyes searching eagerly for each advantage.

Neither Germany nor Austria believed that Italy would honour her treaty obligations if a world war broke out. General Auffenberg of the Austrian Army remarked angrily that he had seen Italian cigarette boxes adorned with maps claiming all the territory from Fiume to the Brenner Pass. The people were so insolent, he said, that they even called their horses and donkeys by the names of Austrian cities. 'In case of war Italy will explode against us like a keg of powder', he declared. The German Foreign Office thought otherwise. Italy would remain neutral – and try to make both sides pay dearly for her non-intervention. She coveted the spoils of war, but shrank from the fighting. Or, as Bismarck had put it: 'Italy has a large appetite and very poor teeth.'

SIX

PARIS

'The first of January 1913 was dark with omen,' wrote Prime Minister Raymond Poincaré, 'and in every effort to preserve peace one seemed to be frustrated by incidents which forbade it. The conference of ambassadors and of the Balkan delegates sat on in London but . . . the diplomats saw no solution.' [1]

[Although the Balkan wars threatened to ignite the whole of Europe many Parisians believed that France's worst enemies were not foreign foes but sinister elements among her own ranks.] That is why the trial of the motor-car bandits which opened at the Palais de Justice in Paris in February attracted so much attention. The twenty young men on trial were not ordinary hooligans, newspaper editors told their readers, but anarchists who had struck their blow as a protest against society. For eighteen months they had terrorized town and countryside by hi-jacking travellers, stealing cars, robbing banks, plundering and killing. They had kept themselves supplied with weapons and ammunition by raiding gunsmiths' shops, and had left in their wake a total of twelve dead (four of their own) and eleven injured.

It is not surprising that the public pictured them as desperadoes of the worst type, nor that the authorities took every precaution to prevent their escape. Troops guarded the public entrance to the Palais de Justice while police guarded the inner corridors. The dock had been altered to cut off any communication between prisoners and public, and gas had been laid on in case the electric light should fail. The Court was also supplied with oil lamps and candles.

When the prisoners filed into the dock a gasp of surprise went up from the spectators, for no one had envisaged pale, under-fed youths still in their twenties, wearing neat suits and polished boots; nor the three demure girls looking like pupils from a convent in dark blue dresses and white collars, accused of being accomplices.

The evidence was even more surprising because it soon became apparent that although most of their crimes had been planned in the office of *L'Anarchie* at Romainville the meeting place had been used purely as a hide-out and no master-mind had guided them. Anarchists believed in 'propaganda by deed', defended their crimes and gloried in them. But the motor-car bandits, far from making impassioned speeches, flatly denied that they had taken part in any of the killings. They accused witnesses of mistaken identification, and even tried to refute the evidence of the fingerprint experts.

Most of them had begun their lives as carpenters, tailors, printers, iron-workers or clerks. Some had had miserable childhoods and fallen into bad ways through hunger; others had taken to crime through boredom, fastening on anarchist argument as a moral justification. It soon became clear that they were not anarchists at all, only anarchistic individuals – 1913 teddy boys in search of excitement.

There was something pathetic about their eagerness to escape the brand of thief and murderer and pose as intellectuals. One of the leaders of the gang, Raymond Gallemain, nick-named 'Raymond La Science' because of his grasp of mathematics, wore a silver pince-nez in court. He had spent three years in prison on a previous charge and had passed the time annotating Renan's *Life of Jesus*. A second, Chosay de Fleury, was described as 'the gentleman of the band'. He had been entrusted with the handling of the money, and had indulged in speculations on the Bourse. A third, Edouard Carouy, a former iron-worker, tried to talk in philosophic language. When he addressed the jury he said: 'I do not recognize your right to judge me. You are neither supernatural beings nor Gods. You are nothing but men and you wish to judge me, an innocent placed here upon this seat of sorrow, who has fallen into the clutches of this formidable apparatus, misplaced justice . . .'

As soon as the public became convinced that the bandits were not professional anarchists, and that it was the habit of the newspaper *L'Anarchie* to offer refuge to petty criminals, the world press lost interest. The manager of *L'Anarchie* tried to intimidate the jury by threatening them with assassination if they pronounced the bandits guilty, and was promptly slapped into gaol for five years. When the sentences were passed four of the bandits, including Raymond La Science, received the death penalty; two of them, including Carouy, were given penal servitude for life; the remaining sentences ranged from a few months to ten years. The three girls were acquitted.

Interest in the case revived for a day when it was learned that Carouy, a few hours after sentence was passed, managed to commit suicide by swallowing a pill. How had the police been so negligent as to allow this to happen? After an inquiry it was established that on the last day of the trial one of the court-room spectators had hurled a wad of paper at Carouy. He had picked it up, examined it and thrown it on the floor. A police officer had also picked it up and pronounced it of no importance. No doubt the cyanide pill had been inside. The day before the verdict Carouy had written to his counsel: 'If my sentence is bearable I should like to see my sister. Last night I lived over again my poor little life . . . All my dreams have always been ship-wrecked just at the moment when I thought they were about to become realities. That is why I shall leave this Kingdom of Atoms without regret . . .'

Despite the tragic circumstances of Carouy's gesture, his defiance struck a familiar chord; for defiance was a characteristic of France in 1913. Sometimes it was sombre; more often it echoed light-heartedly through all the aspects of Parisian life from sport to fashion, from stage to ballroom. It was clearly visible in the Rugby football match played in Paris in January between Scotland and France. When Scotland won by twenty-one points to three the crowd decided that the referee had been too astringent in applying the rules. They mobbed and stoned him, along with several members of the Scottish team. The British *Annual Register* informs us that 'the Scottish Union declined later to play with France'.

Defiance also was apparent in February when the French actress, Madame Réjane, appeared on a stage in Alsace with a skirt slit at the knee, and a gold knee-bangle glinting through the opening. And in March when the great French couturiers showed their spring collections, the new dresses caused an international sensation. The V-lined necks of the afternoon dresses were cut as low as evening gowns, while the skirts were so tight from hip to ankle that they showed the outline of the thighs. (The Americans soon were talking about peek-a-boo blouses and X-ray skirts.) The materials were gossamer thin and many of the skirts were slashed up the middle or the side. Some were buttoned discreetly, others showed half the leg. And as though this were not enough the colours screamed for attention.

We are garbing ourselves like Solomon in all his glory; India, the Orient, all the corners of the world have been scoured for fabrics and ideas [wrote Miss Kate Carew of the New York *Tribune*]. We are to unite every colour of the rainbow on our persons. If we have a yellow skirt we are to balance it with a green coat and a purple hat . . . We are to walk abroad looking like Post-Impressionist pictures, or

Futuristic efforts or Cubist atrocities. Art and Fashion have joined hands and sworn allegiance . . . For the rest our street skirts are modest and discreet. We can walk with ease, and we hide our nether members; our coats are sometimes men's cut-aways, and sometimes granny's dressing jackets but we seem to look all right in them. But the evening gowns and the afternoon gowns! What ho! I blush. We are hobbled, we are slashed, and we are of a tightness! In fact these dresses are distinctly naughty. I shan't be surprised if Senators speak about them disapprovingly in Congress . . . [2]

Each of the big couturiers – Poiret, Worth, Paquin, Lanvin, Cheruit, the Callot Soeurs – presented two hundred models ranging in price from twenty pounds for a day dress to sixty-five pounds for an evening dress. But they did not rest on their laurels when the collection was finished. They were always ready to create an original model for an important customer, always ready to seize upon a new idea. Some derived inspiration from Madame Jane Dieulafoy who, on 30 March, announced proudly that the French Government had accorded her the right to wear men's trousers in recognition of her services to archaeology by her excavations in Persia. (Actually, Madame Dieulafoy had worn trousers on a previous occasion – when she had fought by her husband's side in the war of 1870.) A few weeks later several couturiers pronounced 'les Galluses' the last word in feminine wear. 'Braces will keep the blouses from coming up out of the waist band, and if carried out in the colour of the skirt should make a charming line,' explained the *Tribune* fashion writer. [3]

Other couturiers, such as Paul Poiret, went further, at least as far as the beach was concerned, and Lady Duff Gordon, who had a shop of her own, wrote ecstatically from Venice in July:

The women look absolutely adorable and the costumes are the most becoming things I have ever seen . . . Here is the description of one that I remember particularly: pale flesh coloured tights were worn, then transparent Persian trousers, and a bright coloured tunic, made of fine wool or silk, embroidered in gay contrasting colours, a fez or turban completely covering the hair, and oriental slippers. These were given to the waiting 'femme de chambre' who, when her lady had finished her bath, enveloped her in an ample kimono-shaped brightly coloured Turkish towelling wrap. Thus all the drowned-rat appearance was carefully avoided . . . [4]

The Americans were shocked by the French clothes and the most sophisticated fashion magazines made a point of emphasizing that Parisian 'ladies' did not wear the outré models, but had them altered to comply with the canons of good taste. The English newspapers, on the other hand, pretended to be shocked but tried to raise their circulations at the same time. They

Paris Fashions

The new April fashions.

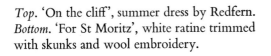

Top. 'On the cliff', summer dress by Redfern.
Bottom. 'For St Moritz', white ratine trimmed
with skunks and wool embroidery.

Top. 'Home from the Bois', *robe de promenade.*
Bottom. Indoor dress in brocaded silk over
pleated linen.

Oriental fancy-dress party at the house of Paul Poiret, the egocentric designer, and leader of café-society.

Poiret's 'Egyptian' dress with 'hieroglyphic' embroidery, typical of the exotic styles which had such a strong appeal in 1913.

Isadora Duncan, the dancer from California, who gave a series of concerts in Paris, and often appeared at Poiret's parties.

Left. *Tableau vivant* with the
Princess Caraman-Chimay,
sister-in-law of Countess Greffuhle,
and her gypsy violinist 'Maître'
Rigo.

Right. Countess Greffuhle, leader of
Parisian society, and the original of
Proust's 'Duchesse de Guermantes'.

Yvette Guilbert, the celebrated
chanteuse.

5ᵉ Année
N° 18
20 Juin 1913

PRIX :
2 francs
52 Pages

COMOEDIA ILLUSTRÉ

Mᵐᵉ IDA RUBINSTEIN
Créatrice de " La Pisanelle "
Habillée par Worth

Portrait par De La Gandara.

Ida Rubinstein, who in 1913 appeared in *La Pisanelle* and *The Martyrdom of St Sebastian*, both written by d'Annunzio and designed by Bakst. This portrait by De La Gandara shows her, in her dress made by Worth, in *La Pisanelle*.

Nijinsky in Debussy's *L'après-midi d'un faune*, the first ballet he choreographed for Diaghilev.

Karsavina, one of Diaghilev's favourite artists, in Stravinsky's *Oiseau de feu*, a rôle which was particularly associated with her.

De Max, the great tragedian, whose name, though without good reason according to Cocteau, 'spelt terror to the mother of any young man'.

Léon Bakst, Diaghilev's designer, who started the oriental craze that swept Europe in 1913.

Igor Stravinsky, whose *Sacre du Printemps* was received with catcalls in Paris in the spring of 1913.

Jean Cocteau, one of the earliest admirers of the Russian ballet, and friend of Diaghilev and Stravinsky.

La Danse de l'ours au Moulin Rouge by Gino Severini, one of the leading Italian Futurists. The *pas de l'ours* was not to be confused with the *grizzly-bear*, one of the new dances imported from America.

printed pictures of French women at Longchamps in tight-fitting, low-cut gowns. 'Would You Let Your Wife Dress Like This?' cried the London *Daily Sketch*. However, the editor soon dropped his campaign, for he was inundated with furious letters from militant suffragettes asking what right a husband had to dictate to his wife, and threatening to cancel their subscriptions if the *Sketch* did not change its tune.

Although the leading French designers were prosperous in 1913 they were worried by 'dress pirates'. In America copies of original models, bearing illustrious labels, were being sold on Seventh Avenue for fifteen dollars apiece. M. Jacques Worth declared in March that 'the fraud was growing to enormous proportions.' However, the USA was not the only culprit; Paris was nearly as bad. The small dressmakers managed to get hold of patterns within a few hours of a collection being sold, and often had copies in the window before the week was out.

The big houses traced the sabotage to the foreign buyers who were making a neat profit by allowing the minnows to copy original models for a high fee. Consequently in 1913 the leading designers informed the foreign buyers that the models they bought would no longer be delivered to their Paris hotels but shipped straight to their business firms. Other security measures were taken. No more strangers would be allowed to view collections, only persons recommended by customers of long-standing. And soon the story was going round that the midinettes were being held incommunicado like jurymen; that cots were put up in the sewing rooms and meals were served on trays. It was not until 1914 that the couturiers formed themselves into a group, known as *Le Syndicat de Defense de la Grande Couture Française* 'to bring to an end that illicit use of their names and the counterfeiting of their labels'.

If Paris fashion created a stir in 1913, the new Diaghilev ballet, *Le Sacre du Printemps*, shown at the Champs-Elysées Theatre on 28 May, caused a storm. The young Stravinsky had tired of turning to Holy Russia for inspiration, and instead looked back to a dark epoch at the beginning of time where people celebrated fearful rites to appease an unknown God. 'To express the dread, hope and frenzy of these brutish folk,' wrote Lydia Sokolova, one of the dancers who took part in the ballet, 'Stravinsky made a music whose rhythms, trembling, pulsing, flickering, thudding and crashing with a maniac piston beat, registered their animal emotions.' [5]

The revolutionary score had the audience in an uproar long before the curtain went up; and Nijinsky's strange and intricate choreography did nothing to lessen the agitation. The derisive laughter and noise from the

audience was so loud that it nearly drowned the orchestra and made it difficult for the dancers to perform. 'We were all terrified that we were doing the
fourth, fifth or sixth steps while somebody else was doing the second,' wrote
Lydia Sokolova. 'Nijinsky was in the wings stamping and trying to count for
different groups all at once. We could see Diaghilev too, walking up and
down, holding his head.' [6] Indeed, Diaghilev was in such a frenzy that he
ordered the lights first on, then off, while Stravinsky in the wings hung on to
Nijinsky's coat collar to prevent him rushing on to the stage. The excitement
combined with the red flannel costumes worn in the first act generated such
heat that the performers were bathed in a sweat.

It was a miracle that the ballet ran to the end, for many of the spectators
regarded it as 'musical anarchy'. The curtain came down to a storm of cat-
calls and boos. M. Camille Saint-Saëns shook his head in disgust, while the
Dowager Countess of Pourtalès warned M. Anstruc, the French producer,
that if he ever repeated such foolery it was the last time she would be seen in
his theatre.

At two o'clock in the morning [wrote Jean Cocteau], Stravinsky, Nijinsky,
Diaghilev and I crowded into a cab, and got it to take us to the Bois de Boulogne.
We were silent; the night was cool and pleasant . . . When we arrived at the lakes,
Diaghilev, muffled in opossum, began to mutter in Russian; I felt that Stravinsky
and Nijinsky were listening and, as the cabby lit his lantern, I saw tears on the
impresario's face. He continued to mumble slowly and without tiring.
'What is it?' I asked.
'Pushkin.'
There was a long pause, then Diaghilev uttered another short phrase, and the
emotion of my two companions seemed so great that I could no longer resist
interrupting them to ask the reason.
'It is difficult to translate,' said Stravinsky, 'really difficult, too Russian, too
Russian . . . It means, approximately: "Will you make a trip to the Islands?" That's
it; and it's very Russian because, you see, with us we go to the Islands just as tonight
we go to the Bois de Boulogne, and it is while going to the Islands that we first
conceived *Le Sacre du Printemps*!'
For the first time they had referred to the scandal. We came back at dawn . . .
and, whatever Diaghilev may have done after, I shall never forget him in that cab,
reciting Pushkin, in the Bois de Boulogne, his plump face wet with tears. [7]

Unlike the majority of hostesses in London and New York, the great ladies
of the Faubourg St Germain liked to associate themselves with the arts. In
1913 the leader of the smartest Parisian society was the beautiful Comtesse
Greffuhle, whose husband was known as 'Veau d'Or' because of his golden

money and golden beard. The Comtesse was a sister of Prince Joseph de Caraman-Chimay, whose American wife, Clara Ward, had run off with a gypsy violinist named Rigo. The Greffuhles had an imposing château near Paris, Bois Boudron, with ten thousand acres of richly stocked game reserves, where they entertained the grandest people in Europe; and a large house in Paris where the Comtesse gave many musical entertainments. As president of the *Grands Auditions de France* she had met Diaghilev and been responsible for raising money to bring his ballets to Paris. She was passionately fond of Wagner and liked to boast that she had taught the French to appreciate him. She wrote operas and sonatas herself and occasionally had them performed for her friends.

In May 1913 the Comtesse assembled an exhibition of French sculpture on board the trans-Atlantic steamer *La France*. The galleries devoted to the display were open to the public for two days when the ship docked in New York on 30 May. Among the collection were works by Rodin, Faliz, Lalique and Bourdelle. Apparently, however, the Comtesse considered her artistic efforts of secondary importance, for when she visited the Phare d'Ailly at Dieppe she described herself in the Visitor's Book as: 'Chimay Greffuhle, dame de qualité.'

The Comtesse led the way; and the social columns of *Le Figaro* record many forbidding soirées given in the name of pleasure. One of the highlights of the season, according to the New York *Tribune*, was a fête in which 'the best dancers of Paris society' performed *Les Dances d'Autrefois*. The evening was arranged by the Comtesse René de Béarn in her home in the Rue St Dominique under the auspices of the Marquise de Ganay, President of the French Red Cross. It was, we are told, 'a subtle manifestation of the dignified Faubourg St Germain against the new rag-time dances from America.' Four hundred spectators sat in the large Byzantine hall to watch the eight or nine tableaux of different epochs, during which quadrilles, waltzes, polkas and mazurkas were danced.

Despite the efforts of the Grandes Dames to uphold the traditions of the Paris *salon* older members of the French *noblesse* felt that 1913 was a regrettable year. Everything in Paris seemed to be changing for the worse; not only music and fashion but manners. Even the impregnable ramparts of the Faubourg St Germain were being undermined by vulgar commercialism. The marriage in February of the Duc de Richelieu, a step-son of the Prince of Monaco, to the rich Miss Elinor Wise of Baltimore, seemed indicative of the times. 'Money is the only thing that counts nowadays,' wrote Princess

Catherine Radziwill under the pseudonym Count Vassili. 'It is so everywhere unfortunately, but in France it seems more potent than anywhere else.'

The aristocracy blamed American millionaires for the deterioration; it was only natural that Frenchmen should wish 'to emulate their luxury'. Some aristocrats married American heiresses; others took what was nearer at hand and wed the daughters of rich Jewish bankers; still others associated with 'persons of a very low social and moral standard' in order to get on the boards of the new automobile manufacturing companies which were springing up everywhere. The salons of the noble ladies of the Faubourg St Germain, people said, were becoming a kind of *succursale* of the 'haute banque and haute finance' not only of Paris but also of France and of New York.

There was no doubt but that 'automobilism' was a craze in 1913. It was popular not only as a money-maker but as a sport. On 12 July thousands turned out to watch the French motor derby, *Le Grand Prix de l'Automobile Française*. Twenty cars took part, racing over the Picardy circuit in the Somme valley. One of the four British Sunbeam cars, driven by Mr Lee Guiness, failed to take a turn at eighty miles an hour, crashed through a fence and plunged into the river. Both driver and mechanic escaped miraculously but a spectator was killed. An Italian car, driven by Signor Moriondo, capsized on a heap of coal dust but driver and mechanic extricated themselves, as black as colliers, righted the machine, changed a wheel and set off again. The final stage of the race evolved into a duel between two Frenchmen, M. Boillot and M. Goux, both driving Peugeots. M. Boillot won, covering the distance of 570 miles in 7 hours 53 minutes 56 seconds. A British driver, Mr Cassagne, came third in a Sunbeam.

There were other uses for cars besides racing. The young bloods of Paris were so enamoured of their Cadillac Torpedoes and Rolls Royce Phantoms that they refused any longer to bring carriages and high-stepping horses into the Bois de Boulogne during the fashionable hours before luncheon. Instead, the leafy roads reverberated to the growl and splutter of engines and young ladies were wooed by the seductive glint of brass horns and intoxicated by the scent of petrol. The Paris Municipal Council tried to preserve the calm of the elegant Avenue des Acacias by banning motors from eleven to one, but the *jeunesse dorée* struck back. In June they collected the most dilapidated carriages and ancient horses that Paris could supply; noisy cabs with iron-rimmed wheels too shabby even to present themselves in the courtyard of the Gare St Lazare. They formed a procession of several dozen carriages and clattered up and down the avenue making a noise that drew hundreds of people to the windows. To make matters worse, they ate lunch on top of the cabs, laughing and shouting to each other and throwing their papers into the street. They won the day, for before long the ban was lifted.

The French not only damned the foreigners for the corruption of society but for the physical changes taking place in Paris. In 1913 the capital was caught up in a fever of demolition and new building. M. Arthur Meyer, the owner of *Gaulois*, the fashionable organ of fashionable Paris, was appalled to see that commercialism was assaulting the Étoile in the shape of dressmaker's shops and automobile showrooms. As for the Place Vendôme, several big firms had installed themselves on the splendid frontage 'and one of these days we may expect to see an advertisement placard in the hands of the Emperor on the top of the column!' That same year the famous Café Anglais closed its doors to make way for an office building, the Bal Tabarin shut down, the Boulevard Haussmann was lengthened and a new street, the Boulevard Raspail, was being forged through one of the most picturesque parts of Paris.

Worst of all was Montmartre. Not only were many famous landmarks being destroyed, such as the house of Berlioz, the dog kennels of Henri Quatre, the flower garden of Gabrielle d'Estrées, but the swarm of cabarets and restaurants that had sprung up had driven away most of the poets and painters. 'Even Montmartre,' wrote M. Meyer in May 1913, 'which seemed to be the last refuge of Bohemianism and of simple and natural loves, has become the crowded thoroughfare of fashionable "night life" . . . Come hither and listen: you will hear chatter and jokes in all the languages of the world. Look! It is Cosmopolis passing by!' [8]

The language most in evidence that spring was Russian, for Montmartre was the favourite haunt of the Grand Dukes. At night they inhabited the *Abbaye* and the *Rat Mort* where they swayed to the sound of gypsy music played by a red-coated band. 'The most beautiful women ever seen used to frequent the *Rat Mort*', wrote Harry Greenwall, an English journalist. 'Russian Grand Dukes poured champagne into grand pianos, and the fun was fast and furious all night long until daylight came; and then one would see women with tremendous cartwheel hats trimmed with ostrich feathers, lace evening dresses with long trains, and ropes of pearls and diamonds, tottering across the pavement to be driven away to rest until the night came again and the fun recommenced.' The Russians often took it in their heads to make a circuit of all the night places; thus the phrase 'La tournée des Grands Ducs' became part of the French language. And for many years, whenever the driver of a horse cab received an unusually generous tip he said: 'Merci, mon prince.' [9]

While the old Frenchmen complained, the young Frenchmen welcomed foreigners. At the famous Bal des Quatres Arts on 13 June the enormous ball-room of the Moulin de la Galette was draped with French, British, American and Russian Flags. The celebrated diseuse, Yvette Guilbert, sang *Les Quatre Etudiants* while Yvonne Yona and Nuibo delighted the audience with several daring cantatas. The students staged a march-past of thirty *meunières* who flung their bonnets over the mill in a competition for the beauty queen. The ball ended in the traditional manner, with intoxicated students ripping each other's clothes and bathing in fountains near the Champs Elysées.

Foreigners were also welcomed by hoteliers. In May the Paris tourist agencies were delighted by an epoch-making expedition from England. A packaged tour of three thousand five hundred trippers arrived in Paris for a one-day sight-seeing tour. This was their itinerary:

Sunday, May 11th. Rose at 6.30 a.m. and travelled all day from Newcastle to London.
Sunday night: Travelled all night to Paris.
Monday: Sight-seeing in Paris from 10 a.m. to midnight.
Monday night: Travelling all night from Paris to London.
Tuesday: To travel all day back to Newcastle.

There are some [wrote the Paris correspondent of the *Daily Mail*] who might think this too severe a programme for a week-end holiday; yet hundreds among the three thousand five hundred English people who arrived in Paris this morning for a day's visit are doing it, and thoroughly enjoying it too. They are of all ages and every class, professional men, clerks, tradesmen, artisans, labourers even. It is democracy on tour. For when you can come over from England to Paris and be fed and driven about there all day, and taken home again for 26/6d there is no reason for anyone not to be a traveller. 'What a week-end!' said an English resident in Paris. 'What powers of endurance! Who shall say that we are a decadent nation?' [10]

The empty ground between the stiff soirées of the Faubourg St Germain and the riotous orgies of the students' balls was occupied by M. Paul Poiret, the star of the French couture and the father of café society. Poiret looked like a music-hall Frenchman, with his waxed moustache and pointed beard. He was small and excitable and an egoist of gargantuan proportions. He took offence easily, and although the smartest women in Europe came to him for clothes he lost many clients by impulsive acts. Once, the Baroness Henri de Rothschild, pronounced by *Figaro* the best-dressed woman in Paris, telephoned to him and asked if he would send some mannequins to her house to show the newest designs. As the Baroness was one of Poiret's richest customers, he agreed. However, the girls returned two hours later greatly distressed. The Baroness had watched the show with several men friends. She and her guests had laughed uproariously and called the clothes ridiculous. When the Baroness bid the saleswoman goodbye she said: 'I knew they were ugly but I could not believe they were as ugly as all that!'

The Baroness made the mistake of turning up at Poiret's salon a few weeks later to see more of his clothes. The room was crowded with customers, and in front of them all Poiret walked up to Madame de Rothschild and asked her to leave. Blushing with chagrin at so public an insult, she first refused to move, and then finally swept out saying: 'You will hear from me . . .'

On the following morning [wrote Poiret], I was with my heads of departments in the glass-walled office whence I dominated all the activities of my house, and which opened on to all its organs. Every morning we had a report and conference, as is customary. The Baroness' saleswoman entered like a hurricane.

'Monsieur, do you know who is there? It is Baron de Rothschild. Monsieur, do not go, he will do you some injury . . .'

I went down at once in order not to keep him waiting and presented myself to him.

'You are Monsieur Poiret?' he asked in an even voice.

'Yes, Monsieur.'

'It is you, isn't it, who put my wife out of your house yesterday?'

'Yes, Monsieur.'

My assurance pleased him, he seemed to reflect, his face lit with a smile, and he said to me gently:

'You have done well. I know someone who adores your dresses but who did not want to meet her . . .' [11]

The next day, Paul Poiret asserted, he had a charming new customer who remained faithful to him for many years.

In 1913 Poiret gave many parties at his house in Paris where aristocrats mixed with the celebrities of the literary and artistic world. Among the guests were Jean Cocteau, Sasha Guitry, Segonzac, Cécile Sorel, Rachel Boyer, and Henri Bataille. An ever-present figure was Count Boni de Castellane whom Poiret described as 'the very reincarnation of elegance'. Castellane was the highest spender and greatest dandy since Beau Brummel. After marrying the American heiress, Miss Anna Gould, he built a palace on the model of the Petit Trianon. Although older members of the Faubourg St Germain thought him 'a terrible little fop' Poiret wrote that no one had a keener artistic discernment. 'He chose in the way one opens the pages of a book with a paper-knife – not at all haphazard, but with implacable certainty and precision. His taste was incapable of betraying him. It was at the performance of *Minaret* that I saw him for the first time, elegant in his black suit, his head high and haughty, with a perpetual shrugging of his shoulders and his elbows pressed into the waist.' But Paris rang with the Count's extravagances and his wife grew so alarmed by the speed with which her fortune was diminishing that she divorced him and married the domesticated Duc de Talleyrand. Although Castellane's circumstances were greatly reduced he amused his friends by writing a book entitled *The Art of Being Poor*.

Poiret was almost as extravagant as Castellane. In 1913 Paris was still talking about the fantastic fête he had given the previous summer at the Pavillon du Butard in Versailles. Nymphs with lighted torches greeted the guests and led them through the woods to their host. There sat Poiret dressed as Jupiter in ivory robes, with golden hair and curling beard. Twenty *maîtres d'hôtel* presided over the mammoth buffet; the table groaned with pomegranates, water-melons and pineapples; the serving maids wore leaves in their hair, and young men dressed as Bacchantes distributed horns in place of wine glasses. The three hundred guests drank nine hundred quarts of champagne before the evening ended.

One of the most remarkable figures at Poiret's parties was the American dancer, Isadora Duncan, who was at the pinnacle of her fame. While still in her twenties this self-taught girl from California had stormed into St Petersburg, the citadel of classical ballet, and given an exhibition of dancing the like of which no one had ever seen before. She cast aside the sacred shoe and danced barefoot in a Greek tunic. The audience applauded wildly but the ballet masters cried blasphemy and thought the world was coming to an end.

However, the great impresario, Diaghilev, did not denounce her; nor did the equally great choreographer, Fokine. And Madame Anna Pavlova invited her to supper. 'I am an avowed enemy of ballet,' Isadora told Diaghilev. 'It is false, absurd and outside the domain of art . . . I thank God that a cruel necessity did not inflict upon me the career of a ballet dancer.' Isadora believed in dancing to the music of great masters, as the mood took her; not dancing to set pieces, adhering to rigid conventions and executing 'tricks'. It was ridiculous to make the toe the focal point of the dance; dancers should use their whole bodies, and allow the music to give them their inspiration. No music ought to be out of their reach.

The Russians listened to the girl from California, and some years after

Paris

'Montmartre, the last refuge of Bohemianism and of simple and natural loves.'

A dramatic moment in the trial of the motor-car bandits in February. Uproar broke out when the prosecuting counsel spoke of threatening letters he had received.

The accident at the Gare des Invalides in July.

Last photograph of handouts distributed in the street, taken the day before this was forbidden by law.

Traditional Shrove Tuesday procession, with the *Char du Bœuf Gras*.

Motor-racing was an important part of the automobilistic craze that swept Paris in 1913.

The start of the Grand Prix de l'Automobile Française. No. 14 in the foreground is the Peugeot of M. Goux, who finished second.

The crowd at Longchamp watching the parade of troops and the take-off of the airship *Commandant Coutelle* at the Bastille day review.

Sardanapale, winner of the Grand Prix du Jockey Club, led in after the race by M. de Rothschild.

Helen, one of the record-breaking aeroplanes of 1913, taking off after refuelling.

Leblanc, winner of the Grand Prix de l'Aero Club de France, with his passenger Mlle Marchal of the Opéra Comique.

The aviator Guillaume and his passenger Max Brugère after their record-breaking flight of 255 miles in four hours ten minutes.

Right. Representatives of the French army: an infantry corporal, an infantry captain and a cavalry brigadier.

Below. Les Grandes Manœuvres: a Blériot monoplane over an army division.

Three girls asleep in the park during the heat-wave.

Pierre Bonnard, *le Pont de la Concorde*.

Fokine's *Scheherazade* had changed the taste of a generation, Diaghilev wrote to an acquaintance: 'J'ai beaucoup connu Isadora Duncan à Petersbourg et j'ai assisté avec Fokine à ses premiers débuts. Fokine en était fou et l'influence de Duncan sur lui était la base initiale de toute sa création.' [12]

Isadora's life was as unconventional as her dancing. She gloried in her body and tried to teach a world of Philistines that flesh and bone was not something to be ashamed of.

There was once a young Scot [wrote an acquaintance], who came to Paris to seek a living, and he heard that Isadora needed a secretary so he asked for and was granted an interview. He arrived, was shown in, and saw the lady entirely nude, lying on a couch and reading the daily newspapers. His first idea was to run, but he stood and coughed apologetically. The lady put down her newspaper, moved gracefully around to her side and said: 'Yes, what do you want?' My young Scotch friend, muttering that he had made a mistake, made for the door and never went back again. [13]

Isadora was used to shocking people. She selected Ellen Terry's son, Gordon Craig, to be the father of her two illegitimate children. Every year she gave a series of concerts and sometimes had as many as thirty curtain calls. Once, when the theatre was empty, she danced for Poiret alone. She asked the organist to play Chopin's *Funeral March*.

My heart swells almost to bursting when I recall what I saw on that evening [wrote Poiret]. Someone must have described somewhere Isadora dancing, and explained the miracle. She came up as if from the earth, as if she were being born, gave herself up to a disordered, pathetic rending, and then fell back into the void with a majesty and a gentleness beyond my power to express. With tears streaming down my face I threw myself into her arms to tell her the profound joy she had given me. She said simply 'It is the first time I have danced this *Marche Funèbre*. I never dared to do it. I feared lest it might bring ill fortune upon me.' [14]

Two weeks later, in April 1913, Isadora's children died in a weird, almost unbelievable mishap. The chauffeur had taken the children, accompanied by their governess, for a ride. On a small rise near the Seine his car had stalled and he got out to crank the engine. He had left the engine in gear, but not put on the brakes. Apparently the gear slipped, for a girl walking along the Seine saw a car hurtle out of the side-street, jump the parapet and plunge into the water. All the occupants were drowned.

The funeral was one of the most remarkable sights Paris had ever seen. 'The bodies of the governess and her two charges lay all together in the mortuary at Neuilly, which was turned into a *chapelle ardente* filled with flowers,' wrote an eye-witness. 'Members of the enormous party of musicians of the orchestra, known as the Orchestre Colonne, were present at the funeral, and played Grieg, Schumann and Mozart. The governess and the children were buried in one common grave, and after the funeral Isadora Duncan made a great gesture in expressing her sympathy and pardoning the chauffeur, who was [later] tried and acquitted of manslaughter.' [15]

Some years later Isadora Duncan met her own death in an equally fantastic manner. She was about to set off on a car journey. She was wearing a long, embroidered scarf, one end of which was flapping in the breeze. The car started forward, somehow the scarf became entangled in the wheel, and Isadora's neck snapped. She died in a few seconds.

Meanwhile the 'soul of France', according to the London *Daily Mail* of 6 March, was undergoing a glorious re-birth. In January M. Raymond Poincaré had exchanged the office of Prime Minister for that of President after a bitter electoral battle. As far as international politics were concerned, the campaign had crystallized into a struggle between the militarists and the appeasers. M. Poincaré's opponents were the Radicals and Radical Socialists, led by M. Clemenceau, M. Combes, M. Caillaux and M. Viviane. On the night before the final ballot was taken Clemenceau predicted that if Poincaré were elected he would deliver the Republic into the hands of reactionaries, and by his provocative diplomacy make war with Germany inevitable.

There is no doubt but that Poincaré's victory acted like a magic wand in reawakening chauvinism. All the forces of the Right took heart and a new belligerency began to blow through France. Of course the fortuitous turn of the Balkan Wars helped. By February the Russian-backed Little Allies had scored stunning and unexpected victories against the Turks, causing France to take a new interest in her alliance with St Petersburg, and to dampen her desire for conciliation with Germany. 'The new President,' wrote the Belgian Ambassador to Paris, Baron Guillaume, on 14 February, '. . . is day by day the object of manifestations of the utmost sympathy. He is invited to banquet after banquet, his praises are sung at the corners of streets, in café-concerts and cinemas, and the appearance of his picture or the mention of his name are the signal for loud applause . . . the popularity is made up of various ingredients; his election was carefully engineered; one knows in the course of his administration he manoeuvred very skilfully for France to be prominent in the European concert; he has expressed himself in some very happy phrases that have caught on. But primarily one must see in all this signs of the old French chauvinism which for many years was away from view . . . M. Poincaré is a Lorrainian and never misses an opportunity of reminding one of it; he was a collaborator and instigator of the militarist policy of Millerand, and his first word after he had been elected President was his promise to maintain all that was necessary for national defence . . .'[16]

The truth was, however, that M. Poincaré went further than national defence. National defence consisted of stepping up French armaments, of extending the two years' military service to three, of issuing loans to Russia enabling the latter to build strategic railways. But M. Poincaré crossed the border-line and began to encourage Russian ambitions. Poincaré was a diamond-hard politician who came from a family distinguished in meteorology, mathematics and physics. He did not share M. Clemenceau's view that conciliation with Germany was practical or even desirable. War seemed to him inevitable and he was determined to see that France fought with full Russian co-operation. He therefore worked hand-in-glove with the Russian Ambassador in Paris, M. Isvolsky, a vain untrustworthy character, whose thoughts were dominated by hatred of Austria and dreams of Russian control of the Turkish Straits. 'Nothing succeeds like success,' crowed Isvolsky in a report to the Russian Foreign Office. 'Under the influence of recent events one notices here a marked change in feeling in favour of the Balkan States and the Russian point of view.' And in a later dispatch he writes that when he inquired as to what France's attitude would be if Austrian intervention could not be avoided Poincaré replied: 'It is for Russia to take the initiative in a question in which she is the most interested party. France's task is to lend her the most effective support . . . In short, if Russia goes to war, France will do the same, for we all know that Germany will stand behind her ally, Austria.' [17]

Although Poincaré claimed later that Isvolsky had twisted his words, he did not demur when the Russian Ambassador told him that he had received a large sum of money from the Russian Foreign Office with which to 'encourage' French newspapers to take a more positive anti-German line. When Isvolsky began to discuss the actual distribution of money Poincaré merely said that he did not wish to know about it.

The French President took an even more drastic step, however, when early in 1913 he brought about the dismissal of the French Ambassador to St Petersburg, M. Georges Louis. Louis was a trained diplomat who feared that Russia's Balkan policy might embroil France in war. He used all his authority to emphasize the purely defensive character of the Franco-Russian alliance.

In 1912 M. Isvolsky, apparently at the instigation of the Russian Foreign Secretary, M. Sazonov, complained to Poincaré that Louis was not trusted by the Russian Government, and hinted that the time was ripe for a more sympathetic character who would be warmly welcomed in St Petersburg. Poincaré took the point and directed the Quai D'Orsay to telegraph: 'The President of the Council has been officially notified that the Russian Government wishes to see France represented by an Ambassador who displays more activity in his political functions and social relations ... M. Poincaré therefore invokes your patriotism to resign your Embassy ...' [18]

Louis was dumbfounded. He was assured by the Russian Prime Minister, M. Kokovtzov, that the Russian Government knew nothing of any request for Louis's recall, and then realized that Isvolsky must be intriguing against him. He hurried to Paris to defend himself; the press got hold of the story and raised an uproar against Isvolsky's unwarranted interference in French affairs; and Georges Louis remained at his post.

Poincaré, however, was more nettled than relieved. For shortly after he assumed the Presidency, and the tide of French opinion was visibly hardening in favour of firm action, Poincaré dismissed Georges Louis and replaced him by the belligerent M. Delcassé.

The sudden revival of patriotic fervour manifested itself in many ways: by the huge throngs at the air displays; by an article in the *Echo de Paris* by Count de Mun entitled *The Decisive Hour*; by the thunderous applause for the cavalry display at the International Horse Show; by plays such as *Alsace* and *Servir* which brought the audiences to their feet cheering wildly. *Servir* was written by Henri Lavedan of the French Academy. Lucien Guitry played the part of a retired French Colonel who had become a spy, unbeknownst to his family, in order to serve his country. The son was an artillery officer who had discovered an appalling new explosive which could blow up the world. As the son was a socialist as well he decided to destroy the formula; but when he went to carry out his resolve, it was not there. The Colonel, of course, had stolen it and sent it to the French General Staff. The highlight of the play was the dialogue which took place between son and father, one arguing for humanitarian internationalism, the other for France ...

The great issue which divided Left and Right was the bill introduced in March to extend compulsory military service from two years to three. Poincaré travelled the country urging the adoption of the measure. Although his speeches always contained the word 'peace' he aroused the emotions of his audience by emphasizing 'a great and strong France'. 'If France shrinks back she loses her proud place.' As the weeks passed, however, it seemed unlikely that France would retreat. In a survey entitled *Les Gens Jeunes d'Aujour d'hui*, published in 1913, one of the investigators wrote:

There are no longer any students in the high schools who call themselves anti-patriotics. In the Ecole Polytechnique, in the Ecole Normale where the anti-militarists and the disciples of Jaurès were formerly so numerous, even in the Sorbonne, which contains so many cosmopolitan elements, humanitarian doctrines no longer have any followers . . . The word 'War!' has attained a sudden prestige. It is a young, entirely new word, tricked out with the seductive fascination which the eternal warrior instinct in the heart of man keeps reviving. These young people invest it with all the beauty for which they long and which their daily life does not give them. War, in their eyes, is above all the opportunity for the display of the virtues which they feel to be supreme, energy, leadership, devotion to a cause that matters more than themselves. [19]

However, there was another young France, the France of the Left, which the survey ignored. Socialists, Syndicalists, Anarchists and Communists had joined together to fight the military service bill. They organized mutinies in various regiments; brought out a blueprint for a general strike in the event of mobilization; and held meetings and processions all over France. As these parties were represented by one-third of the deputies on the Chamber they were not to be taken lightly. Their biggest rally took place on 8 June on the vast wasteland known as the Pré Saint-Gervais near the north-east gate of the city. The crowds were estimated at anywhere from one to one hundred and fifty thousand people, and ten thousand troops stood by in case of disorder. The fifteen rostrums were draped with red cloth, but the law forbade the unfurling of a red flag or the singing of the *Internationale*.

Jean Jaurès, the Socialist leader, was the most striking figure present. He wore a black Derby hat, a dark jacket and trousers. Around his neck was a red kerchief, and hanging from his shoulders the red, white and blue sash of a Deputy. 'With his red face and his red beard,' reported a newspaper man, 'he presented a picturesque notion of "the red sceptre of the Commune".' Dozens of speakers harangued the crowd, many of them paying honour to the mutineers of the Seventeenth and 153rd Infantry Regiments. One orator began with the word '*Patrie*' but shouts of 'There is no *patrie*' ended his speech.

Jean Jaurès was the hero of many French intellectuals. He preached that international socialism could prevent war, even after a war had been declared by 'capitalist' leaders. All that was needed was organization; the sort of organization to fire the workers of the world to rip up the railway lines, blow the bridges, desert the armament factories, ignore the call to the colours.

It was not yet a panic [wrote Stefan Zweig, the young Austrian writer who lived in Paris in 1913], but there was a constantly swelling unrest; we sensed a slight discomfort whenever a rattle of shots came from the Balkans. Would war really come upon us without our knowing why and wherefore? . . . We writers, too, stood up against the war, although, as always, individuality isolated instead of united and determined . . . We thought we were doing enough when we professed in our sphere the ideal of peaceful understanding and intellectual brotherhood beyond language and frontier . . . [20]

Many of the young French writers were ardent pacifists: Jules Romains, who was to address the great poem to Europe during the war; Georges Duhamel, Charles Vildrac, René Arcos, Jean-Richard Bloch and Romain Rolland, the author of *Jean-Christophe*. Rolland lived up five winding flights of stairs near the Boulevard Montparnasse. For hours he wrote in his tiny room, eating little, scarcely even taking time for a walk. When friends dropped in to see him, he lectured them, and tried to goad them into making a positive contribution. There was a task for each to do, in his own country, in his own language. The powers of hatred, he said, were more vehement and aggressive, because of their baser nature, than those of reconciliation. Obscurantism was visibly at work, and the battle against it was even more important than art. 'Art can bring us consolation as individuals,' he told Stefan Zweig, 'but it is powerless against reality.'

The painters took little part in the political battle, perhaps because their own struggle for survival was too acute. Matisse was recognized as the leader of the modern school, and in 1913 was working on his famous sculpture of 'The Backs'. The thirty-three-year-old Picasso was experimenting with Cubist abstraction, as were thirty-one-year-old George Braque and thirty-seven-year-old Duchamp-Villon. The critics found Cubism incomprehensible but Picasso refused to be discouraged. 'The fact that for a long time Cubism has not been understood,' he wrote some years later, 'and that even today there are people who cannot see anything in it, means nothing. I do not read English, an English book is a blank book to me. This does not mean that the English language does not exist, and why should I blame anybody else but myself if I cannot understand what I know nothing about?' [21]

Although they held exhibitions in London and New York that year they either were ignored or derided. And when they sent their pictures to the Paris Autumn Salon which opened in November, they were upset to find that they were not hung in one section, where they could be studied to the best advantage, but scattered among the conventional works. An American paper reported that Picasso had submitted to the exhibition a board on which he had stuck a news clipping, two buttons and a piece of red glass and that the 'picture' had been returned. In the spring Picabia gave an interview to the New York *Tribune* defending the *Nude Descending a Staircase* by Marcel Duchamp, which had caused such a furore at the Armory Exhibition. It was useless, he said, for people to peer at the picture trying to find the nude or the staircase. Neither was there. It was simply what an artist felt when he saw a nude descending a staircase.

Perhaps it was the uncertainty over war; perhaps it was the changeable weather; but more duels were fought in Paris that year than in any other capital in Europe. Most of them had a common factor: they were fought against journalists or friends of journalists because of unfavourable newspaper comment; and in the majority of cases the journalists triumphed. In January M. Lagrosillière, the Deputy for Martinique, challenged M. Lionel, Honorary President of the Court of Appeal, who he said had inspired an article against him. As M. Lionel was sixty-one years old the son fought the duel in his father's place and was slightly wounded. That same month M. Postel du Mas challenged journalist Bernard Grasset to a duel with swords. M. Postel du Mas received a wound in the forearm but insisted on continuing the fight until a second wound rendered him *hors de combat*.

In April M. Ceccaldi, the Radical-Socialist Deputy of the Aisne, challenged M. Georges Berthoulat, the director of *Liberté*, for describing those who voted in the Chambre in favour of clemency towards the anti-militarists as 'renegades'. The seconds were unable to decide whether or not a duel was called for, and appointed M. Georges Clemenceau and M. Gaston Jolivet as arbitrators. These gentlemen failed to agree and appointed a supreme arbitrator in the person of General Dalstein who pronounced that the duel should take place. The duel was fought with swords. Ceccaldi was pronounced *hors de combat* after receiving serious wounds in the shoulder and chest.

The duel which attracted the greatest number of spectators was fought at the Château d'Orly in May between M. Georges Breittmayer and M. H. G. Berger, two of the best fencers in Paris. The encounter was described as 'extremely keen'; M. Berger received a wound which penetrated his chest and was thought to have affected the pleura. He was declared to be in a state of absolute inferiority and the combat was stopped.

The Duc Decazes, President of the Cercle Hoche, was worried about the publicity given to duels and their increasing popularity. In June he sent a circular to members of the Club asking them to sign a pledge not to give information to the press. This provoked a cartoon in a Paris journal in which one man says to another: 'The seconds say we are to have only one paragraph in the paper.' 'Then let's chuck it. It's not worth the effort.' [22]

The Duc's intervention had little effect. Outraged citizens continued to challenge journalists, and journalists continued to demonstrate that the sword could be as mighty as the pen.

If it was too dangerous to be a journalist in 1913 it was even more dangerous to be an unfaithful lover. Between 1908 and 1913 it was estimated that three hundred and fifty murders of the *crime passionnel* variety had been committed in France. In January alone seventeen people had been shot, stabbed or poisoned.

The case that attracted the most attention that year came in August. It was the trial of Alice Crespy, a beautiful thirty-three-year-old poetess who was accused of murdering a handsome young priest, the Abbé Chassaing, when he tried to part with her after a three-year love affair.

Madame Crespy told the court that she had first met the priest at a confessional shortly after she had obtained a divorce from her husband. When she told him that she had a lover he begged her to renounce the man and return to the embrace of the church. Shortly after this meeting the Abbé became her lover.

The Abbé and Madame Crespy wrote love poetry to each other. 'What matter heaven itself or Destiny, if thine arms hold me not.' However, this mood began to change, and the priest grew tired of Madame Crespy's possessiveness and jealous rages. He was delighted when the Bishop of Agen appointed him as curé at Montastruc. A greengrocer, a cobbler and a watchmaker testified that the priest came into their shops to make purchases on the afternoon of his departure and spoke happily of the new life before him.

Madame Crespy, however, claimed that Chassaing was distraught at the thought of parting with her. He came to bid her goodbye.

He seemed [she told the court] more than ever haunted by my former lover and asked me to destroy a poem which he had written to me entitled *Les Harpes Lointaines*, an analysis of the sentiments which united us. I refused and we had a quarrel. However, the thought of my book *Mort des Heures* which entered the minds of both of us restored peace. He asked me to fetch it. As soon as I left the room I heard the sound of a shot. I ran back to find the Abbé lying on the floor with a bullet hole in his left temple.

Feeling ran very high in the court. Almost everyone in the village was hostile to Madame Crespy. The 'Women of Agen' sent a letter to the foreman of the jury threatening him with death if Madame Crespy was acquitted. One witness after another stepped forward to relate how the accused pressed her attentions on the priest; how she spied on him, harrassed him, and how relieved he was when he learned of the transfer that would free him of her attentions.

The evidence about the gun was conflicting. Apparently the police had failed to examine the revolver for fingerprints. Although one medical man gave evidence for the defence saying that in his opinion it was physically impossible for the Abbé to have shot himself, other experts stated the opposite. The priest was not left-handed yet the wound in his temple was on the left-hand side. Furthermore, the pistol, which belonged to Madame Crespy, was defective and would have blackened the hand of anyone who used it; yet there were no marks on the Abbé's hand.

When the Prosecuting Attorney made his final plea to the jury he emphasized these points, but the climax of his case rested on the fact that a few seconds after the shooting, Madame Crespy's mother and sister had inadvertently called. Although they heard the priest groaning Madame Crespy refused to let them into the room and bundled them out of the house. 'When you heard his revolver go off did you call for help?' the prosecutor asked Madame Crespy. 'No, you did nothing. Even worse, your mother and sister arrived . . . they heard the groans. But you wouldn't let them go near him, because as long as he was alive he could tell them that you had shot him. You got rid of them because you were guilty!'

However, the lawyer for the defence, M. Dauzol, had sensational evidence up his sleeve. He had letters written from the Mother Superior of a Convent stating that the Abbé Chassaing had betrayed two nuns. One of them was a sister of mercy who had attended him while he was ill. 'He committed the worst crime a priest could commit,' the lawyer solemnly told the jury. [23]

Apparently the jury thought so too for they took less than an hour to reach a decision. The verdict was 'Not Guilty'.

The acquittal emphasized a trend which had been going for some time. Juries refused to find men and women guilty who had killed because of passion. The law did not distinguish between the various kinds of murder, and death or life imprisonment struck the ordinary jurymen as far too serious a punishment for a crime committed under the duress of deep emotion. The matter had been taken up by the Chamber of Deputies and earlier in the year a *Crime Passionnel* bill, which allowed the judge to give a minimum sentence of five years, had been introduced, and eventually became law.

Another dangerous activity which Frenchmen indulged in that year was flying. In February the French aviator, M. Perreyon, established a new air record at Buc Aérodrome by reaching a height of 19,686 feet. In August M. Pegout thrilled spectators by doing a parachute jump; and in September tested the theories of M. Bleriot by flying to a height of three thousand five hundred feet in a Bleriot monoplane, turning it upside down, and gliding one thousand five hundred feet. Later that month M. Garros reached the headlines for flying across the Mediterranean from Fréjus to Tunis. And in December the French airman M. Leganeux established a new world record by reaching a height of 20,305 feet.

At Rheims the air race in September drew large crowds. Although it was billed as an international race only three Frenchmen and one Belgian took part. It was won by M. Prevost, in a Deperdussin monoplane with a 160 horsepower Le Rhône engine, who established a new world record by flying a hundred and twenty-five miles in a few seconds under the hour.

A far more spectacular event, however, was the balloon race sponsored by the owner of the *Paris Herald*, James Gordon Bennett. It started from the Tuileries in Paris on 18 October, and had eighteen participants representing France, Great Britain, Italy, Germany, Austria, Belgium, Switzerland and the USA. A grandstand had been erected close to the Orangerie and was packed with members of the Aéro Club of France. Among the celebrities were Princess Marie of Greece, Prince Roland Bonaparte and M. Léon Barthou. Ten thousand spectators gathered on the Place de la Concorde and five hundred thousand lined the banks of the Seine. While the balloons were being inflated the participants darted in and out of the tents which had been set up in the gardens collecting supplies and checking on weather reports, and making last-minute preparations. The balloons required thirty-eight thousand cubic feet of gas; special conduits had been run from the mains on the Rue de Rivoli and the Place de la Concorde.

The object of the race was to see who could fly longest and fastest. The winner of the previous year's competition was M. Maurice Bienaimé of France who had flown from Stuttgart to Moscow, a distance of some eight hundred miles in forty-six hours.

This year the competitors hoped to do better. The English competitor, Mr Francis, told reporters that he was hoping to penetrate Russia at great depths. The food he was taking for himself and his aide was as follows:

> 6 fowls
> 2 hams
> 2 tongues
> veal and beef sandwiches
> 2 lbs. grapes
> 1 dozen pears
> 1 dozen apples
> raisins, bread, chocolate, biscuits, tea, coffee

Mr Francis reckoned that he and his aide could last a week on their food supplies. No doubt his calculations were correct but, alas, Mr Francis had underestimated the elements. And so had all the other balloonists. The winds were not favourable. They were strong and rebellious and threatened to sweep every one of the competitors far out into the Atlantic. So one by one the balloons came down on the coast of Normandy and Brittany. Only one balloon managed to cross water, and that was the Goodyear balloon piloted by Mr Ralph Upson of the USA. He flew six hundred miles and landed near Scarborough in Yorkshire. He was duly declared winner.

Even the stay-at-homes experienced the adventure of air and sea in 1913. A spectacle entitled *Champion d'Air* produced by M. Emile Cody and shown at the Châtelet Theatre in February consisted of twenty-five sensational tableaux. The audience was treated to the sight of a British-Indian steamship sinking after a terrific explosion, and to the hysterical passengers being saved by lifeboats and, as if this were not enterprising enough for the stage, the show ended with a real aeroplane landing before the footlights.

Less vicarious excitement was experienced at the Théâtre Populaire in Belleville where a play entitled *Dévoré* was given. The villain was condemned to die by being torn to pieces by a wild beast; and in order to provide the necessary realism a flesh-and-blood lioness, snarling through the bars of its cage, was wheeled on to the stage. But one night in January the lioness pushed open a side door and came padding on to the stage unattended. As she stood blinking at the audience a stage hand lost his head and lowered the curtain. The lioness, finding her path of retreat cut off, jumped into the stalls. The audience fled screaming. The lioness then leapt into a box and surveyed the pandemonium with dignified interest. When her keeper approached, she meekly allowed herself to be collared and led away. The angry spectators returned to pick up the hats, bags, gloves and umbrellas which littered the floor.

There were plenty of bedroom farces that year but serious plays, most of which dealt with current problems, were the most popular. *La Femme Seule* by M. Brieux revealed the difficulties facing a young unmarried woman who tries to earn an honest penny; *Les Requins* by Dario Niccodemi attacked the greed of the upper class; *Alsace* beat the drum of patriotism.

Although a few sentimental plays were produced they were not successful. Gabriele d'Annunzio's musical drama *La Pisanelle* was regarded almost as a period play. Although Bakst designed the costumes, Ildebrando di Parma wrote the music and the beautiful Ida Rubenstein played the leading role, the notices were not favourable. It was the story of a beautiful courtesan of the Middle Ages, captured by pirates and taken to Cyprus; while dancing she was smothered to death in roses. At the end of the performance ex-Prime Minister Georges Clemenceau told a reporter: 'D'Annunzio is the last of the troubadours.'

That Autumn Parisians talked a great deal about the tango. All the year it had been a subject of controversy. Although the clergy denounced it as 'a disgusting dance of low origin', tango teas were being given in private houses, and even the gypsy music of Montmartre was retreating before the new rhythm. At the end of October M. Richepin, a member of the French Academy, created a sensation by reading a paper on the tango at the annual meeting of the Five Academies. Many fashionable ladies attended hoping for exciting revelations.

M. Richepin, however, was disappointingly erudite. He scoffed at the charge that the tango was indecent. He had seen the tango danced by Princesses who were models of distinction, he said: he had also seen 'the insipid polka and other respectable dances danced in a way *à faire rouger des singes*.' Nor could he condemn the tango on account of its Negro origin since the graceful old court dances of France, including the minuet and gavotte, had developed from dances of rude peasantry in Brittany and Poitou, where the dancers clattered on the floor with their sabots. The popular bourée was still danced in Auvergne and even in Paris to the music of the *musette* and was perhaps more complicated in its movements than the tango.

Apparently some critics considered M. Richepin's theme unworthy of the Institute. The press pointed out that only four of M. Richepin's colleagues at the Académie Française thought it worth while to be present. Nevertheless,

the London *Times* plucked courage from M. Richepin's talk and finally came
off the fence; it pronounced the tango a perfectly respectable dance for
perfectly respectable people.

During the last weeks of 1913 Parisians also talked about the novel by
Marcel Proust *Du Côté de Chez Swann*; about the International Automobile
Show; the centenary celebration in Neuilly in memory of Antoine Parmentier
who popularized the potato in France; the fall of the Barthou Ministry and
the formation of a new Government by M. Gaston Doumergue; the award
to Professor Richet of Paris of the 1913 Nobel Prize for Medicine; and about
the international boxing match in London at which the French champion,
nineteen-year-old Georges Carpentier knocked out the British hope,
Bombadier Wells, in the first round after only seventy-seven seconds of
fighting.

They also talked about the coming European war. Some talked about it
eagerly, some angrily, some sadly. Anatole France, who was the guest of
honour at a dinner in London on 10 December presided over by Lord
Redesdale, had made his position clear: 'If there is any honour still left in the
nations, it is a strange way of upholding it to go to war, and so to commit all
the crimes, arson and robbery, rape and murder, which bring a private
citizen to dishonour.' Marcel Sembat, in a new book, *Faites un Roi sinon
faites la Paix*, echoed the same pacifist arguments. 'If we were victorious, we
should be able to re-take the lost provinces and impose an appalling war
indemnity on the Germans; but that is all. We shall be unable to destroy
German unity . . . defeat would cement this unity even more firmly than
victory . . .' [24]

Parisians forgot their worries on the last day of December. The hotels,
dance halls and night clubs overflowed with people who welcomed the New
Year with vintage champagne and danced the tango with the blessing of the
French Academy.

SEVEN

NEW YORK

Thousands of New Yorkers greeted 1913 with a stupendous mass rendering of *Nearer My God to Thee* and *The USA Forever*. The hymns and patriotic songs were organized by Major Gaynor who had launched a campaign for a 'safe and sane' New Year. At 11 p.m. Commander Evangeline Booth led the Salvation Army Band to Union Square, while more bands and choral societies took their stands at City Hall Park, Herald and Madison Squares. The words of the songs were flashed on to mammoth screens by stereopticons so that the dense crowds could join in. Everything was going nicely until throngs of revellers in paper hats began to intervene. 'There were jars and discords when Young America chose the "unsafe and insane" method of mere noise,' commented the New York *Tribune*. 'The screeching hand-grinders, the rattling ding-dong of the improvised tin-pan bells and the deeper tones of the gilded cowbells and ear-splitting blasts of tin horns ... marred the solemnity of the occasion.'

The clash between the two groups seemed to reflect Manhattan's schizophrenic mood, for New York, like London, stood poised on the brink of the irreverent twenties, seven years before its time. Although the established order still prevailed, there were plenty of straws in the wind. Jazz and the protection racket had made their debut, while surrealism, birth control, socialism, female suffrage and even 'free love' were ideas that might be resisted but could no longer be ignored.

Perhaps even more significant was the fact that 1913 arrived to find the Wall Street millionaire under attack. This gargantuan figure, visible proof that the New World was the land of truly golden opportunity, had commanded nation-wide respect and admiration for over fifty years. Yet on New Year's Day the Fifth Avenue residence of oil magnate William Rockefeller was in a state of siege, surrounded by congressional clerks, reporters, police, detectives, cameramen and ordinary citizens out to see the fun.

The clerks had travelled from Washington, on the instruction of the House of Representatives' Sergeant-at-Arms, to serve a subpoena on Rockefeller which would force him to give evidence before the Pujo Committee. Rockefeller, however, declined to accept the subpoena. His doctor said that he was suffering from a serious throat complaint and was in no condition to appear in public. The clerks refused to be fobbed off and hired detectives from the Burns agency to make sure that their quarry did not escape from his house, whereupon Rockefeller retaliated by hiring his own detectives from the Pinkerton agency.

Only firearms and clanking sabres were needed to complete a picture of the feudal days when outlawed barons held at bay the forces of a kingdom [reported the *Tribune* on 2 January]. The Pinkerton men had been put in service for Rockefeller for the purpose of preventing the Government's men from gaining access to the house, or learning whether the master of the house was "at home". In their eagerness to catch a glimpse of Mr Rockefeller the Burns detectives crept to the roofs of adjoining houses and tried to peer into the windows of the upper stories . . . the shades were gently drawn. Charles F. Riddell, Sergeant-at-Arms of the House of Representatives . . . was in the forefront of the battle line last night.

What was it all about? A Congressional Committee, headed by Arsène Pujo, had completed an investigation of 'money trusts'. It had issued a report declaring that little more than a dozen men, headed by J. P. Morgan, James Stillman, George F. Baker and the Rockefeller family, controlled the money markets of the USA. These men and their co-directors, the report stated, together held 'a hundred and eighteen directorships in thirty-four banks and trust companies having total resources of $2,679,000,000; thirty directorships in ten insurance companies having total assets of $2,293,000,000; a hundred and five directorships in thirty-two transportation systems having a total capitalization of $11,784,000,000; sixty-three directorships in twenty-four producing and trading corporations having a total capitalization of $3,339,000,000; twenty-five directorships in twelve public-utility corporations having a total capitalization of $2,150,000,000. In all, 341 directorships in a hundred and twelve corporations having aggregate resources of $22,245,000,000.' (This amount, it was pointed out in London, was four times the size of the British national debt.)

The struggle between Congress and Mr Rockefeller continued for four days. Finally Rockefeller's lawyer announced that his client would accept the subpoena and appear before the Pujo Committee when his doctor declared him fit. But where was Mr Rockefeller? Reporters and detectives lingered on, prowling about on neighbouring roof tops and keeping watch on doors and windows. Much to their chagrin, it soon leaked out that the old fox was sunning himself in Nassau. How had he slipped through the net? Had he used the bridge that connected his house with the McAlpine residence, or had he escaped in the suspicious-looking Consolidated Gas car that had drawn up before his door on 3 January? Or had he never been at the Fifth Avenue house at all? The mystery was not revealed. But in February the elusive millionaire finally agreed to be questioned by Mr Samuel Untermyer at the Jekyl Island Club in Georgia. It was soon obvious that his illness was not feigned, for in the middle of the interrogation he had such a severe coughing spasm that the session had to be cancelled. 'Mr Rockefeller's physical breakdown,' a newspaper lashed out angrily, 'is its own sufficient commentary of Mr Untermyer's demagogic vindictiveness in persisting, despite the warnings of Mr Rockefeller's physician, in pushing this inquisition to dangerous extremes...'[1]

Nevertheless many other financiers testified in Washington. George F. Baker denied that the directors acted as a consortium; Henry Davidson said that it was harmful that the country should gain the erroneous impression that such staggering sums were at the disposal of a small group of men; and J. P. Morgan said that a clumsy and outworn banking system was to blame rather than the schemes of men.

On 31 March it became apparent that the charges hurled by the Pujo Committee had not succeeded in undermining America's faith in her great tycoons. On that day a newspaper from Rome announced the death of J. P. Morgan, who had gone to Italy for his health. Newspapers all over the USA deplored the passing of 'the greatest financier in the world – the greatest financier who ever lived.' His obituaries were fit for a monarch, at least in length and breadth. The New York *Tribune* devoted the first seven pages of the paper, in their entirety, to the story of his life. Some of the headlines ran: Forehead of a Thinker and Jaw of a Fighter; Morgan Menage Goes On – Gardeners Remain at Work; His Library the Expression of a Mind Imperial in Scope; Art World Mourns its Patron; London Market Steady; Morgan Intensely Patriotic Afloat As Well As On Shore. His death, however, was not interpreted as the passing of an era, for his son, J. P. Morgan Junior, had already donned his father's mantle.

Although the Wall Street financiers were abused by Congress, no-one ever dared to attack their wives. These ladies ruled the social world of New

New York

Fifth Avenue, 1913.

President-elect Wilson and
his predecessor William Taft
before Wilson's inauguration
in Washington.

Elizabeth Gurley Flynn
addressing strikers at Paterson,
N.J.

Mrs Oliver Belmont, a leader
of Newport Society, and of the
American Suffragette
movement.

Procession of thirty thousand suffragettes in New York.

Coffee in the Onyx Hall of the Vanderbilt residence. The servants who waited on the family and guests had their own fleet of servants, who waited on them at meals.

After-dinner recreation at the Vanderbilt house in New York: smashing precious Nymphenburg and Copenhagen china.

A concert at the Vanderbilts'. Caruso is singing, Franz Léhar conducts and the orchestra includes Mischa Elman, Fritz Kreisler, Eugène Ysaye and Bronislav Hubermann.

Above. St Caruso – enshrined by the ladies of society.
Right. Mrs Stuyvesant Fish and Mrs James Gerard at Newport. During 1913 Mrs Cornelius Vanderbilt, the Queen of Newport society, spent many months in Europe, and Mrs Fish ruled in her absence.

Alfred Vanderbilt, with his famous equipage, which dominated the Coaching Season.

Mrs W. Lippett's *château*, one of the great variety of extravagant residences in Newport.

The middle-classes were given mobility by the Model T Ford.

John D. Rockefeller's
New York residence.

John D. Rockefeller on his way to the monopoly investigation.

York with unruffled assurance and iron authority. They were national figures, characters from a fairy story, for they lived on a scale that even Russian Grand Dukes found impressive. Their jewels, their yachts, their palaces, servants, clothes and carriages were of breathless interest to thousands of Americans who dreamed of success on the same terms. As Hollywood was in its infancy, and the stage not wholly respectable, these social figures had few competitors in the field of glamour. Newspapers ran daily columns on their activities while the public flocked to the weddings of their sons and daughters in such thousands that battalions of police had to be on hand to maintain order. They lived up to what was expected of them by breath-taking extravagance, and preserved themselves as a côterie by merciless snobbery.

The ascendancy of these very rich ladies was not of long standing. Most of them had secured their positions only thirty years earlier, in a palace revolution engineered by the Vanderbilts. The clash between the old aristocracy, consisting of middle-class Dutch and English families who had settled in Manhattan in the eighteenth century, and the new giants thrown up by industry and banking – the Vanderbilts, Whitneys, Rockefellers, Goulds Morgans, Harrimans, Bakers, etc. – had come in 1880 when the exclusive Academy of Music had refused to allot any of their boxes to the newcomers, despite the fact that sums as large as thirty thousand dollars had been mentioned. The Academy had only eighteen boxes and all of them were taken by the old guard.

The Vanderbilts, smarting with defeat, decided then and there to build a new opera house that would give the millionaires of New York ample opportunity to display their fabulous jewels. Consequently the Metropolitan Opera House opened its doors in 1883. Its gala first night sounded the death knell of the 'Faubourg St Germain' aristocracy, for it had two tiers of thirty-six boxes each (a top tier was built originally but torn down soon after) known as the Golden and Diamond Horseshoes. Although the *Dramatic Mirror* reported acidly that 'the Goulds and the Vanderbilts and people of that ilk perfumed the air with the odour of crisp greenbacks,' and went on to say that 'the tiers of boxes looked like cages in a menagerie of monopolists,' it was obvious that no other hall could offer such a magnificent parade ground. [2] Within two years the Academy of Music had closed its doors leaving its patrons to get on to the best terms they could with the new overlords.

Mrs William Astor, known as 'the Mystic Rose', accepted the advice of her social mentor, Mr Ward McAllister, and came to terms with the new millionaires. Her quick decision was well rewarded. Hailed as queen, she ruled over New York until her death in 1908. Mrs Astor turned Monday night at the Opera into a ritual. On that evening every lady worth a million donned her most spectacular dress and jewels and sallied forth to be eyed by an enthusiastic populace. The worrying problem was how to wear the jewels so that everyone in the vast audience could see them. Mrs John Drexel solved the dilemma by devising a sort of Sam Browne belt. Her jewels were reset on a wide band which she wore around her waist, diagonally crossing her imposing bosom and shoulders. Mrs Frederick Vanderbilt was even more original. She had been told that Venetian beauties in the Renaissance liked to toy with a single jewel at the end of a chain. So she walked majestically through the lobby with a string of pearls that went to her ankles, kicking before her a huge uncut ruby.

Mrs Astor died in 1908 and the sceptre passed to Mrs Cornelius Vanderbilt, whose brother, Orme Wilson, had married Mrs Astor's daughter, Carrie. Mrs Vanderbilt followed the pattern laid down by Mrs Astor with scrupulous care. Society must not be looked upon as a pleasure, but a duty. Its task was to establish a tradition of elegance and refinement which the nation could follow. If it lowered its standards for the sake of amusement (such as inviting stage celebrities or politicians or intellectuals to its parties) it would soon cease to exist. The mystique of aloofness practised by European royalty was deemed the quality most essential to its well-being. Indeed, many Americans (including the great ladies themselves) regarded New York 'society' as the equivalent of royalty.

Father [wrote Cornelius Vanderbilt Junior] . . . had been reared by his parents in the firm belief that they were America's aristocracy, embodying in their lives and actions all that was fine, honourable, and Christian. Theirs was a sacred God-given trust to maintain these standards. My sister and I were brought up like European royalty; indeed my mother grew to think of herself as a kind of American royalty. 'Dear, poor Marie Antoinette,' she once remarked. 'I feel so sorry for her. If the revolution ever came to this country, I would be the first to go.' [3]

The New World royals were seldom relaxed, however, for they competed savagely with each other in clothes, jewels and general splendour. The battle raged fiercest at Newport, the summer capital. Here the *élite* built huge palaces which astonished European eyes, for they were erected side by side on only an acre or two of ground, like a row of giant Garden City villas.

Into those six or seven weeks were crowded balls, dinners, parties of every description, each striving to eclipse the other in magnificence [wrote Elizabeth Drexel]. Colossal sums were spent in the prevailing spirit of rivalry. I remember Mrs Pembroke Jones telling me that she always set aside three hundred thousand dollars at the beginning of every Newport season for entertaining. Some hostesses must have spent even more. A single ball could cost a hundred or even two hundred thousand dollars. No-one considered money except for what it could buy.

The mornings were always spent at Bailey's Beach, Newport's most exclusive club, or on the Horse Shoe Piazza at the Casino. Here the ladies had an opportunity to display their Paris clothes.

Different dresses for every occasion, eighty or ninety in a season, worn once or twice and put aside . . . How they swished and rustled! . . . Parasols to match every dress, enormous flopping feathered hats assorted to every costume. White gloves to the elbow, three or four new pairs every day, priceless lace ruffles at throat and wrists, yards of lace flouncing on underskirts, thousands of dollars worth dragged over the Casino terrace. [4]

Society women not only were expected to vie with one another in extravagance but to fight a rear-guard action to prevent newcomers, new millionaires who seemed to spring up like mushrooms, from crashing into the sacred circle. 'I know of no profession or work for women more taxing on mental resources than being a society leader in society,' sighed Mrs Oliver Belmont, mother of the Duchess of Marlborough.

The pressures were great. 'A few women seem to head the concourse like sheep and there is a most riotous struggle of getting in and keeping other people out,' observed a society reporter wearily. Rich aspirants rented vast villas and splashed their money recklessly. They cooed and kowtowed and came up smiling from repeated humiliations. There was no way to hide defeat, for outsiders were not permitted to bathe at Bailey's Beach, to yacht at Hazard's, to join the reading room or the Casino Club. Their children might win the tennis tournaments and their thoroughbreds carry off the prizes at the Horse Show, but not a single society leader would be 'at home' when their wives called.

Occasionally an outsider met success through the hostility of rival factions. When the Tin Plate King, Mr William Leeds, and his pretty wife rented 'Fairholme' for the season from Mr John Drexel, Mrs Edith Wetmore protested vehemently. 'How can you lease to those horrid, vulgar people? Why the whole house ought to be disinfected after them!' This remark was repeated to Mrs Oliver Belmont, who was thirsting for a diversion to relieve her boredom. She decided to pit her strength against that of the Wetmores, and promptly issued an invitation to a ball 'in honour of Mr and Mrs William Leeds'. The recipients were in a dilemma for although they opposed the advance of the Tin Plate King they did not want to be struck off Mrs Belmont's list for the remainder of the season. So no one replied. Mrs Belmont knew her Newport, for she countenanced no change of plan and day by day the preparations for her mammoth ball continued. Her iron nerve was rewarded, for a few days before the party the herd of sheep thundered forward. Letters of acceptance poured in by the shoal. Mr and Mrs Leeds had arrived.

Mrs Cornelius Vanderbilt, on the other hand, rarely paved the way for an outsider. The daughter of a handsome, ruthless adventurer (whom some people said was the model for Rhett Butler) who had begun life selling tobacco across the counter and made a fortune dealing in arms in the Civil War, she had little pity for eager aspirants. At tea-time, when she sat before her silver urn in a hostess gown, acquaintances not wholly acceptable sometimes made the mistake of calling upon her. She always said to her butler: 'Please say that Mrs Vanderbilt regrets that Mrs X is not on her calling list this afternoon.'

In 1913 people were still talking about the magnificent Oriental Ball that Mrs Vanderbilt had given in Newport the previous summer. The lawns of Beaulieu gleamed with flowers and myriad lights, and a huge theatre tent was silhouetted against the sky. *The Merry Countess*, a musical comedy version of *Die Fledermaus*, which was playing in New York, was to be performed. 'I can give you the entire second act,' J. J. Schubert had written, 'which includes a new ballet, a very remarkable dancing number done by the Dolly Sisters and some solo dances by Mlle Dazie. I will send the entire scenic equipment, stage manager and orchestra conductor.' [5] All the guests appeared in exotic dress; there were gypsy and Persian and Russian quadrilles; and the *New York American* pronounced it 'the most extravagant affair of its kind ever seen in Newport'. But what pleased Mrs Vanderbilt most of all were the comments on her selectivity. 'Mrs Vanderbilt's guest list,' someone remarked, 'is a victory in vacuums. No-one is here who ought not to be.'

Mrs Vanderbilt entertained with equal grandeur and precision in New York; but in 1913 she spent many months abroad, taking the cure at Bad Nauheim, visiting her niece, the Duchess of Roxburghe; and cruising with her husband on his vast steam yacht the *North Star*. In her absence that year the role of Queen was played by Mrs Stuyvesant Fish, a formidable woman in her late forties, whose sharp tongue terrorized society.

Once, as her fifty guests sat down to dinner she swept the huge table with a glance and said: 'Here you all are again. Older faces and younger clothes.' On another occasion she referred disobligingly to Mrs John Drexel who was rumoured to be having an affair with her secretary. 'I have been looking everywhere for Aunt Alice,' said one of Mrs Drexel's relations. 'Have you seen her?' 'No,' replied Mamie Fish. 'Have you tried under the secretary?' On another occasion she crossed swords with her bosom companion, Mr Harry Lehr, the Court Jester of society who had married a Philadelphia heiress. They both attended a party where people amused themselves by guessing each other's favourite flower. 'I know yours, Mamie', said Harry rashly. 'The climbing rose.' 'And yours, pet,' retorted Mamie. 'The marigold.'

'My mother', wrote Cornelius Vanderbilt Junior, 'could not abide Mamie and her breezy, brash, cruel wit, her breaking with the traditions of the past. It was Mrs Fish, she always claimed, who created the nucleus of what later became café society.' [6] Mrs Fish, however, insisted that she was merely trying to liven things up when she invited John L. Sullivan and Marie Dressler to dinner; when she dined at Sherry's one Sunday night in an evening dress; when she dispensed with dinners three hours long and instructed her footmen to serve the guests in forty minutes.

If Mrs Fish had not had a weakness for pranks she might have grasped the sceptre herself from Mrs Astor, rather than letting it fall to Mrs Vanderbilt. But schoolgirl escapades were her undoing. Encouraged by Mr Harry Lehr, Mrs Fish invited people to dinner to meet Prince del Drago, then produced a monkey in a white tie and tails. The guests, afraid to offend their hostess, solemnly sat down to dinner with the little creature. On another occasion she sponsored a dinner party for dolls where everyone talked baby talk; and on another, helped Harry Lehr to send out invitations for a Dogs' Dinner. A hundred dogs arrived with their owners and were served a sumptuous meal on a trestled table. The highlight of the evening was provided by a dachshund who over-taxed its capacities to such an extent that it fell unconscious on its plate and had to be carried home. These stories leaked into the press, and newspapers, who took their society seriously, lashed out angrily against the jokesters. 'It is dreadful to think of distinguished foreigners coming over here and judging us by Mrs Stuyvesant Fish's entertainments, arranged with the assistance of Mr Harry Lehr. New York society represents America in the eyes of the foreign world, and we should behave with a becoming sense of dignity.' [7]

Nevertheless, Mrs Fish had started a fashion. Mr Henry Clews Junior sent out invitations to a ball on which was printed 'No one admitted unless wearing servants' dress'.

When the evening of the party arrived [wrote Mrs Lehr], no-one had the courage to face their servants dressed in what appeared to be clothes purloined from their own wardrobes, with the result that Freebody Park was thronged with maids and menservants who had been given an unexpected evening off so that they should not witness their master and mistress's departure for the ball.

I donned the black dress and white apron of a ladies'-maid; Harry Lehr was a pompous butler.

The door of 'The Rocks' was opened by Henry Clews attired as a valet and holding a duster in one hand and a kitchen pail in the other. Behind him was Mrs Oelrichs with a large mop, industriously polishing the floor. Oliver Belmont, a little feather dusting brush stuck into his cap, was acting as cloakroom attendant, taking charge of coats. The funniest part of the evening was the dinner, cooked by the guests. Everybody made his own speciality, and the result was a weird assortment of dishes. Mrs Fish made scrambled eggs, Mrs Pembroke Jones a salad, Elisha Dyer cooked lobster à l'Americaine, Mr Van Alen, spaghetti. Those who could not contribute to the menu spread tomatoes and sliced onion on toast and laid the table. Harry Lehr acted as butler and poured out the wine.[8]

In 1913, with Mrs Vanderbilt on the other side of the Atlantic, Mrs Fish had things her own way. That summer it was she who gave the great fancy dress ball at Newport. Arrayed as a Fairy Queen in shimmering white satin, she received her guests at the foot of the marble stairway at her house, Crossways. Mrs Hermann Oelrichs came as Mother Goose with a live bird under her arm, while Mrs Elsie Vanderbilt French drove up as Snow White in a wonderful yellow coach. The ballroom was decorated with witches on broomsticks, black cats, sheaves of wheat and hobgoblins.

But Mrs Fish was in the news that year not only because of her parties. In 1913 she startled her friends by paying a visit to the East End, which was featured in all the papers. Mrs Stuyvesant Fish knew nothing of politics and social work but she adored publicity. So when she received a letter from her literary friend, Miss Elizabeth Marbury, asking her to help the women and girls used as sweated labour in the garment industry, then on strike, she responded. She sailed forth in her imposing limousine with liveried chauffeur and footman on the box, and pulled up at Oddfellows Hall, 67 St Mark's

Place. A public relations officer, Miss Barnum, joined her and took her to several tenement houses. Then they returned to the Hall and Mrs Fish addressed the workers.

Mrs Fish was elegantly gowned and veiled and wore an exquisite corsage. There was a great craning of necks among the pinched girls in shabby dresses who assumed that Mrs Fish must be a shop forelady. 'I am not a suffragette and I am not a socialist,' the great lady told them, 'but I do think you ought to get seven dollars a week and I am here to urge you to keep up the fight, though I don't really believe in strikes. And I think it is a pity that there's so much bitterness among the poor against the rich. But you ought to get seven dollars a week.'

Miss Barnum murmured that the Consumers' League stood for a minimum wage of nine dollars for women and Mrs Fish amended her estimates accordingly. 'Good gracious,' she commented. 'We spend that much for a bunch of flowers or a box of candy.' She told the girls to save their money so that they could strike successfully but Miss Barnum murmured that they could not save much out of four or five dollars a week. 'I suppose not,' conceded Mrs Fish. As she left she warned the girls not to read Ibsen, not to support woman suffrage and above all to resist the sinister appeal of socialism. [9]

Concern with this revolutionary creed was not surprising, for in the winter of 1913 Socialism appeared to be making alarming progress, particularly among intellectuals; and as the intellectuals also supported female suffrage Mrs Fish and her friends inevitably bracketed the two together. This tendency was strengthened by the Socialist Costume Ball held at the Murray Hall Lyceum on 17 January. The star turn consisted of two English girls, one dressed in suffragette attire, the other as her jailor.

The ball was sponsored by rich, plump, middle-aged Mrs Mabel Dodge who had returned to America after a long sojourn abroad to establish herself as the queen of Greenwich Village. Mrs Dodge lived in a house at Fifth Avenue and Ninth Street, with a snow-white drawing room furnished with delicate French furniture and an elaborate Venetian chandelier. Her evenings soon became famous both for bodily food and spiritual succour. Mrs Dodge was amazingly intense. Causes were her life-blood and she championed them indiscriminately. She loved people, she said, who 'believed in life' and championed everything from Freud to sabotage.

Among her many distinguished guests were 'Big Bill' Hayward, President of the International Workers of the World, and Elizabeth Gurley Flynn, the Jeanne d'Arc of the movement. The I.W.W. (referred to by hostile New Yorkers as 'I Won't Work') was a militant syndicalist-anarchist organization which advocated violence. In Mrs Dodge's drawing room Elizabeth Flynn planned the waiters' strike which took place in January, and gave many late diners the fright of their lives.

The strike was about overtime pay. Evening waiters were asking for a three-and-a-half-hour day, day waiters for seven hours, with overtime pay and one day off every two weeks. Kitchen employees were asking for a ten-hour day, a six-day week, and overtime pay ranging from twenty-four to fifty cents. The employers refused to meet the demands, so after midnight on 24 January disgruntled workers downed tools and swept out of New York's smartest hotels and restaurants. One hundred and fifty waiters departed from the Folies Bergères in a group, leaving the diners gasping in amazement. They gathered near the Hotel Knickerbocker, two thousand strong. Some of them peered through the lighted windows,terrifying the guests. The I.W.W. organizers equipped them with stones and brickbats and then the mob, con-sisting of chefs, pantrymen, kitchen boys, valets and waiters, all in their working uniforms, smashed the windows of the Knickerbocker, formed into a parade and swept up Madison Avenue to the Hotel Belmont at Forty-Second Street where they did more damage. They broke windows at the Waldorf Astoria, the Astor, the Ritz-Carlton and Delmonico's. The police were sent for but for some unexplained reason failed to arrive.

The disorder continued for nearly twenty-four hours. 'Scenes comparable to the Commune took part in the hotel and café zone all day,' reported the *Tribune*. [10] However, this time the law surfaced and many of the rebels were bundled away in police cars. Meanwhile in the abandoned restaurants headwaiters and receptionists were peeling potatoes and washing dishes. The strike petered out; the waiters lowered their demands; but many managers refused to take them back. Their places were filled by those who believed that high tips were a recompense for long hours.

The I.W.W. was not unduly despondent, insisting that their demon-strators were teaching the working classes solidarity. In February they organ-ized a far more effective strike among the silk workers at Paterson, N.J., which lasted over four months and ended in partial victory. Once again Mrs Dodge's drawing room played a part. In her house plans were drawn up for a giant pageant to be held at Madison Square Garden dramatising the strikers' plight. Young John Reed,who was destined to play a part in the

Russian Revolution, wrote the script while his Harvard classmate, Robert Edmund Jones, designed the scenery.

It was performed on 7 June before an audience of fifteen thousand who bought tickets at one dollar fifty. Two thousand workers took part. The scenes showed women and children picketing in the early morning; the arrest and trial of their leaders; the funeral of Modesto Valentino, who had been shot by a detective as he stood on the doorstep with a baby in his arms. The crowds sang the *Internationale* and 'Viva Tesca, Hayward and Flynn'; a huge banner saying 'No God, No Master' decorated one of the walls. The climax came when huge red electric light bulbs, high above the audience, suddenly blazened forth forming the letters 'I.W.W.'

Fortunately Mrs Dodge's activities were artistic as well as political. At one of her 'Evenings' the decision to put on a show of modern painting at the Sixty-ninth Street Armory was taken. Mabel was an ardent supporter of the 'Ashcan School', the name given to eight American painters whose pictures scandalized the public and were derided by the critics. The painters gloried in their martyrdom; they detested the chocolate box covers of the fashionable artists of the day. Robert Henri flung out the clarion call: 'Don't imitate; be yourself.' Other members of the select coterie were John Sloan, William Glackens, George Luks, Everett Shinn and Arthur Davies.

Sixteen hundred paintings by American and European artists were shown at the Armory in March. The emblem of the exhibition was a pine tree, symbolic of the American revolution. Yet it was not the American rebels who created the uproar, but the European dissenters. Conservative New York stormed and shouted in protest.

Outrage and protest flared up in newspaper headlines [wrote Lloyd Morris]. Cubism, futurism, post-impressionism became issues in a battle that engaged the general public. Critics blasted at the baffling *Nude Descending a Staircase* by Marcel Duchamp; Constantin Brancusi's roughly hewn block *The Kiss*; the distorted, crudely-coloured nudes of Henri Matisse; the incomprehensible vagaries of Pablo Picasso and Francis Picabia. Obviously these were the work of degenerates or impostors... [11]

Theodore Roosevelt condemned all 'modernists' as lunatics, while the famous tenor Enrico Caruso drew caricatures of cubist art which he scattered to a boisterous crowd. Critics described the exhibition as 'bedlam in art', likening the cubist drawings to the cave ornamentation of prehistoric man. However, a poet of the day, Harry Kemp, reflected the disturbing impact that the pictures had made on many visitors:

> I cannot shake their wild control.
> Their colours still go roaring through my soul . . .
> Strange cubes evolving into half-guessed forms,
> Cyclones of green, and purple rainbow storms.
> Thus artists on huge Jupiter might paint
> (Or some mad star beyond the earth's constraint) . . . [12]

Shortly after the Armory Exhibition another picture caused a furore almost as great as all the post-impressionists lumped together. A naked, startled girl, standing in a pool, painted by a Frenchman, Paul Chabas, and entitled *September Morn* was displayed in the Fifth Avenue gallery of the French art dealers, Braun & Compagne. A member of the Baptist Church across the street complained. When the manager, Mr Ortiz, returned from lunch the picture was no longer in the window. His assistant told him that Anthony Comstock, president of the Society for the Suppression of Vice, had visited the shop with a warrant for his arrest.

Ortiz replaced the picture and telephoned to Arthur Brisbane, the editor of the New York *Journal*. Within an hour the gallery swarmed with reporters; and the next morning newspapers hailed Ortiz as 'one art expert with the courage to stand up against Comstock and his dictatorship'. The publicity made *September Morn* famous all over the country, and no more was heard from the anti-vice society.

Despite Mrs Stuyvesant Fish's insistence on coupling Socialism and Female Suffrage the two movements had nothing in common. Most suffragettes were ladies from prosperous conservative families. They were proud of the fact that Mrs Oliver Belmont was one of their leaders, and who could accuse Mrs Belmont of subversion?

Compared to their English sisters the American suffragettes were positively mouselike. They refused to adopt militant tactics and contented themselves with parades, rallies, or quaint ideas that would get their pictures into the paper. One young lady told reporters that she inter ded buying an orange grove in Oregon; that she would market the fruit herself and stamp every orange with 'Votes for Women'. And in January a group of suffragettes strolled down Fifth Avenue ringing the door bells of all the imposing mansions. They gave their cards to the butler who always returned with the same reply. Mrs Hermann Oelrichs was not at home; neither was Mrs William K. Vanderbilt; nor Mrs Reginald Vanderbilt; nor Mrs Ogden Mills; nor Mrs

Borden Harriman. Mr Andrew Carnegie was very much at home, but he made it clear that he was unalterably opposed to female suffrage and would be obliged if the young ladies left his doorstep. Mr John D. Rockefeller was also opposed to the idea, although he was prepared to help women in other ways. In January he gave ten million dollars for the establishment of two thousand Magdalen Homes throughout the USA for the rehabilitation of prostitutes.

Almost every day the newspapers ran pictures of suffragettes drilling in Central Park in preparation for the great parade scheduled to take place in Washington the day before the inauguration of President Woodrow Wilson. When it finally came, it was a heart-breaking failure. Although nine thousand women took part in the procession crowds of hooligans and jeering throngs of spectators surged across the path of the marchers and scattered them far and wide. The Washington police were too few to control the mob and although cavalry from Fort Meyer was rushed to the scene it arrived too late. 'I have marched in London; I have marched in New York; I have marched in Chicago,' said the Rev. Anna Howard Shaw. 'Never have I received such insults, never have I seen such incompetence on the part of the police.' But in the end the suffragettes decided that the national publicity given to them was ample compensation.

While the New York *élite* shuddered at such anti-establishment ideas as Socialism, a far more drastic revolution was taking place beneath their noses. It had started eighteen months earlier when a young East Side immigrant, Irving Berlin, had written *Alexander's Ragtime Band*. The new beat not only had taken Manhattan by storm, but had encouraged the Negro musician, Jim Europe, to give New York a public demonstration of jazz. In the spring of 1912 the Clef Club rented Carnegie Hall, the citadel of classical music, and played syncopated rhythms to an audience that went wild with enthusiasm.

By 1913 Manhattan was dance-mad. One by one hotels and restaurants bowed to the craze, introducing 'dinner dances' where men and women snatched cold mouthfuls of food between their gyrations. The tea-dance, from four to six, became an institution which was to last a generation. Scores of new dances were invented, most of which were named after animals: the Turkey Trot, the Grizzly Bear, the Fox Trot, the Bunny Hug, the Kangaroo Dip, the Chicken Scratch, the Crab Step.

Moralists all over the country protested. Propriety had deserted the dance floor. Men clutched their partners, bent them backwards, flung them about in the most suggestive ways. Gone were modesty, reticence, restraint, femininity! The *New York Sun* asked: 'Are we going to the dogs by rag-time route?' Hearst's *New York American* referred to the 'disgusting and indecent dance known as the Turkey Trot' while H. E. Krebbiel, a distin-guished critic, wrote that 'in this year of our Lord 1913 the rag-time dances are threatening to force grace, decorum and decency out of the ballrooms of America.' [13] Mr Bok, the editor of the *Ladies' Home Journal*, sacked fifteen girls who danced the Turkey Trot during their lunch hour, while a Paterson, N. J., court fined a young woman twenty-five dollars for indulging in the same dance on the pavement.

The humorous magazines had a field day. The *Harvard Lampoon* printed a cartoon of a young man saying: 'Shall we bunny?' and a girl replying: 'No, let us just sit down and hug.' The Grizzly Bear inspired a popular song '*I Would Like to Try It*' in which a maiden repines:

> But mother said I shouldn't dare
> To try and do the Grizzly Bear.

The *London Spur* gave a whole page to a drawing of New York couples indulging in wild rhythms, while the hit song *Everybody's Doin' It* became parodied to *Everybody's Overdoin' It*. In June 1913, *Life* printed a poem which summed up the state of affairs:

> Oh, the rag-time of the present
> Is in many ways unpleasant . . .
> It is not in music solely
> That its Influence unholy
> Is exerted the proprieties to balk
> But it permeates existence
> With insidious persistence
> And it gets into our thinking and our talk.

Meanwhile the puritanical mayor of New York, Mr Gaynor, found him-self caught between conflicting pressures. The public was dance-mad, yet the churches and anti-vice leagues were urging him to close down the public halls. The mayor sent a squad of plain-clothes men into restaurants and dance-halls to report what was happening. They came back saying that everyone was dancing the Turkey Trot and Grizzly Bear; that men and women were drinking gin fizzes; and that one girl had unbuttoned the slashes in her skirt to get more freedom of movement. 'The lascivious orgies going on in the so-called respectable dance-halls in this city . . . have grown to be intolerable,' fulminated the mayor. However, his bark was worse than his bite. Although he closed the public dance-halls between one a.m. and noon the next day, he did not touch the hotels or restaurants. 'The public dance-hall,' he explained, 'is open to all who pay. In no sense is a hotel ballroom a public dance-hall.'

A month later he introduced more restrictions. The anti-vice societies claimed that white slavers were flocking to tea dances with the sole object of plying unattended girls with liquor and luring them into a life of sin. The very phrase 'White Slavery' sent a shiver down the maternal spine for in 1913 the country was caught up in a popular hysteria which believed that white slavers lurked everywhere; that they carried poisoned needles which they jabbed into innocent girls on street cars, rendering them instantly pliable to their sinister designs. A novel by Elizabeth Robbins, *My Little Sister*, sold by the thousand that spring and heightened the alarm. It told the story of two English girls who travelled to London and were met by a supposed relation who took them to an elegant house from which there was no escape. Once more the mayor bowed to the pressure of the anti-vice societies and warned restaurant managers that if they allowed 'pick-ups' their establishments would be shut down. Consequently all dance places were placarded with 'Don'ts' for waiters.

1. It is absolutely forbidden under penalty of instant dismissal for any waiter to take a gentleman's card or a message of any kind to a lady patron.
2. Head waiters must prevent gentlemen who are alone from going to any other table to speak to any lady unless invited by the gentleman accompanying her.
3. Should any lady be left alone temporarily the head waiter and waiters must see that no gentleman addresses her until her escort returns.
4. It is absolutely forbidden for a lady to speak to a gentleman who is alone. Any ladies doing so will be reported to the management and refused admission in the future.

The fashionable ladies of New York did not know how to handle the dance craze. At Newport that summer people practised the new steps at private parties but not in public. Then Miss Elizabeth Marbury, the fat jolly literary agent, and Miss Elsie de Wolfe, the interior decorator, who shared a flat in Greenwich Village, and whose friendship with Miss Anne Morgan, daughter of the late J.P., gave them entrée into the best society, came to the rescue. Thin, blond, sinewy Vernon Castle and his pert, wholesome wife, Irene, were working with Jim Europe inventing new dances to his syncopated music. They danced with grace and elegance, never clutching each other, often with only their fingertips touching. They were delighting audiences at Louis Martin's Cabaret with the Castle Walk and the Texas Tommy. Why not open a club where the Castles could coach the best people? Miss Marbury and Miss de Wolfe persuaded Mrs Stuyvesant Fish, Mrs William Rockefeller, Mrs Anthony Drexel, Mrs Hermann Oelrichs, and Mrs Oakley Rhinelander to support their project, and in the late autumn of 1913 Castle House, near the Ritz-Carlton, opened its doors. Prices were high. The cover charge for tea-dancing was three dollars on Fridays, two dollars on other days. Instruction was extra.

The Castles saved the dignity of New York Society. After a few lessons the grandest ladies could dance to jazz tunes without censure. Their favourite haunts that winter were the Plaza, the McAlpin, the Vanderbilt, Delmonico's or the *Sans Souci*, the Castles' own establishment, which was modelled after a restaurant in the Rue de Caumartin in Paris.

Now that syncopation had come to stay many New Yorkers described it as the 'true expression' of the American spirit. Although London, Paris and Rome had gone tango-mad, very few Europeans danced the Grizzly Bear or the Bunny Hug; and the Turkey Trot which had enjoyed a mild vogue was already on the wane. When it was announced that Madame Pavlova would visit New York in the autumn an enterprising reporter interviewed her at her house in London and asked her what she thought of America's contribution to the art of dancing. The great ballerina looked thoughtful and said that all dancing was for only two motives – 'for one's own pleasure and to give pleasure to the spectator. One of my objections to "trotting" is that, although enjoyable to the dancer, it is so *hugly* to the spectator. But,' she said doubtfully, 'it may be *rem*-edied, changed, made more beautiful . . .' [14]

Meanwhile New Yorkers eyed their new President, Woodrow Wilson, with considerable reserve. The Republican Party had been split in half by Taft and Roosevelt, and Wilson, the Democrat, had been elected on a minority vote.

Although Wilson had written a book attacking the great trusts which came out in February 1913, the New York financiers were not unduly worried. Everyone knew that Wall Street, not Washington, was the true seat of power. What depressed the fashionable world was the provincial strait-laced outlook that the Wilsons brought to the White House. Exuberant Theodore Roosevelt and plump smiling William Taft had exuded an atmosphere of *bonhomie*; but Wilson was tight-lipped and schoolmasterish – an idealist and an intellectual – two qualities which were regarded with deep suspicion by the world of high finance.

The great ladies of New York found Washington politics unutterably boring. Not only were politicians (except for Roosevelt) completely below the salt, but the issues they discussed were dreary and unintelligible. 1913 was taken up with currency reforms, tariff legislation, discussions on labour laws, and a long wrangle with Mexico. The only simple piece of legislation that year, promoted by the Senator from Iowa, was a bill abolishing Washington's famous red-light district. For fifty years this institution had flourished on the site where General Hooker's division had pitched camp in the civil war, and was known throughout the capital as the 'division'.

President Wilson had the disconcerting habit of behaving as though he were still a schoolmaster. Five days after the inauguration he announced that the White House would go 'dry'. His Vice-President, Mr Marshall, and his Secretary of State, William Jennings Bryan, obediently followed suit. President Wilson received the press once a week; the morning papers at 3 p.m. on Thursdays and the evening papers at 10 a.m. on Tuesdays. The London *Daily Mail* found him chilling, 'a professor again with a class of eager students around him'. He came in from the garden wearing white trousers and rubber soled shoes. While the newsmen moved in and formed a half circle before him he looked down at the neatly arranged papers on his desk, rearranged the jar of carnations and the green shaded lamp before him. He smiled frostily with an odd little twist of his mouth, and then asked for questions.

'If the US . . .' someone began.
'We won't deal with ifs . . .'
'Will you tell me what action you will take if Mexico . . .'
'When the time comes.'
'Do you think . . .'
'I prefer not to speculate.'

The conference continued in this vein for half an hour, then the class was dismissed. When the newsmen left the White House they went to the nearest bar.

Mrs Woodrow Wilson was scarcely more sympathetic than her husband. Two weeks before the inauguration she gave an interview to women reporters who questioned her on her wardrobe. The outgoing First Lady, Mrs Taft, had told a friend that no President's wife could dress on less than

$6,640 a year. The list Mrs Taft compiled was as follows:

10 evening gowns at $300 each	$3,000
4 street dresses each season for 4 seasons at $50	800
2 afternoon dresses each season for 4 seasons at $100	800
3 afternoon reception gowns each season for 4 seasons at $45	540
Hats and gloves	1,500
	$6,640

When this list was shown to Mrs Wilson she was appalled. 'I would never dream of spending such a sum,' she gasped. 'What sort of sum were you thinking of? A thousand dollars?' persisted one of the reporters. 'A thousand dollars!' ejaculated Mrs Wilson. 'I have never spent a thousand dollars in one year on clothes and have no intentions of starting now. I like to be tastefully gowned but I do not think', and here she paused and eyed her audience reprovingly, 'that extravagance brings a woman happiness. Happiness only comes in more worthwhile pursuits.' [15]

Although the White House encouraged economy and savings, the American press was amazed by Secretary of State Bryan's announcement that he had signed a lucrative contract to embark on a nationwide lecture tour. It was unheard of for a Cabinet Minister – particularly the Foreign Secretary – to undertake work of this nature. However, Mr Bryan explained that for the past seventeen years he had saved ten thousand dollars a year, and he did not wish to alter the habit. As his salary was only twelve thousand dollars a year, a lecture tour was unavoidable. He would carry it out in his holiday.

The press lashed out against him, for Mr Bryan was noted for his miserliness. Indeed, most people felt that this mode of life was undignified for a Foreign Secretary. Reporters pointed out that he saved at least two thousand five hundred dollars a year by serving guests fermented fruit juice instead of wine; that he rented a house in the most unfashionable section of Washington; that his horses and carriages were provided by the Government; and that although he and his wife had bought a motor car they ran it themselves without a chauffeur. The London *Daily Mail* quoted a jingle from an American paper:

Artistic Sensations

The Armory Show, March 1913.

Marchel Duchamp's *Nude Descending a Staircase*, which was the most controversial painting in the Armory Show.

Sunday, Women drying their hair, painted in 1913
by John Sloan, one of the Ashcan School.

The poster for the Armory Show, announcing
an impressive list of 'guests'.

INTERNATIONAL EXHIBITION
OF MODERN ART
ASSOCIATION OF AMERICAN
PAINTERS AND SCULPTORS
69th INF'T'Y REGT ARMORY, NEW YORK CITY
FEBRUARY 15th TO MARCH 15th 1913
AMERICAN & FOREIGN ART.

AMONG THE GUESTS WILL BE — INGRES, DELACROIX, DEGAS,
CÉZANNE, REDON, RENOIR, MONET, SEURAT, VAN GOGH,
HODLER, SLEVOGT, JOHN, PRYDE, SICKERT, MAILLOL,
BRANCUSI, LEHMBRUCK, BERNARD, MATISSE, MANET, SIGNAC,
LAUTREC, CONDER, DENIS, RUSSELL, DUFY, BRAQUE, HERBIN,
GLEIZES, SOUZA-CARDOZO, ZAK, DU CHAMP-VILLON,
GAUGUIN, ARCHIPENKO, BOURDELLE, C. DE SEGONZAC.

LEXINGTON AVE.–25th ST.

Irving Berlin, the composer of *Alexander's Ragtime Band*, which achieved immense popularity in 1913.

Two stills from Zukor's sumptuous film version of *Quo Vadis*, made in 1913.

Mr and Mrs Vernon Castle, who coached elegant society in the tango and the other novel dances of 1913.

Five of the latest dances: one-step, tango, maxixe, rag and step-over. Besides
Alexander's Ragtime Band, other popular tunes for these dances were: *Mysterious Rag,*
Belle of the Barbers' Ball, Botsford's Black and White, Grizzly-bear, Chatterbox Rag,
Peaceful Henry, and *Temptation Rag.*

September Morn by Paul Chabas.

> While the cost of grapefruit may be soaring
> We all pay the same price for beer.
> If Bryan can't live on a thousand a month
> Can we on nine hundred a year? [16]

The rhyme was signed 'Department of Justice'.

Nevertheless Mr Bryan got his way, and in the autumn carried out his lecture tour.

New York found more amusement in Washington Society than in its political life. Rich Mrs John Henderson, a lady who lived in Henderson Castle at Sixteenth Street, was frequently in the news. A few years earlier she had become an ardent prohibitionist, smashed every bottle in her husband's cellar and emptied the contents into the street. Her popularity as a hostess was on the wane for recently she had become a vegetarian as well. Guests were disappointed to find that the juicy quails and succulent pheasants put before them were made entirely of cornmeal. In the early months of 1913 Mrs Henderson was brought before the courts for cutting down a dead tree outside her house, which she found depressing. But she was let off with a light fine, as everyone knew she was a lady of impulse.

Even more amusing were the antics of the fabulously rich Mrs Evalyn Walsh McLean, whose father had struck gold in Colorado in 1896, and whose son, Vinson, was known as 'the hundred million dollar baby'. The McLean family owned the *Washington Post*, and the young McLeans had houses in Palm Beach and Newport. In the winter of 1913 their friends were fascinated to learn that Mrs McLean had adopted a Negro boy, Julian Winbush, as a companion for her three-year-old Vinson.

Somehow [wrote Mrs McLean] my husband got the idea that Vinson would be spoiled by too much attention from his elders. 'Say,' Ned exclaimed to me one day . . . 'I had a Negro boy to play with when I was little. Vinson needs a change from this association with detectives, nurses, and others. He does not see enough of children. He'll be a snob if you're not careful.'

We could not buy a coloured boy, of course [continued Mrs McLean], although it was our habit to buy anything we wanted. But Ned made arrangements with a little five-year-old named Julian Winbush to let him come and live with us . . . The Winbush boy was shiny black with teeth that anyone would envy. I dressed him up to match Vinson, and then we headed South in the private car . . . In winter and in summer most of Vinson's little things came from Paris, from Worth's – like his little carriage robe, his hat, his coat, all made of ermine. I liked that little coloured boy, at first; but I could not bring myself to a point where there was pleasure for me in dressing him in clothes from Paris. Yet, since Vinson played with him, he must be clean and sweetly scented. He was playful, friendly, roguish. His big eyes that rolled like agates in his little head gleamed with amusement when I placed him and Vinson in a wicker rolling chair at Palm Beach and pushed them, seated side by side. [17]

Apparently Vinson finally rebelled at having a playmate forced upon him and the McLeans finally returned Julian Winbush, plus a large sum of money, to his parents.

Throughout 1913 American enterprise displayed itself in many and original forms. In the winter New Yorkers were shocked to learn that arson had become big business. Fire Commissioner Johnson declared that insurance companies were being defrauded of millions of dollars a year by an organized network of 'firebrokers' who encouraged people to over-insure their premises on the understanding that professional fire-setters would offer them their services.

At the end of January Izzy Steinkreutzer turned State's evidence and blew the gaff. Izzy claimed that in the past five years over five thousand East Enders had asked him to burn up their property.

They would come to me when I was standing on the street corner or walking along the street [he told the court]. They would say to me, 'Izzy', or maybe they would say, 'Mr Steinkreutzer, do for us a great favour and make a fire in our house.' I would say to them: 'How much insurance have you got?' And when they told me, I would tell them what I would charge for the job – anywhere from twenty-five dollars to seventy-five dollars. But sometimes I would tell them I wouldn't do it. Then they would say 'Well why shouldn't you do it? Ain't you set a fire for So-and-So? I'm as good friend of yours as So-and-So and ain't my money as good?' Then sometimes they would tell if I shouldn't make a fire for them they would tell the police. [18]

Izzy's testimony led to the arrest of several fire brokers who were believed to be the brains of the outfit. Izzy himself was let off with a light sentence as a reward for his co-operation.

More commendable enterprise that spring revealed itself in the announcement that fifty families in Montclair, N. J., had banded together to launch a mass cooking experiment that would 'eliminate household bother and propagate a spirit of brotherly and sisterly love'. And, of course, save money. Hitherto the yearly expense of each family for domestic labour was: one

servant three hundred dollars; cost of keeping servant a hundred and fifty
dollars; extra help fifty dollars. The cost of the new scheme would be:

Rent of kitchen in a central locality	$1,200
Stoves and dishes	1,000
General Manager's salary	1,200
Chef's salary	3,000
Ten under cooks	3,000
Ten Males at $9 a week	4,680
Incidental expenses	500
Operating two motor cars	2,500
Total	$17,080

In addition, the spokesman said, two motor cars and vacuum cleaners
would have to be purchased.

Enterprise that ended in tears was displayed by a group of ladies whose
fashion sense was titillated by the Balkan Wars. They appeared on Fifth
Avenue in 'Bulgarian Bloomers' over-lapped by 'X-ray skirts'. As they
strolled along women passers-by began to cry 'Shame'; soon a crowd of outraged citizens had gathered behind them. Their walk broke into a run, and
soon it was a chase with the mob in full pursuit. A policeman intervened and
took the fashion plates, who by this time were sobbing hysterically, to the
nearest police station. The sergeant in charge could find no reason for
booking them and ordered their release.

This incident inspired the Right Rev. Monsignor O'Hara to inveigh
against feminine indecency. Not only did he object to the vulgar dress but to
the shameless way women were beginning to paint and powder. 'We are
living today', he told a group of Brooklyn mothers, 'in a pandemonium of
power, a riot of rouge, and moral anarchy of dress.' The London *Daily Mail*
commented chirpily on his speech by printing the jingle:

> Then powder your nose, powder your nose,
> For history shows that a certain repose
> Is acquired by the lady who powders her nose. [19]

There was no doubt but that the world of 1913 offered a feast of new ideas.
New Yorkers talked about the giant stadium being built at New Haven,
which would hold sixty thousand and be known as 'the Yale Bowl'; about
the lectures on interior decorating being given at the Colony Club by Miss

Elsie de Wolfe; about the use of a 'dictaphone' to trap a group of black-mailers; about the dish-washing machine that had come on to the market and the lectures in kitchen efficiency being given by Mrs George Frederick; about the record price of a hundred and thirty thousand dollars paid by Knoedler & Co. for Rembrandt's *Lucretia Stabbing Herself* at a sale at the Plaza Hotel; about the defection of heiress Miss Rosalind Guggenheim who preached Socialism and every month returned unopened a letter from her father containing a cheque for five hundred dollars.

They also talked about the rise of Hollywood. Cinemas were springing up all over the USA and by 1913 the investment in the new industry totalled a billion dollars. Mary Pickford, described as the Maude Adams of the films, was hailed as the 'Queen of the Movies'. The craze for Westerns was so great, said Mark Sullivan, 'that cattlemen suffered a labour problem due to cowboys trying to get into the movies. When "Billy Broncho", a cowboy character, appeared on the streets of Cleveland he started a riot.'

Broadway, however, still retained its glamour and prestige. That year New Yorkers saw Douglas Fairbanks in *Hawthorne of the USA*, Jane Cowl in *Within the Law*, Ethel Barrymore in *Tante*, Laurette Taylor in *Peg o' My Heart*, Elsie Ferguson in *The Strange Woman*, Billie Burke in *The Land of Promise*, Al Johnson and Gaby Deslys in *The Honeymoon Express*, Elsie Janis in *The Lady of the Slippers*, Pauline Frederick in *Joseph and His Brethren*, Grace George in *Divorcées*, De Wolf Hopper in *The Beggar Student*, Mrs Fiske in *The High Road*.

The favourites of the literary world were almost as plentiful. In 1913 New Yorkers were reading *The Reef* by Edith Wharton, *Roast Beef Medium* by Edna Ferber, *Daddy Longlegs* by Jean Webster, *A Preface to Politics* by Walter Lippmann, *The Rich Mrs Burgoyne* by Kathleen Norris, *New Leaf Mills* by William Dean Howells, *A Personal Narrative of Political Experience* by Robert LaFollette.

Sometimes American enterprise took a nasty turn and became nothing less than unreasoning aggressiveness. So thought the fashionable foreign ladies who embarked from the steamship *Loraine* on 5 October. When they descended the gangway they were amazed to hear customs inspectors saying: 'Your hat, if you please, madam, we must have your hat'. It was the first day of a new tariff – the life-long work of Dr William Hornaday, director of the New York Zoological Gardens – which forbade the importation of all feathers plucked from wild birds. As feathers were the height of fashion in 1913, the chic Frenchwoman, Madame Bevalagua, came to grief. She was wearing a small velvet hat decorated with a valuable aigrette. She was so intimidated by the burly customs inspector that she meekly handed it to him. To her amazement she saw him rip off the feathers. 'My milliner never told me,' she gasped furiously.

Although a dozen more ladies wept and implored, the inspector was adamant, plucking away feathers with savage abandon. However, the next day it became plain that he had grossly exceeded his terms of reference. General Nelson Henry, surveyor of the Port of New York, declared that the law aimed at the importation of feathers as merchandise and did not apply to individuals wearing aigrette-plumed hats. Although the General apologised deeply to the ladies concerned, it was not a happy beginning to a pleasure trip.

Another angry visitor in October was Marie Lloyd, the famous English musical comedy queen. She was travelling with her lover, Bernard Dillon, the jockey, to fulfill a forty-week contract at a thousand dollars a week. To her amazement she was refused entrance under the White Slave Act which called for the deportation of any woman travelling with a man other than her husband. Although she stormed and argued, explaining to the officials that she was planning to marry Mr Dillon as soon as her divorce from her actor husband was final, they forced her to spend three nights at Ellis Island. Finally Washington again intervened and she was allowed to put up bail and proceed on her trip.

Enterprise that no one could quarrel with was displayed by the motor car industry. At the end of 1913 more than half a million Model T Fords were on the roads of America: and the Ford joke was part of every vaudeville show in the country. 'Does this car always make this racket?' 'No, only when it's running.' 'Why is a Ford like a bath tub?' 'Because you hate to be seen in it.' Or limericks such as this:

> There was a fat man of Fall River
> Who said as he drove his Ford Flivver,
> " This bumping and jolting
> To me is revolting.
> It's hell, but it's good for the liver."

Henry Ford operated on a simple theory. Make a good car; stick to a few models and cut out all non-essentials so that you can sell it at the lowest price then increase sales and reduce prices in an ascending spiral of expansion. These tactics brought Henry Ford a record profit of twenty million dollars in 1913.

His workers received the standard wage of two dollars a day, but Ford decided to do better. Consequently that December he took a decision that was destined to revolutionize America's outlook. On 5 January 1914 he announced that he would pay his workers five dollars a day. The announcement stunned the *New York Times* which commented almost angrily. 'The lower paid employees, the sweepers, who in New York City may claim one dollar to one dollar fifty a day, are now to receive five dollars a day in Ford's plant.'

'It was,' said the *New York Sun*, groping for a suitable simile, 'a bolt out of the blue sky, flashing its way across the continent and beyond, something unheard of in the annals of business.' 'An epoch in the world of industrial history,' said the *New York Herald* crisply.

And that was exactly what it was.

NOTES

CHAPTER 1   *London*

1   *Queen Mary* p. 439: James Pope-Hennessy
2   24 February
3   26 February
4   *Lord Crewe* p. 141: James Pope-Hennessy
5   *Queen Mary* p. 471: James Pope-Hennessy
6   Ibid p. 426
7   *Grace and Favour* p. 103: Loelia, Duchess of Westminster
8   *A King's Story* p. 104: The Duke of Windsor
9   Ibid p. 100
10 *Queen Mary* p. 481: James Pope-Hennessy
11 *The Life and Letters of Walter H. Page* p. 134: edited by Burton J. Hendrick
12 Ibid p. 153
13 Ibid pp. 155-7
14 *Lost Splendour* p. 154: Prince Felix Yusupov
15 *Daily Mail*, 17 June
16 Ibid, 3 June
17 *It was such Fun* pp. 185-6: Mrs Hwfa Williams
18 *The Rainbow Comes and Goes* pp. 88-9: Lady Diana Cooper
19 *Diaghilev* p. 240: Arnold Haskell
20 27 May
21 *Daily Mail*, 16 July
22 *The Rainbow Comes and Goes* pp. 51-2: Lady Diana Cooper
23 *Daily Mail*, 16 July
24 4 July
25 *Twenty-five Years* p. 268: Viscount Grey of Fallodon
26 *Daily Mail*, 7 April
27 *Lord Carnock* p. 389: Sir Harold Nicolson
28 *Die Grosse Politik der Europäischen Kabinette* Vol. XXXIV: edited by Johannes Lepsius
29 *Lord Carnock* p. 388: Sir Harold Nicolson
30 *Female Pipings in Eden* p. 285: Dame Ethel Smyth
31 *The Suffragette Movement* pp. 468-9: Sylvia Pankhurst
32 Hansard, 6 May
33 *My Own Story* p. 158: Emmeline Pankhurst
34 *The Times*, 22 January
35 *F.E.* p. 159: The Earl of Birkenhead
36 *Daily Mail*, 30 April
37 *Female Pipings in Eden* p. 285: Dame Ethel Smyth
38 *The Times*, 29 April
39 *F.E.* pp. 187-8: The Earl of Birkenhead
40 2 September
41 5 September
42 *The Life and Letters of Walter H. Page* p. 158; edited by Burton J. Hendrick
43 Ibid pp. 158-9
44 *Tempestuous Journey* p. 256: Frank Owen

CHAPTER 2   *Berlin*

1   *William of Germany* p. 353: Stanley Shaw
2   Ibid p. 234
3   *Betrachtungen zum Weltkriege*: T. von Bethmann-Hollweg
4   *German Diplomatic Documents* Vol. IV p. 126: edited by E. T. S. Dugdale
5   *Die Grosse Politik der Europäischen Kabinette* Vol. XXXIV: edited by Johannes Lepsius
6   *Men Around the Kaiser* p. 168: Frederick William Wile
7   *William of Germany* p. 211: Stanley Shaw
8   *My First Fifty Years* p. 155: Paul Poiret
9   *Germany and the Germans* pp. 260-1: Price Collier
10 *Memories of the Kaiser's Court* p. 85: Anne Topham
11 *Germany and the Germans* p. 357: Price Collier
12 *Assize of Arms* p. 97: Brigadier-General J. H. Morgan
13 *Daily Mail*, 16 June
14 *German Life in Town and Country* p. 105: William Dawson
15 *Daily Mail*, 23 May
16 *Vanished Pomps of Yesterday* p. 43: Lord Frederick Hamilton
17 *Memories of the Fatherland* p. 5: Anne Topham

18 *Memories of the Fatherland* pp. 287–8
19 *Further Pages from My Life* p. 287: Rt. Rev. William Boyd Carpenter
20 *Daily Express*, 9 July
21 *The Eve of 1914* p. 320: Theodor Wolff
22 *New York Tribune*, 19 October
23 *Daily Mail*, 19–23 September
24 *History of the English People* p. 581: Elie Halévy
25 *The Memories of the Crown Prince of Germany* p. 114
26 *Daisy, Princess of Pless* p. 253: by Herself
27 *The Annual Register 1913* p. 321
28 *From Bismarck to the World War* p. 474: Erich Brandenburg
29 *Walter Rathenau* p. 164: Count Harry Kessler

21 Ibid p. 86
22 *Out of My Past* pp. 346–7: Count Kokovtzov
23 *The Origins of the First World War* p. 446: Sidney Fay
24 *The Reign of Rasputin* p. 98: M. V. Rodzianko
25 *Lenin* p. 186: Ralph Fox
26 *The Crucifixion of Liberty* p. 125: Alexander Kerensky
27 Ibid p. 162
28 *Lenin* p. 189: Ralph Fox
29 Ibid p. 190
30 *Lost Splendour* p. 164: Prince Felix Yusupov
31 *The Last Grand Duchess* p. 97: Ian Vorres
32 *Once a Grand Duke* pp. 248–9: Grand Duke Alexander

CHAPTER 3   *St Petersburg*

1 *The Letters of Czar Nicholas & Empress Marie* p. 283: edited by Edward J. Bing
2 Ibid p. 284
3 8 February
4 *The Reign of Rasputin* pp. 75–7: M. V. Rodzianko
5 *Dissolution of an Empire* pp. 36–7: Meriel Buchanan
6 *Memories of the Russian Court* pp. 93–4: Anna Virubova
7 *Life and Tragedy of Alexandra Feodorovna* p. 175: Baroness Buxhoeveden
8 *Out of My Past* p. 361: Count Kokovtzov
9 Ibid
10 Ibid
11 *Daily Mail*, 8 February
12 15 May
13 *Life's A Gamble* p. 91: F. H. Cripps
14 *Dissolution of an Empire* p. 20: Meriel Buchanan
15 *The Vanished Pomps of Yesterday* pp. 156–157: Lord Frederick Hamilton
16 *Lost Splendour* p. 89: Prince Felix Yusupov
17 *At The Court of the Last Czar* p. 79: A. A. Mossolov
18 *Life's A Gamble* p. 85: F. H. Cripps
19 *The Origins of the First World War* p. 433: Sidney Fay
20 *The Reign of Rasputin* p. 81: M. V. Rodzianko

CHAPTER 4   *Vienna*

1 *Lord Carnock* p. 390: Sir Harold Nicolson
2 *The Fall of the House of Hapsburg* p. 366: Edward Crankshaw
3 Josef Redlich's diary, 29 April 1913
4 *Sarajevo* p. 25: Joachim Remak
5 *Modern Austria* p. 193: Virginia Gayda
6 *The Vanished Pomps of Yesterday* pp. 64–5: Lord Frederick Hamilton
7 *A Wife in Many Lands* Vol. II pp. 256–7: Mrs Hugh Fraser
8 *Scenes & Memories* pp. 219-20: Walpurga, Lady Paget
9 16 March
10 *Scenes & Memories* pp. 223 and 231: Walpurga, Lady Paget
11 *The World of Yesterday* p. 28: Stefan Zweig
12 Ibid
13 *Memoirs of Michael Karolyi* p. 40
14 *Lord Carnock* p. 403: Sir Harold Nicolson
15 *Sarajevo* p. 27: Joachim Remak

CHAPTER 5   *Rome*

1 *Glimpses of Italian Court Life* pp. 212-4: Tryphosa Bates Batcheller
2 *My Italian Years* pp. 5–6: Richard Bagot

3 *Italian Life in Town & Country* p. 23: L. Villari
4 *Social and Diplomatic Memories* pp. 172-3: Sir James Rennell Rodd
5 Ibid p. 174
6 *The Rainbow Comes and Goes* pp. 93-4: Lady Diana Cooper
7 *Memoirs of an Aesthete* p. 37: Harold Acton
8 *It Was Such Fun* p. 148: Mrs Hwfa Williams
9 *Memoirs of an Aesthete* pp. 38-9: Harold Acton

CHAPTER 6   *Paris*

1 *Memoirs* Vol. II p. 11: Raymond Poincar
2 30 March
3 10 August
4 *Harper's Bazaar*, July
5 *Dancing for Diaghilev* p. 42: Lydia Sokolova
6 Ibid p. 44
7 *Diaghilev* p. 244: Arnold Haskell
8 *Daily Mail*, 10 May
9 *Paris Calling* p. 129: Harry Greenwall
10 13 May
11 *My First Fifty Years* pp. 114-6: Paul Poiret
12 *Diaghilev* pp. 185 and 190: Arnold Haskell
13 *Paris Calling* pp. 212-3: Harry Greenwall
14 *My First Fifty Years* pp. 204-5: Paul Poiret
15 *Paris Calling* p. 214: Harry Greenwall
16 *Memoirs* Vol. II p. 33: Raymond Poincaré
17 *Un Livre Noir* Vol. II pp. 14-15
18 *The Origins of the First World War* p. 333: Sidney Fay

19 *The Eve of 1914* p. 276: Theodor Wolff
20 *The World of Yesterday* p. 155: Stefan Zweig
21 *Masters of Modern Art* p. 77: Alfred Hamilton Barr
22 *New York Tribune*, 29 June
23 *Daily Express*, 8 August
24 *The Eve of 1914* pp. 281-2: Theodor Wolff

CHAPTER 7   *New York*

1 *New York Tribune*, 28 February
2 *Incredible New York* p. 192: Lloyd Morris
3 *The Vanderbilt Feud* p. 200: Cornelius Vanderbilt, Jr
4 *King Lehr and the Gilded Age* p. 126-7: Elizabeth Drexel Lehr
5 *The Vanderbilt Feud* p. 215: Cornelius Vanderbilt, Jr
6 Ibid p. 171
7 *King Lehr and the Gilded Age* pp. 138-9: Elizabeth Drexel Lehr
8 Ibid p. 212
9 *New York Tribune*, 8 February
10 25 January
11 *Incredible New York* p. 304: Lloyd Morris
12 *Our Times* Vol. IV p. 112: Mark Sullivan
13 Ibid p. 254
14 *Harper's Bazar*, October
15 *Daily Mail*, 15 October
16 29 July
17 *Father Struck It Rich* pp. 226-7: Evalyn Walsh McLean
18 *New York Tribune*, 20 January
19 30 July

INDEX